Writing Your Thesis

→SAGE Study Skills

Writing Your Thesis

Third Edition

Paul Oliver

Los Angeles | London | New Delhi
Singapore | Washington DC

Los Angeles | London | New Delhi
Singapore | Washington DC

SAGE Publications Ltd
1 Oliver's Yard
55 City Road
London EC1Y 1SP

SAGE Publications Inc.
2455 Teller Road
Thousand Oaks, California 91320

SAGE Publications India Pvt Ltd
B 1/I 1 Mohan Cooperative Industrial Area
Mathura Road
New Delhi 110 044

SAGE Publications Asia-Pacific Pte Ltd
3 Church Street
#10-04 Samsung Hub
Singapore 049483

Editor: Marianne Lagrange
Assistant editor: Kathryn Bromwich/Rachael Plant
Project manager: Jeanette Graham
Production editor: Nicola Marshall
Copyeditor: Carol Lucas
Proofreader: Isabel Kirkwood
Indexer: Paul Oliver
Marketing manager: Catherine Slinn
Cover design: Wendy Scott
Typeset by: C&M Digitals (P) Ltd, Chennai, India
Printed and bound by CPI Group (UK) Ltd,
Croydon, CR0 4YY

Library of Congress Control Number: 2013932301

British Library Cataloguing in Publication data

A catalogue record for this book is available from
the British Library

ISBN 978-1-4462-6784-4
ISBN 978-1-4462-6785-1

To

Moses Joseph

Contents

About the Author

Paul Oliver is an academic writer and researcher. He has either authored or edited 19 books in the areas of Research Methods, Education, Philosophy and Religion. He has had books translated into seven languages. For many years a lecturer at the University of Huddersfield, he was course leader there for the Doctor of Education programme. He has wide experience of both supervising and examining master's and doctoral theses.

Acknowledgements

The author and publisher would like to thank:

Dr Gwendolen Bradshaw for permission to reproduce pages 30 and 234 from her Doctor of Education thesis 'Involving service users in the assessment of the performance of pre-registration student midwives – an interpretive study of the perceptions of key stakeholders' (The University of Huddersfield, 2003). See page 87.

The University of Huddersfield for permission to reproduce the abstract from the above thesis. See page 190.

Part 1

The Process of Academic Writing

1

The Research Thesis

In this chapter you will learn about the different forms which a research thesis can take, and explore the criteria which help to distinguish a master's from a doctoral thesis. We look at the broad characteristics of academic writing, along with some of the features which characterize a well-written thesis. We also examine the formal university procedures and requirements for academic theses.

Study Strategies

- Visit a university library, and select several examples of the type of thesis you intend to write.
- Read the titles. Do they give an unambiguous indication of the nature of the thesis?
- Read the abstracts. Do they provide a clear summary of the thesis?
- Locate the aims of the thesis. (You may find these near the end of the first chapter.) Are they precise and clearly worded?
- Look at the contents pages and overall structure of the thesis. Is it easy to find your way around the thesis?
- Examine a few sample pages of the thesis at random. Is the page layout 'easy on the eye' and is the text easy to read?

Getting the most out of yourself – why do you want to write a research thesis?

This book is designed to help postgraduate students with the process of writing a thesis. For many people engaged in master's or doctoral research, collecting and analysing data is interesting and exciting. In the social sciences, the research process often involves interaction with other people, and as you begin to amass your data there is a real feeling of progress. However, the time comes when all of this data and analysis has to be converted into a thesis. Writing is a largely solitary process, and progress may seem very slow. The task seems to stretch away into infinity. This book will help you with writing your thesis, from the moment you type your first word, to when you walk into the viva voce examination to defend the completed work! The book is divided into two parts. The first provides help on the broad issues of academic writing which are useful when preparing a thesis. The second part is a template for writing your thesis. It takes you through the process, step by step, from the title page to the final examination. Although there is no single way of using the book, one idea would be to read Part 1 during the early stages of your research, and to save Part 2 for when you actually start writing your thesis.

Motivation

We can start by exploring one or two aspects of personal motivation in terms of academic writing. Most students write a thesis as part of an academic qualification such as a 'taught' master's degree, or a research degree such as a Master of Philosophy or Doctor of Philosophy. There is often a natural tendency to be thinking continually about the final qualification, and to treat the thesis writing simply as a means to that end. This is a pity, because academic writing is a very creative activity. It is an opportunity for you not only to describe your research, but also to reflect on your own intellectual world view. Thesis writing is not merely an instrumental activity, but an opportunity to express your understanding of the world in a fresh and novel way. If you can concentrate on this creative dimension to academic writing you will probably enjoy the process much more.

Communication

More than this, a thesis is also a means of communication. On the one hand, you might see it as being written primarily for the examiners in the oral examination. However, you should also think of the thesis as finally resting on the library shelves, and being consulted by many future students who are struggling with their own research. Students from overseas may study your thesis and take ideas back with them when they complete their course. Part-time students who are in work may be influenced by the thesis, and incorporate ideas at their workplace. In short, the act of writing is an opportunity to convey interesting and sophisticated ideas to an untold future audience. This can make academic writing a very exciting prospect.

Process

There is also, in the process of writing, a sense of being part of the development of ideas. Writing a thesis involves building upon the ideas of researchers and thinkers who have gone before, and helping to lay a foundation for future students. A thesis usually involves reviewing and analysing the background literature to a subject, and showing how current research adds incrementally to the sum of human knowledge. The process of academic writing is here not only part of the transmission of culture, but also of providing a new perspective on the world. The doctoral thesis has traditionally involved the generation of an original contribution to knowledge, but writing any thesis provides an opportunity to create fresh insights into the social world.

This book provides practical advice in the successful writing of a thesis. Although this is very important, I hope it will achieve more than suggesting useful strategies to maximize success. I hope it will enthuse you with the feeling of excitement inherent in the writing process, and its potential for conveying fascinating and complex ideas. Above all, I hope this book helps you to gain pleasure and enjoyment from the writing process.

The nature and varieties of a research thesis

Before we start discussing the thesis in detail, we should clarify some of our terminology. The terms 'dissertation' and 'thesis' are sometimes used interchangeably in everyday academic conversation, although there is perhaps a tendency for 'dissertation' to be used more frequently in relation to master's degrees, and 'thesis' in connection with doctorates. However, to avoid any possible confusion in relation to different institutional practices, the word 'thesis' will be used throughout this book. Where there are differences between master's and doctoral levels, these will be clearly stated.

In the briefest possible terms, a thesis is a piece of formal academic writing which reports on a research study. However, both the structure and content of theses are diverse, and it would be helpful briefly to survey some of this variation. Theses in the social sciences generally tend to use empirical data as the basis of the research. This is data derived from sources such as questionnaires, interviews, measuring instruments or, perhaps, the analysis of documents. In philosophical terms, empirical data is often defined as data which is collected through the use of our senses. Probably a minority of theses, however, employ data which is based upon the analysis of concepts. That is, the researcher explores ideas which are used in a particular subject area, subjecting those ideas to critical scrutiny and examining the meanings and understandings inherent in those ideas. Whatever the type of data used, a thesis generally extends our understanding of a subject, takes the subject further in some way or makes an additional contribution to knowledge. This will, of course, be a more significant feature of a doctoral than a master's thesis.

5

Example – Empirical and Conceptual research

One thesis may involve examining the possible effects of social class on educational achievement in schools. A second thesis may be concerned with whether social class *should* have an effect upon educational achievement.

   The first topic requires empirical data to examine whether class and achievement are linked in any way. The second topic requires conceptual analysis to explore whether we *ought* to try to eliminate any connection between the two.

Master's theses

Most master's degrees such as an MA or an MSc consist of a taught element followed by a thesis. The thesis can vary considerably in length, depending on the type of course and institution, from say 12,000 words to around 30,000 words. Some students find that they have to attend an oral examination, or viva voce, to answer questions on their thesis, although this is not a particularly common practice with master's degrees. Once the thesis has been approved by the examiners, a copy is usually placed in the university library or repository. This may be a traditional bound copy or an electronic copy.

   A Master of Philosophy (MPhil) degree is classified as a research degree, rather than a 'taught' degree, and does not normally have a taught element of modules and assignments. This degree is awarded on the basis of a longer thesis, typically up to about 40,000 words in length. With the MPhil degree, a viva voce, or 'viva', is a more frequent occurrence.

Doctoral theses

The traditional doctoral thesis such as the PhD is a much more substantial piece of work, of 80,000 words or more. There is usually a viva which is regarded as an integral part of the assessment process. Some PhD programmes include a course in research methods. This course may be additional to the thesis and not assessed, or it may be an integral part of the programme, formally assessed and result in a reduction in the length of the thesis. This pattern is fairly typical of the Doctor of Education, where an assessed course in research methods, or aspects of educational research, is combined with a shorter thesis of perhaps 50,000 words. The Doctor of Education or EdD is sometimes referred to as a 'taught' or 'professional' doctorate. Such taught doctorates are also available in some other subject areas, such as the Doctor of Business Administration (DBA), or Doctorate in Clinical Psychology (DClinPsy). Some university regulations permit the inclusion of creative work, or journal articles which have been written and published, as part of the research for the thesis.

Whatever the variation in structure and format of a thesis, there are certain common-alities which are usually present in one form or another. The research problem or issue should be described clearly, and contextualized within the relevant literature of that subject. There would also usually be an explanation and justification of the research design, and of the data collection and analysis methods. As part of this one might also expect an explanation of the way in which the study is located within a specific theoretical tradition or perspective. Finally, there would be a careful analysis of the data, and a summary of the conclusions drawn.

It should be added that there are other methods for obtaining a doctorate, including the method based on publications. Here the candidate submits a collection of research publications, along with a relatively short critical commentary on these articles or books. The publications and the commentary together constitute the doctoral submission. This process is normally only relevant to fairly experienced academics, and as the critical commentary is typically much shorter than a thesis, it will not be discussed in this book. Aspects of the process of working towards a doctorate are discussed in Leonard (2001, pp. 69–71).

Shorter doctoral theses

The new types of doctoral structure, often known as professional doctorates, typically have a much shorter thesis than is the norm with a PhD. Although this may be appealing to potential students it does pose a possible difficulty. In the case of a long, traditional thesis there is generally plenty of scope within the word length, to develop sophisticated arguments and to examine all aspects of issues. This is important, since during the final oral examination, or viva, the examiners will want to assure themselves that the student is thinking, analysing and writing at doctoral level. If there are constraints in terms of word length placed upon you, it may be difficult to decide where to make reductions in length and what to eliminate. You may reasonably feel that by reducing certain sections the final thesis may appear too superficial.

Traditionally one of the marks of good academic writing has been considered to be the ability to examine the different aspects of a question. In so doing one acknowledges that academic and research issues are very complex, and that in order to reveal this complexity, one has to discuss the range of perspectives which one might take on a particular question. If however the student is constrained in terms of length, then it may not be possible to achieve this in the same degree of detail.

As the range of new types of doctorate expands, it is becoming more and more important that both students and supervisors reflect carefully on their strategies to assure the doctoral level of the thesis while adhering to the word length requirements. Possible strategies for achieving this are discussed towards the end of Chapter 2.

Similarities and differences between a master's and a doctoral thesis

One of the results of the diversification in structure of postgraduate programmes is that some doctoral theses are not very much longer than some master's theses. It therefore becomes increasingly important to be as clear as possible about the differences. First, it should be pointed out that individual universities have their own regulations in this regard, and it is essential that you read carefully the regulations for the institution at which you are studying. Nevertheless, there are general similarities and differences between the two kinds of thesis.

The similarities are largely in terms of overall structure. They typically have the same overall content, consisting of a review of the literature, a discussion of methodology, an analysis of data and a conclusion, and a list of reference materials. The theses are written in the same fairly formal academic style, divided into appropriate chapters, and use an accepted form of academic referencing. In addition, the theses incorporate a fairly standard pattern of preliminary pages, including a list of contents and perhaps a list of abbreviations or technical terms being employed. There is thus a broad area of commonality, particularly in terms of structure, although students exert their own individuality in terms of the format of their particular thesis. However, despite these similarities, the elements of the thesis are treated differently at doctoral level compared with at master's level.

Literature

In the doctoral thesis, the review of the research literature is treated more thoroughly. The literature is subdivided into sections, and treated either thematically or in chronological order within themes. Concepts from the literature which are in some way philosophically problematic are discussed separately, and an attempt made to clarify some features of their use. In the doctoral, compared with the master's thesis there is a much wider use of current research from academic journals, in order to contextualize the subject matter. Although as much contemporary material as possible is used, the thesis may also trace the historical development of ideas.

Methodology

The treatment of methodological issues is much more detailed in a doctoral thesis. Typically, a master's thesis places the research conducted within a particular approach, such as case study research or survey research. At doctoral level, however, the treatment goes beyond this. The overall methodological approach is carefully related to the aims of the study. If, for example, a case study approach is selected, then there is normally a discussion of epistemological issues, explaining the way in which the particular types of data collected are expected to reveal knowledge about the issue being investigated. The discussion also extends further into questions of ontology, and whether or not the researcher perceives the social world as consisting of external, observable realities. These considerations lead into a description of the data collection process, and a careful analysis of the reasons for adopting this approach. The doctoral thesis also contains a much more detailed discussion of the ethical issues implicit in the research.

Data

The scope of the data collected is inevitably much greater in a doctoral thesis. In the case of a survey, the questionnaire typically is distributed to a much larger sample of the research population. In an ethnographic study, more interviews are conducted, and in a longitudinal study the research is conducted over a greater period of time. A master's thesis has to be completed in a matter of months, which limits a longitudinal study. However, in the case of a doctoral thesis it is feasible to collect data over a period of two or three years. Quite apart from the magnitude of the data collected, the actual process of data collection is conducted in a more sophisticated manner. A questionnaire is more complex, collecting a wider variety of data, which are subjected to more advanced statistical analysis. Careful checks are made of potential threats to validity and reliability. Both the volume and complexity of the data collected might necessitate the use of computer packages to analyse the data, whether the latter was quantitative or qualitative. The ability of the student to use such packages is likely to result in the data being subjected to a much more detailed analytic procedure. As a consequence, any theories generated from the data are more sophisticated, and any hypothesis testing more rigorous. Through the influence of these and other factors, there are firmer grounds for any generalization from the sample to the research population. The normal assumption is that the doctoral thesis encapsulates an 'original contribution to knowledge'. The master's thesis may well add to our level of understanding, but the findings are more dependent upon, and embedded within, existing knowledge.

However, it would be wrong to assume that there is a clear division between the master's and the doctoral thesis, in the sense that a characteristic is always present in one type of thesis, and never in another. It might be perfectly possible to find one master's thesis where ethical issues are much more thoroughly discussed than in a specific example of a doctoral thesis. Generally, however, the features outlined in the previous paragraphs are a reasonable guide to distinguishing the two levels of thesis. Think of master's and doctoral theses not as two entirely separate levels of academic writing, but rather as lying on a continuum, with some measure of overlap depending upon the overall quality of the research and writing. The broad content of a thesis is discussed in Cryer (1996, pp. 178–9).

9

The thesis as research training

From one point of view, your thesis may be regarded as a major element on the way to achieving a particular qualification. In addition, it is a means by which you can gain an understanding of research methods and procedures in order to be able to follow the thesis with some original research which may lead to publication in an academic journal. In master's degree programmes, there is often a module or course in research methods which is delivered prior to commencement of the thesis. The 'taught' element on EdD and some PhD programmes also fulfils this function of preparation for the thesis.

For most theses, however, the usual requirement is that the student prepares a research proposal. This is a synopsis of the proposed research, and is usually submitted for approval before the data collection for the research can be started. In the case of a master's degree, it is often the supervisor who approves the proposed research. In doctoral programmes the research proposal may have to be submitted to a committee of experienced supervisors for their comments, and may, in addition, be sent anonymously to academic referees.

Research proposal

A research proposal sets out very clearly the research which is intended, and the methods which it is anticipated will be used. There is no rigid structure for a proposal, but it explains, in a succinct manner, the key aspects of the research:

- A brief introduction explains the subject of the research, and the reasons for considering it a suitable topic to investigate.
- Enumerate briefly the aims of the research.
- An indication of some of the relevant research literature enables the reader to understand the context of the research. It is not necessary to do more than suggest some of the principal sources of literature, and some of the most recent and relevant research studies on related themes.
- There must be a clear summary of the proposed research design, and of the intended means of collecting and analysing data.
- It is also helpful to discuss the ethical issues which have been taken into account in developing the design.
- The reader is also interested in seeing a broad plan of the projected timescale for the research. This need only be approximate at this stage, but it at least indicates that some thought has been given to this area.
- The proposal concludes with a list of references.

There may be other features which it would be sensible to include, but those already mentioned provide a reasonable synopsis of the intended research. The proposal is not usually for very long; between 1,500 and 3,000 words should suffice.

The idea of submitting a research proposal has a number of advantages both for you as the research student and for the institution in which your research is being carried out. Most importantly, it enables you to receive feedback and advice on the proposal. It can be viewed as a form of quality check to help ensure that you are not embarking on an ill-advised project. Experienced researchers will provide advice on ways in which the research design can be improved. They might provide guidance on such issues as sampling or contacting possible respondents. This advice will help you to reflect on the proposal and to adapt and improve it where necessary. This process is an important stage in your development towards becoming an experienced and autonomous researcher. Finally, the review process also helps to give you confidence, in the knowledge that experienced supervisors and researchers have seen and approved the research design. There is also a significant advantage for the institution in which you are working, in that it is aware of the research which is being conducted in its name. For example, if the research is in some way ethically sensitive, it enables special care to be taken in monitoring the research.

Summary – The research proposal

A research proposal should contain:

- A summary of the subject and aims.
- A justification for the research.
- An overview of the context and related literature.
- A summary of the anticipated research design, methodology, and ethical issues.
- The anticipated timescale.

Quite apart from receiving feedback on the proposal, many other aspects of the research process provide learning opportunities for you. One of the major roles of the supervisory team is to integrate a process of learning and training in research methods with the writing of your thesis. In commenting upon drafts of the thesis, supervisors are also engaged in creating learning experiences for you. During the writing of the thesis, there may be opportunities to attend seminars by experienced researchers, training courses in research methods, and research conferences, all of which contribute to your training. The role of the thesis supervisor is discussed in Brown (1997, p. 50).

> ## Example – Research aims
>
> Consider the following aims for a thesis:
>
> 1 To consider the way in which employees receive instructions in an organization.
> 2 To analyse the management style adopted in an organization for the transmission of instructions.
>
> If reviewers were asked to comment on these aims in a proposal, they might point out that the first is rather general, while the second is more precise, including, for example, the concept of 'management style'. The second aim might therefore be more suitable for a doctoral thesis. This is the kind of advice which can be very useful in the early stages of a research project.

The characteristics of a good thesis

In Part 2 of this book we examine systematically the structure of the thesis, but it may be helpful here to explore some of the broad features of a well-written thesis. It is important when writing a thesis to consider those who will eventually read it. In the immediate future these may be the examiners, but later, when the thesis is bound and in a library, many future students may read it. A thesis is a long and complex work, and it is helpful if it can be written and structured in such a way that readers are able to navigate their way through it reasonably easily. It should be written in a clear style which, while doing justice to the academic requirements of the subject, does not use unnecessary jargon. It often helps if the thesis is subdivided into chapters and sections so that the reader can readily follow the developing argument. There should be an easily followed thread of argument running through the thesis, so that readers never reach a point where they are unsure how one section has led to another. To sum up, the thesis should be coherent. The issue of writing for a specific reader is discussed in Northedge (1990, p. 166).

The thesis should have clear aims which are enumerated near the beginning and which provide a rationale and framework for the remainder of the work. The thesis then sets out to explain the way in which the research meets those aims. If some aims are only met partially, then this also is explained. Finally, the conclusion reviews those aims, and discusses the ways in which they have been addressed. In a sense, the aims act as an integrating link throughout a good thesis, setting out the intentions of the research at the beginning and providing a focus for the results and conclusion at the end.

The aims are also very important in influencing the choice of theoretical perspective and methodology. The overall research design should be appropriate to the aims. For example, if the aims of a study are to examine broad trends across a number of different high schools, then the research design needs to use survey techniques, possibly using questionnaires. On the other hand, if the research intends to explore the social context of a group of teachers in a single school, then a case study, ethnographic or interactionist perspective may be more appropriate. Unstructured or semi-structured interviews may be selected as the data collection procedures. In terms of writing the thesis it is important to make these connections clear, and to demonstrate the way in which the research design has evolved from the need to address the aims.

Within the thesis there should be an adequate review of the relevant literature. The literature selected should be sufficiently contemporary to demonstrate the way in which the thesis is building upon recent research. While there will undoubtedly be extracts from different studies and articles, these should not be so numerous that they obscure the prose you write. You therefore need to achieve a balance between the number and length of quotations, and the main text of the thesis. Quotations and extracts should supplement the arguments of the thesis.

While these macro issues in writing are important, you should also pay careful attention to detail. Small errors can be very noticeable. Proofread the thesis carefully, to reduce typographical, punctuation and grammatical errors to a minimum. Check referencing carefully so that details of works cited match in different parts of the thesis. Consistency is very important in a thesis. In a good thesis, there will be consistency in the way the thesis is written and structured. This applies, for example, to the spelling of technical terms, to the use of acronyms, and to the way in which subsections are set out and numbered.

Start the thesis with a clear and well-written abstract. Many readers in a library will read the abstract before deciding whether or not to read the whole thesis. The abstract should provide a succinct overview of the whole research project described in the thesis. It should summarize the context of the research, the aims and research design, the results and the conclusion. Finally, it is important not to forget the title. Rather like the abstract, this encapsulates the nature of the thesis. Writing a good title is almost an art form in itself. The title should not be excessively long, but it should describe precisely the nature of the thesis, and ideally include some of the key words associated with the subject of the research. Although we will revisit many of these issues later, it does help at this stage to have an idea of some of the broad features of a well-written thesis. A typical structure is described in Barnes (1995, p. 130).

Summary – Characteristics of a well-written thesis

A well-written thesis should have:

- A clear title and abstract which accurately and succinctly reflect the nature of the research study.
- A structure and format which help the reader to absorb the subject matter.
- An intellectual coherence which starts with precise aims, from which follow the research design, and a clear conclusion.
- Accuracy in grammar and punctuation.
- Consistency in referencing, presentation and the use of terms.

The title of the thesis

As the title of a thesis is likely to be the first aspect read by someone else, it is worth giving considerable thought to how best to phrase it. The title needs to convey quickly and succinctly the subject matter and nature of the thesis. Consider the series of potential titles in the following example box.

Example – Thesis titles

- Elderly patients.
- The care of elderly patients.
- The care of elderly patients in hospital.
- The care of elderly patients with psychological problems in hospital.
- An ethnographic study of the care of elderly patients with psychological problems in hospital.
- A comparative ethnographic study of the care of elderly patients with psychological problems in hospital and in the community.
- A comparative ethnographic study of the care of male elderly patients with psychological problems in hospital and in the community.

Each successive title has one element of detail which is omitted from the previous title. We could continue with the list, adding successively more and more information about the thesis, but the title would become increasingly cumbersome. Common sense suggests that a point is reached at which the title contains sufficient detail to be informative, but not such an excess of information as to be off-putting to a potential reader. The choice of level of detail is to some extent a subjective matter. My personal choice from the list is the fifth option. The word 'ethnographic' tells us about the methodology; 'hospital' informs us of the location of the study; the term 'psychological' indicates the theme of the study; and, finally, the term 'elderly patients' makes clear the subjects of the research. This title includes the key elements of the research, without becoming excessively complex.

Having decided on the key concepts to include, you may wish to reflect on the structure of the title, in order to make it as elegant as possible in a literary sense. The title above could be amended to read for example 'An ethnographic study of the hospital care of elderly patients with psychological problems'.

Academic writing as a genre

There are many different genres of writing, including poetry, short-story writing, formal legal English and business writing. These different styles of writing each have their own characteristics. In much the same way, academic writing is a particular genre, with its own distinctive style, forms of expression and vocabulary. The skills of academic writing can be learned, and anyone who wants to improve their academic writing can acquire such skills. We will look in detail at academic writing skills in Chapter 5, but in the meantime we can explore some of the broad features of the genre.

Academic writing needs to be very clear and precise. In a research context you are writing about complex ideas and these have to be expressed with great precision. Moreover, in research, it is frequently the case that one idea follows from another, or that when analysing data, one procedure follows another. For example, when analysing a group of questionnaires, the researcher first allocates numerical codes to the different alternative responses, and then inputs the raw data into a statistical analysis package. The researcher then computes certain statistical tests, and analyses the results. One process tends to follow logically from another, and this should be reflected in writing about that process. Academic writing thus tends to proceed very logically and systematically, describing first one process, then explaining how this relates to the next issue, and then describing the second process. Good academic writing makes clear the linkages between the different aspects of the subject being described or analysed.

Objectivity

As a general rule, academic writing tends to avoid mentioning the personal feelings or attitudes of the researcher. The emphasis is normally upon considering the research process in an objective manner. It is for this reason that the traditional approach to academic writing uses the third person singular rather than the first person. However, many interpretative approaches to research, typically using qualitative data, tend to take the view that the researcher almost inevitably has an effect upon other research participants during the collection of data. Hence interpretative researchers often feel that it is permissible, and even desirable, to write at least partially in the first person, in order to explain the particular orientation which they bring to the research process. Such reflexive accounts are often a very desirable element in accounts of interpretative research. Thus, as in all genres of writing, conventions are not fixed and rigid, but are evolving, in parallel with developments in newer approaches to research.

Justifying arguments

When writing a thesis it is normal to include a variety of arguments, inferences, deductions or propositions. These may be based upon an analysis of the relevant literature, an analysis of data which has been collected or, even, upon personal experience. However, it is the norm in academic writing to provide some form of justification for these assertions. A typical justification is to point to previous research and to argue that the new assertion can be seen as reasonable in the light of that. A variant of this type of justification is to refer to previous literature on the topic being considered. This literature may include research articles, or perhaps the writing of a noted authority in the field. However, it is perhaps not always a satisfactory justification to rely solely upon a noted authority, without ensuring that those comments or writing are clearly derived from research data. Finally, the writer makes assertions based upon the data which have been collected specifically for the thesis. Although the appropriate substantiation of assertions is a key feature of academic writing, a related feature is the manner in which such assertions are made.

Signpost to success – Justification of arguments

Check the arguments you are making, and ensure that they are soundly based on logic and evidence.

Academic writing tends to be characterized by the rather provisional manner in which assertions and claims to truth are made. Even though the evidential basis of assertions is clearly established, there is still a reluctance to be too definite in terms of claims to truth. Hence in a thesis, it is more desirable to use phrases such as 'the evidence would appear to suggest that . . . ' or 'one might wish to argue that . . .' in preference to more definite claims. The reason for this approach is ultimately based upon ideas from the philosophy of knowledge. It is generally considered in the social sciences that it is very difficult to know anything with absolute certainty. No matter how much apparently overwhelming evidence there is for something being true, you can always conceive that in the future, some contrary evidence might appear. The general approach to the writing style for a thesis thus tends to be one of caution, and using expressions which reflect this tentative position.

Using specialist vocabulary

Inevitably, academic writing employs a great deal of technical vocabulary. It is quite understandable that a thesis should contain a number of specialist terms. However, it is always worth reminding ourselves that arguably the prime purpose of writing is to communicate, and hence we should be very careful about the necessity of employing highly specialized terms. If a specialist term is the correct and widely accepted form of referring to a concept, then its use is completely justified. However, it is important not to stray into the practice of using complicated terms in the hope that they will make the thesis sound more impressive! If we do this, we are likely to be open to accusations of using jargon.

These, then, are some of the features of academic writing. We explore these in more detail in later chapters, but for now we can examine the ways in which some of these features are reflected in typical university requirements for a thesis.

General university requirements for a thesis

Before discussing these, it is perhaps worth reminding ourselves of the variation in university regulations regarding theses. There is no such thing as a 'standard' master's or doctoral thesis, as each university may have slightly different requirements in terms of such aspects as length, style of binding, or the formal wording to be included on the title page. In addition, on some 'taught' courses, there may be a recommended structure for the thesis, in terms of the names and order of the chapters. Generally, however, the differences between university requirements are relatively minor, especially when compared with the large number of similarities. Universities usually make their requirements clearly available to students, and such requirements often include some of the following features.

There are usually specifications concerning the length of the thesis, the font size for the typing and the spacing between lines. The thesis normally should be typed on only one side of the paper. The length of the thesis can have a considerable effect upon the writing style. For example, in taught doctorates, such as the EdD, which often have a shorter thesis, a more succinct writing style is needed, which is less discursive than in a PhD.

Normally the thesis has to have an abstract which is typically placed immediately after the title page. The abstract is regarded as an important summary statement. Prior to the examination procedure, the thesis is usually temporarily bound, although this binding may be more formal for a doctoral thesis than a master's thesis. After the thesis has been assessed and approved, it is permanently bound ready for being placed in the library. Alternatively, universities are increasingly employing virtual repositories, where theses are stored electronically. If you need to have the traditional book binding, it is important that you check the sequence of procedures for temporary and then permanent binding, as institutions do have different requirements. For permanent binding, there are individual regulations governing such matters as the colour of the cloth for the binding, and for the presentation of the lettering on the front and spine of the thesis. Sometimes the quantity of material in the appendix may necessitate the thesis being divided into two volumes to be separately bound. Again, check that this is acceptable. The assessment process may involve passing the thesis subject to some minor corrections. Once these have been made and officially approved, then usually the thesis may be permanently bound. The making of the award by the university may be subject to the submission of a copy of the permanently bound thesis. The precise formalities of these final stages of the process may differ between institutions, and it is important that you ensure you are familiar with them.

Quality and funding bodies

When you embark on a thesis or a research degree, you probably hope and expect that there is a certain amount of consistency between universities in the way they teach you and look after you. You hope that two different universities have similar standards, in order that their qualifications are comparable. It is clearly in the interests of universities generally that there exist systems to assure this type of comparability. In the United Kingdom (UK), the body which specifies the standards expected of postgraduate research programmes is the Quality Assurance Agency for Higher Education (QAA). This organization publishes a code of practice, which details in broad terms what is expected of universities. It covers such aspects of research degree programmes as the admission of students, the supervision of research and of theses, the development of research skills and mechanisms by which your progress as a research student can be monitored (QAA, 2004). The code of practice does not try to specify the exact mechanisms by which its standards will be met, but instead concentrates on rather broad principles.

When universities receive funding to support the postgraduate research students on their courses, there is an assumption that the university concerned is meeting the requirements of the code of practice. Universities in England receive income from the Higher Education Funding Council for England (HEFCE). The income received by a university depends on factors such as the number of research students enrolled, and the quality of the academic research conducted at the university. The latter has been measured in the UK, through the Research Assessment Exercise; although this is to be replaced in 2014 by the Research Excellence Framework. These procedures use academics from a variety of universities to evaluate the research being conducted in a particular institution. Some students also receive financial support from one of the seven UK Research Councils (see Research Councils UK, 2012).

While you are working on your thesis, you will probably be unaware of this complex administrative system which is operating behind the scenes. However, it is there to give you confidence that you are being taught and supervised to agreed standards.

Consulting research theses

One of the most useful exercises when you are planning to write a thesis is to read existing theses in the general area of your research. Quite apart from issues about content and subject matter, it is often very helpful to see the way in which other research students have approached both the structure and writing of their theses. It is probably too time-consuming to read a great many from cover to cover, but it is possible to look quickly through a few for ideas on broad presentational issues.

Most theses are written to a general pattern of discussing the literature and methodology first, and then analysing the data. However, within this broad pattern, there are many different ways of dividing a text into chapters and then into subsections. It is always interesting to see the ways in which different students have achieved this. In some, subsections are numbered using a hierarchical numbering system, and it is often interesting to see how this is approached in different theses. Charts, diagrams, tables and illustrations are also presented in different ways, and it can be very helpful to get ideas on ways in which these may be successfully integrated into the text.

Writing style

In terms of writing style, it is always useful to read a number of different abstracts. The writing of a successful précis demands considerable skill, and reading a number of examples can help enormously when it comes to writing one yourself. When discussing the background literature to a research study, it is not always easy to integrate extracts from the literature with your own discussion. It is often necessary to write sentences which link together the quotations with your own discussion, in order to create a flowing prose style. If this is not done, artificial disjunctions occur between the quotations and your analysis. It is useful to examine whether other writers have been successful in achieving a coherent style.

It can also be very instructive to read the conclusion to a thesis. It is here that the writer has the task of summarizing the results and findings, and it is interesting to read the way in which different writers approach this task. It is often a good idea in the conclusion to reconsider the aims which were delineated at the beginning of the thesis. This is an opportunity for the writer to assess the extent to which the aims have been achieved. It is also interesting to analyse the linguistic style used by the writer in summarizing any claims to new knowledge. Sometimes this is done using provisional expressions in order to indicate the tentative nature of the claims, and on other occasions you might find that a writer makes rather more definite claims. It is, first, a matter of academic judgement about how strongly one can make assertions and, secondly, a matter of linguistic style concerning how those assertions may be appropriately expressed.

This chapter has been an introduction to some of the main features of academic writing in the context of theses. There now follows a list of further reading which may be helpful in extending your knowledge of this issue. Each subsequent chapter also has a list of relevant further reading.

Further reading

Craswell, G. (2004) *Writing for Academic Success: A Postgraduate Guide*. London: Sage.

Delamont, S. (1997) *Supervising the PhD: A Guide to Success*. Buckingham: Open University Press.

HEFCE (2010) *Guide to Funding: How HEFCE Allocates its Funds*. London: HEFCE.

Punch, K. (2006) *Developing Effective Research Proposals*. 2nd edn. London: Sage.

Research Excellence Framework (2012) *Submission System: Pilot User Guide* (REF 2014). London: HEFCE.

Thody, A. (2006) *Writing and Presenting Research*. London: Sage.

Wilkinson, D. (2005) *The Essential Guide to Postgraduate Study*. London: Sage.

2

The Intellectual Content of the Thesis

This chapter deals with strategies for writing about the academic content of a thesis. You will learn about the role of the thesis in making an original contribution to knowledge, and consider the incorporation of data within the thesis. We explore some of the fundamental philosophical terms which may be employed, and discuss strategies for integrating them in the text. Finally, you will learn about different approaches to the presentation of arguments and claims to knowledge.

Study Strategies

- Keep a record of phrases which academic writers use to express the provisional nature of their findings. You will find such phrases in theses, research-based books and academic journal articles. Analyse such phrases, and then try to develop new ones to use in your own writing.
- Keep a record of the kinds of evidence used by academic writers to support their arguments. Look carefully at the way in which they express their argument, and then integrate their supporting evidence. Try to develop your own writing style to achieve this.
- Look at the concluding chapter of a variety of theses, and gain an idea of how the researcher has expressed their 'original contribution to knowledge.'

The thesis as an original contribution to knowledge

When you are first designing your research and, in particular, when you are thinking of a potential title for your thesis, one concern is whether someone else has investigated the same topic before. Specifically, has another student written a thesis with the same, or a very similar title? Underlying this concern is usually that you do not wish to be thought of as repeating someone else's research, and hence not be able to draw any new conclusions or add anything to the sum total of human understanding. This raises the rather complex issues of, first, the nature of the concept of new knowledge and, second, the nature of our ideas of originality.

Let us imagine a situation where a research student wishes to explore the attitudes of some high school students to course work assignments, as opposed to examinations, as a form of assessment. During the preliminary design of the research, she discovers that during the previous academic year, another researcher had conducted an investigation into the same topic, in the same school, with a different cohort of students. The researcher immediately considers whether she should abandon the project and develop a new idea. However, even though the theme of the research is the same, there are a number of significant differences which suggest that the new research project is still capable of generating new knowledge. First, the students are not the same, and for a variety of reasons may have different attitudes to those of the previous cohort. The researcher, too, is different, and brings different research skills and approaches to the research. There may well be a different type of interaction between researcher and respondents which will generate new data. In addition, and importantly, the students this year will have had a different range of educational experiences from the students last year. They may not have had the same discussions on assessment with their teachers; they may have read articles on assessment procedures in newspapers which have helped to form their attitudes; and they will probably have had discussions among themselves on these issues. In short, the research context this year will almost certainly be very different from the research situation last year. Even though the subject of the enquiry may be the same, the contextual issues are very different, and hence it does not seem unreasonable to conduct the research this year as originally planned.

Example – Original contribution to knowledge

An original contribution to knowledge does not need to be something which has a sweeping, worldwide impact. More often it may appear rather limited in scale. For example, in a study of undergraduate student attitudes to assessment grades, it may be found that: 'In the sample, it appeared that students generally preferred to receive a percentage grade, than a more general descriptor such as "satisfactory" or "very good". The lecturers in the sample, on the other hand, appeared to prefer to give general descriptors. More research is needed to explore this issue further, both in different institutions, and across different subject areas.'

Not only may a contribution to knowledge be fairly limited, but it does not represent an end to enquiry in the area. It may merely point the way to the need for further research.

Distinguishing between data and knowledge

Of course, it is important in this and other situations to distinguish between new data and new knowledge. New data does not of itself constitute new knowledge. The data has to be analysed and interpreted before it can be said to have yielded fresh insights and understanding. This kind of discussion provides us with a further way of conceptualizing the distinction between a master's and a doctoral thesis. They both involve the collection of broadly the same kind of data, such as questionnaire or interview data. Although the doctoral thesis will almost certainly involve the collection of a more substantial amount of data, there is no essential difference between the nature of the data. However, it is in the process of data analysis that a distinction is likely to emerge. The analysis of the data for the master's thesis is more superficial. It concentrates on summarizing and describing the data. The latter may be grouped into categories, or summarized by using descriptive statistics such as percentages or standard deviation.

The doctoral thesis is likely to employ a more sophisticated form of analysis. For example, if the data is qualitative, there may be an attempt through a process of induction to develop a new theory which is grounded in the original data. If the data is quantitative, then inferential statistical methods will be employed to try to develop possible causal connections between variables. This is the reason for the use of the term 'original contribution to knowledge' in the context of the doctorate, but not in the context of the master's degree. Master's theses tend to present the empirical data in a summary form which describes the nature of the world. The doctoral thesis, on the other hand, attempts to go further, and explains the reasons for the world existing as it does. The analysis may look for explanations, reasons, influences, causes and generalizations. The doctoral thesis will try to develop a novel way of looking at the world, and of making sense of our surroundings. Such a thesis is 'original' because it tries to enable us to view a topic in a new light.

The different kinds of data and evidence which can be included in a thesis

A research thesis is based upon many different kinds of data. Each type of data is normally associated with one or more approaches to analysis. Questionnaire survey data, for example, is associated with statistical analysis; interview data may be analysed using the techniques of grounded theory; and conversational data may be analysed using ethnomethodological techniques. These links are not exclusive. There are a variety of other possible connections between type of data and approach to data analysis. Of particular importance for this book is that each pairing of data and analysis technique is associated with a particular approach to academic writing.

Survey data

We start by considering survey data and statistical analysis. Many students like to employ a self-completion questionnaire in their research, and often devote a great deal of time to the questionnaire design and to piloting the questionnaire. When the completed questionnaires are returned, students often feel that they have collected a great deal of data. In one sense, of course, this is true. However, once the questionnaires have been coded and the data entered into a statistics package, it gradually becomes evident that the data may become condensed into a very brief summary of statistics. Not only this, but in reality, it may be rather difficult to write a particularly long commentary on a few statistics. In other words, the research student may have put in a great deal of work, yet the end result may not provide very much material on which to write a full-length thesis. The situation can be improved slightly, by ensuring that the questionnaire includes some open-ended questions which require written commentaries, rather than exclusively 'closed' questions requiring simply a box to be ticked. This may appear to be rather a trivial issue in the elevated academic concerns of writing a thesis but, on a very basic level, you need sufficient data upon which to comment in order to write, say, 80,000 words for a PhD. This is an important issue, and can easily be overlooked.

In terms of writing style when discussing quantitative data, it is even more than usually important to be very precise in what one says. The techniques of inferential statistics are fundamentally based upon probability theory. They do not indicate whether or not something is true, but they provide us with evidence of the likelihood of something being true. It is therefore very important when discussing statistics to qualify any assertions which we make. For example, it would not be seen as desirable to write that 'the result of the chi square test shows that . . .', or perhaps even less desirable, 'the result of the chi square test proves that . . .'. It would probably be better to say that 'the result of the chi square test appears to suggest that. . .'. Furthermore, a word which can easily be used in a misleading fashion in writing about statistics is the word 'significant'. This word has a specific meaning in discussing statistics, and refers to a measure (expressed as a percentage) of the confidence we may have in accepting or rejecting a hypothesis. Of course, the word also has an everyday sense of indicating that something is of importance or relevance. When discussing statistical results it is preferable to avoid the word in its everyday sense, otherwise some confusion may result.

Qualitative data

As a general rule, qualitative data is much more voluminous than quantitative data. Whereas quantitative data may be condensed into several short tables, qualitative data can often seem to be so extensive that the major problem is deciding on the sections to omit. The sheer quantity of qualitative data can make it unmanageable. The first time students transcribe a tape-recording of a fairly short interview, they are usually astonished at both the magnitude of the task, and at the quantity of written data which results from a short recording. Examples of different research methods deriving from qualitative and quantitative data are discussed in Anderson (1998, pp. 85–93).

One of the first issues which can arise in the use of qualitative data is the process whereby some data is selected to be included in the thesis, and other data is omitted. It is clearly important to have precise methodological criteria for selecting some data and rejecting others, but in the context of the writing process, it is also important to have a policy on the inclusion of extracts from the data.

The usual strategy with, say, interview data, is to include verbatim extracts from the interviews in the text. These extracts are employed as the evidential basis of the arguments developed in the thesis. However, because there is usually a great deal of data available, there is often a natural tendency to include rather too much data. It is essential in a thesis to strike a reasonable balance between the number of extracts from the data, and the amount of discussion by the writer. At one extreme, if there are too many extracts and quotations then the data assumes a disproportionate importance, and there is insufficient room for analysis. On the other hand, if the writer provides insufficient quotations, then the arguments in the analysis will not be adequately supported. As with many issues, it is really a question of finding a suitable compromise. An approximate guide might be that the total number of words of analysis should be double the total number of words of quotations. People may differ in opinion, but this would be a reasonable guide.

What is essential, however, is that the quotations and the analysis are combined into an integrated whole. It is here that the style of writing matters a great deal. It is very easy to add extracts from interview data in such a way that they appear as isolated sections of text, disembodied from the main writing. Sentences can be added in such a way that they link the analysis and the extracts. For example, just before an extract from the data, you could write, 'In the following extract from the interview with the chemistry teacher, she highlights the problem of technician resources in the laboratory'. This kind of linking sentence provides the reader with an idea of what is to come, and enables the reader to adjust to thinking about the content of the extract.

It is relatively straightforward with extracts from interview data to ensure that the reader is clear that these are quotations. The usual convention is to indent the quotation, and use either a smaller font, italics, closer line spacing or a combination of these. The quotations are then clearly separated from the main text. Some kinds of data, such as observational data, field notes and ethnographic data, may be relatively similar to the main text, because they have been written by the author of the thesis, and hence contain, for example, some preliminary analysis. It is important to make sure, when extracts from field notes are used specifically as data, that this is made clear by the manner in which the data is inserted in the main text.

Reflexive accounts

An interesting addition to the process of analysing qualitative data is to include a reflexive or reflective account. This is essentially an attempt by researchers to reflect upon their own intellectual background and perspective which have provided the context for their analysis of the data. Academic writers often acknowledge the value of making their own academic perspective clear. For example, an author might write in the introduction to a book that 'this is written from the perspective of a committed Marxist' or 'I have written this book within the framework of my belief in the virtues of a free market economy'. Such open and public declarations enable the reader to set any truth claims and assertions within the book in context. Readers are able to attribute more weight to some arguments than to others, depending upon their understanding of the arguments within the stated perspective.

The reflexive or reflective account, to some extent, serves this purpose in a thesis. It acknowledges that while students do try to write their thesis in an unbiased and balanced manner, complete objectivity in research, as in life, is not easy to achieve. In the reflexive account the researcher tries to discuss, in as open a manner as possible, the various influences which have formed his or her particular academic perspective. The assumption, then, is that the reader will be able to take this into account, in reading and evaluating the analysis in the thesis. The reflexive account is often placed at the end of the thesis, although it can be positioned wherever it would be of most use to the reader.

A reflexive account can contain a variety of material, depending upon the significance attached by the researcher to the various intellectual influences in his or her life. There may be an account of the courses of study they have undertaken, and mention of the institutions where they have been students. Books which the researcher has found particularly helpful or informative may be mentioned, along with conferences attended or countries visited. If relevant, the researcher may also include such issues as the influence of family or friends, various aspects of employment, or the influence of spare-time activities. In short, the reflexive account is an opportunity to outline the personal and subjective perspectives which the researcher brings to the data collection and analysis process. Issues of reflexivity are discussed in Steier (1991).

Example – A reflexive account

In a comparative study of social influences in a state school and a fee-paying school, it would probably be relevant for the researcher to provide at least some detail of his or her own schooling. If the researcher had attended, say, a private school, it would be helpful to discuss how they perceived socialization in that school. In addition, they could describe how they attempted to set these influences on one side, in order to try to achieve an objective and balanced account in the thesis.

Conceptual analysis

Some data may derive from the analysis of the concepts used in the research, and may be described as analytic data. In the early stages of a thesis, for example, it is often necessary to try to define the key concepts which are at its heart. Such definitions will rarely be complete, but will at least map out something of the parameters of the terms. For instance, in a thesis devoted to the theme of 'teacher autonomy' in terms of determining the curriculum, it would be desirable to establish a working definition of autonomy, in order to illuminate the later discussions.

The problem with a concept such as autonomy is that one person may feel that they have more or less complete freedom of action, whereas another person may feel constrained and restricted under exactly the same circumstances. One way of proceeding in such a case is to identify a number of different situations in which the word 'autonomy' is used in education, and then to explore the characteristics of the use of the word in the different contexts. However, following such analysis, it is unlikely that there will be any truly empirical means by which it can be argued that one definition of 'autonomy' is superior to another definition. You might point to the apparently logical consistencies or inconsistencies of the use of the concept in different situations, but it is unlikely that you could reasonably assert a final definition of autonomy. You would be left with a range of situations within which the term appears to have significant inter-subjective meanings for human beings, and some idea of the logical foundations of those meanings. It is therefore important in a thesis to be able to recognize those issues which are susceptible to empirical verification, and those which require an analysis of concepts.

Example – Empirical and conceptual questions

Sometimes the aims of a thesis may be superficially similar, but one may be empirical while the other is conceptual. Consider the following two aims:

1 To analyse the views of people as to whether capital punishment is right or wrong.
2 To analyse the issue of whether capital punishment is right or wrong.

The first aim will require the collection of data on people's views, and the subsequent analysis of that data. The second aim will require an analysis of the terms 'right' and 'wrong' in the context of capital punishment, and does not necessarily require any empirical data.

Summary – Types of data in a thesis

- The arguments in a thesis may be based upon the analysis of empirical data, or upon the analysis of concepts.
- Empirical data may be qualitative or quantitative.
- Quantitative data may be collected by such methods as questionnaires or rating scales.
- Qualitative data may be collected by methods such as interviews, life history accounts or discussion groups.

Working within a paradigm and incorporating a theoretical perspective

One of the most important elements of a research thesis (and particularly of a doctoral thesis) is the incorporation within it of a theoretical foundation. At master's level it may be sufficient in a minority of cases to discuss the collection and analysis of some data, without setting this process within a theoretical framework. Generally, however, it is preferable to employ a theoretical framework of some kind at both master's and doctoral level. The theoretical framework employed would normally be more sophisticated at doctoral level.

One of the unfortunate problems with terms such as 'theoretical framework', 'theoretical perspective' and 'paradigm', is that they tend to be used by different writers in slightly different ways. However, the problem can be resolved by first employing a working definition of the terms used and secondly, employing the terms consistently throughout the thesis. The term 'paradigm' is normally used to refer to the broad world view which informs an approach to research. For example, you might refer to a scientific paradigm, suggesting that you are working within the broad tenets of the scientific approach. This would probably imply adherence to such principles as the provision of rational arguments to support assertions, the collection of evidence in a systematic manner, and the making of truth claims in such a way that it would be clear on what basis they might be rationally refuted. Research theses within the social sciences would be written usually within such a paradigm, and it may not be necessary for you to discuss their theoretical approach at this level of generality. The nature of a paradigm is discussed in Creswell (1998, p. 74).

The term 'theoretical perspective', however, is used to refer to the more specific assumptions made in terms of conducting research. For instance, you might write of operating within an interpretative perspective. This would indicate to the reader that you are making certain assumptions about the nature of the data which have been collected, and also about the process of analysis to which the data has been subjected. Within this particular perspective, for example, the researcher is not seen as the determinant of the nature of the social world; rather, a focus is placed upon the way in which the research respondents view the world and the research issue in question. Similarly, the way in which respondents see the world, and provide data about it, is not necessarily perceived as having a permanent nature. It is accepted that respondents may change their views on issues, and that to some extent the data which is provided by participants depends upon the changing interactions between human beings. Within the interpretative perspective, it is not assumed that there are predetermined social facts which can be collected and analysed, but rather that the social world exists in a state of fluid interaction, and that it has to be interpreted to be at least partially understood.

It is generally important then that such assumptions are made clear in a thesis, and that the particular perspective which has been adopted is explained to the reader. This helps the reader to understand better the ideas behind the research design and the data analysis process. The thesis will not only have a stronger theoretical basis, but is likely to be more easily understood by the reader.

Example – Theoretical perspectives

- A positivist perspective tends to assume that the research methods of the natural sciences may generally be applied to the social sciences, including education.
- Positivism tends to be associated with the use of quantitative data.
- Interpretivism is associated with a number of perspectives used in research including phenomenology, interactionism, feminism, ethnography and action research. Such perspectives tend primarily to employ qualitative data.

The relationship between ontology, epistemology and methodology

These three concepts are closely related to the previous ideas of paradigm and perspective but are used in different ways. Ontology and epistemology are both important terms in philosophy, and are used by students to varying degrees when discussing theoretical issues in their thesis. The term 'ontology' may be used to refer to the fundamental nature of the world and what it means to exist in that world. One of the basic ontological distinctions, for instance, is about the possible nature of the entities which researchers seek to measure. For example, you may perceive the world as being made up of entities which exist in the world, independently of human existence and of human thought. Alternatively, you might consider the world as being basically a function of human thought, analysis and perception. Although ontological issues have considerable theoretical importance, many students, even at doctoral level, would probably not feel the need to discuss their research in these terms. Nevertheless, ontological concerns are connected with the epistemological basis of research.

Epistemology, in philosophical terms, is the study of the grounds on which we claim to know something about the world. In the sense that a doctoral thesis should make a contribution to knowledge, then it is important that you should be able to indicate, at least in broad terms, the basis for making any claims to truth. The term 'epistemology' may be used, for example, in the context of a 'positivist epistemology', indicating that the truth claims in the thesis are based upon the broad tenets of the natural sciences. In such a case, the epistemological assumptions might be, for example, that the proposal and testing of a hypothesis, involving the collection of empirical (and perhaps specifically quantitative) data, would be a satisfactory means for generating new knowledge. We can see, therefore, that the ontological assumptions which you make about the world, and the nature of measurable reality, do to some extent have implications for the selected epistemological position. If you adopt the ontological position that the world consists of entities which are outside the human mind, then you might feel that a positivist epistemology would be the most appropriate basis for the research. A discussion of the concept of a hypothesis is contained in Punch (1998, pp. 39–41).

Finally, the term 'methodology' may be used in many ways. It is used most commonly for the title of the chapter in a thesis which describes both the design of the research, the theoretical orientation and the approach to data analysis. In this sense, it is a very general term used to refer to the research procedure adopted. However, it is also used to refer more specifically to the data collection process of the research. In this sense, it exists on a logical continuum starting with ontology and epistemology, and ending with methodology. On this interpretation, a particular epistemology might imply the adoption of certain data collection methods. For example, a positivist epistemology might suggest the use of survey methods and questionnaire data to be analysed quantitatively. On the other hand, a non-positivist epistemology implies the use of such methods as unstructured interviews or participant observation.

Example – Definitions of key terms

It may help if you have a succinct statement of the meaning of the above three terms.

Ontology: the study of the fundamental nature of the world. Does the world consist, for example, of independent entities, or are the latter dependent upon human consciousness for their appreciation?
Epistemology: the study of the grounds upon which we make truth claims about the world.
Methodology: the type of data collection and analysis method which follows from a particular epistemological perspective.

In the last two sections, we have explored several different terms which are used to discuss the theoretical aspects of a thesis. On one level it is important to be aware of them, because they are all part of a group of concepts concerned with research theory. However, in many theses, ontology and paradigm are concepts which are rarely used, probably because of their level of generality. On the other hand, epistemology, theoretical perspective and methodology are much more widely used. Nevertheless, it is important in a thesis to do more than simply describe the research design and the data collection methods adopted. The selection of one data collection method implies the rejection of other methods, and in turn, that decision is likely to be based on at least some theoretical basis. It is important to explain that basis, and its associated assumptions in order to allow the reader to appreciate the logical thought process of the researcher.

Signpost to success – Theoretical dimension

Include a theoretical dimension in your research. Make sure you are clear about the reasons for selecting that dimension.

Testing a hypothesis or developing a theory

One means of comparing theses in education or the social sciences is to examine the overall purpose of the thesis. Broadly speaking you can identify theses whose research design is fundamentally concerned with testing a hypothesis and theses which are concerned with the generation of theory. In the former category, the research design typically involves developing a hypothesis from a pre-existing theory, and then testing that hypothesis in order to examine whether the theory appears to retain an explanatory function. Alternatively, some research designs start with the collection of data, and seek to develop a theory which arises out of, and is grounded in, that data.

Whichever approach is adopted in the research design, it is important that it relates to the aims of the research. A hypothesis is not always easy to express, and it should be written in such a form that, first, is clearly testable and, second, is clear as to the nature of the data which would be needed in order to either support or refute it. As a general rule, research designs involving the testing of hypotheses tend to operate using a positivistic epistemology, while designs involving the development of a theory tend to be within an interpretive epistemology.

When testing a hypothesis it is possible to collect data which seems to support it. On the other hand, we may collect data which appears to support the hypothesis now, but yet we may be well aware of the logical possibility of further data which may refute the hypothesis. Another dimension of the issue is that we may only have been able to collect data from a small sample of the entire research population. Thus, even though the data from the restricted sample may appear to support the hypothesis, we need to estimate the likelihood of this result being typical of the whole research population. Such an estimate will almost certainly involve a statistical calculation, and the result will be expressed as a degree of probability. The language used to explain this degree of probability will need to be carefully expressed.

In the case of developing a grounded theory, it is typical of the approach that a great deal of qualitative data is collected, from which broad themes are identified. These themes gradually become more focused and further data is collected, finally resulting in a theory which expresses some of the relationships between the themes.

In writing about such a theory, however, it is important that it is seen as a provisional expression of the nature of the social world, and not as a final statement. The general assumption behind the development of grounded theories is that there always remains the possibility of extending and adapting the theory, so that it reflects more accurately the nature of newly collected data. An analysis of grounded theory is contained in Glaser and Strauss (1967).

Exercising caution in making truth claims

Throughout a thesis, it is important to exercise care in making statements which suggest an absolute or universal validity, or which make claims for which it is difficult to provide substantiating evidence. For example, in the introduction a student may rather incautiously write that 'the subject for this thesis has been chosen because there have been no other studies on this topic'. Unless the subject selected is extremely esoteric, this claim seems rather unlikely. Most subjects will have been studied previously in one form or another. Even though there may not have been previous studies with these exact aims and research design, it is still a very sweeping claim to make without a long and extensive review of the literature on a scale which is probably outside the time and resources of the average research student. It would be much more appropriate to claim that 'there have been few other studies on this particular facet of the subject', or 'although there have been a number of studies on this topic, the particular sample and context of this study gives it a distinctive character'. Such claims are not as far-reaching, and leave scope for the revelation of other studies which, while similar, may not be identical.

In the chapter exploring the relevant literature, it is very easy to make claims which are too extensive. When you have invested a great deal of time in searching for relevant literature on the subject of the thesis, you may be tempted to write that 'the literature on this topic is very sparse'. What you probably mean is that the searches you have made have revealed very little relevant literature. An alternative would be to write that 'following a detailed search, the following sources have been identified'. Not only does this express the issue in a more positive light, but it also avoids making a claim which may be untrue.

Discussing methodology

Methodology is a complex area to write about, and one where it is relatively easy to make unsubstantiated assertions or value judgements. A student might write that 'ethnomethodology is an approach which is rarely used in educational research'. Of course, the use of the word 'rarely' is a little problematic here. The relevance of its use depends very much upon the approaches being compared. Ethnomethodology may not be used as frequently as field research, ethnography or interactionism, but that does not necessarily merit its description as 'rare'. In another case, the researcher might claim that 'a random sample size of forty is adequate for most statistical tests'. You might wish to amend the use of 'adequate' here since it does not take into account such important issues as the size of the sample when compared with the size of the research population.

When relating the aims of the study to the research design chosen, the student might be tempted to write that 'this data collection method has been chosen as the only appropriate method for addressing the aims of the study'. In the case of research aims which have been written in a very precise style, it may well be true that this narrows considerably the research design and methodology which may be used to meet them. However, if there was only one method which could be used to address a set of research aims, then the latter would be expressed in an extremely precise manner. In most cases, it would be much more likely that several possible data collection methods might be suitable. Avoiding the suggestion of absolute certainty is discussed in O'Hara (1998, p. 115).

Presenting alternative viewpoints

Just as it is important to be cautious about making sweeping statements, it is also advisable to present alternatives to the specific line of argument which has been adopted. As an initial illustration we consider the manner in which much interview data is analysed in research studies. When interview data has been transcribed, the researcher begins to analyse and interpret the data, either developing concepts which emerge from the data, or employing concepts from a previous theoretical orientation. It is an almost inevitable part of this process that certain sections of the transcribed data are selected for use in the developing argument, while certain parts are omitted and discarded. Nevertheless, it is often the case that within the discarded elements, there exist potential concepts which could support an evolving argument. Hence, although it may be that the principal part of the data supports a particular line of argument, there may be alternative, potential arguments which are embedded in the data. It is important to articulate these alternatives, as it demonstrates that the data in its entirety is being employed to develop theory.

The act of presenting alternative viewpoints is a reflection and acknowledgement of the multifaceted nature of the social world. In any research issue it is very often possible to explore it from a number of different research perspectives. Each different approach is potentially capable of shedding fresh light on the research issue. For instance, we might consider the research issue of teacher attitudes to discipline in the classroom. If we undertook a major survey of a large number of teachers, we may be able to identify broad trends in opinion, but the deeper feelings of teachers about this issue would probably not be disclosed through this approach. On the other hand, if we treated a small group of teachers as a case study, and collected detailed interview and participant observation data, then we may very well identify many different facets of the research issue. Other methodological approaches may reveal their own distinctive insights.

If we then sought to argue on the basis of only one method of enquiry that an all-embracing understanding of an issue had been reached, then this would appear to be illogical. It would be more appropriate to argue that while one methodology had suggested certain insights, other approaches may result in different provisional conclusions. It would not be unreasonable for the writer to indicate a preference for one form of argument compared with another, provided that reasons were articulated for this preference.

There are various strategies for expressing the existence of alternative viewpoints. To take the above example of classroom discipline, you might write that '84 per cent of teachers in the sample considered that there were insufficient sanctions in place to deter indiscipline in the classroom. However, this would appear to be a far from simple issue, as preliminary interviews suggest that teachers have a diversity of views on the nature of appropriate sanctions'. This does not try to assert that there is a single straightforward analysis of the issue, but rather that there are alternative perceptions, all of which have some relevance.

Developing a coherent argument

A thesis should gradually develop a coherent argument which is apparent to readers as they progress through it. The starting point for this argument is the aims of the thesis. These lead logically to a set of theoretical assumptions reflected in a particular perspective, and subsequently to a strategy for collecting data. The theoretical assumptions will probably suggest a specific approach to the analysis of the data, which will finally affect the manner in which the conclusions are drawn.

For example, if the aims of a thesis are primarily concerned with exploring the feelings of school pupils about the careers education which they receive, then it may be that these would suggest an interpretative approach to the research. This, in turn, may result in a case study method being used, collecting data using interviews and a life-history approach. The data may then be analysed inductively to try to generate a theory which explains the attitudes towards career education. Perhaps the key issue here is that the reader should be able to discern this approach throughout the thesis.

A thesis, particularly a PhD, is a very long document to read, and it is easy for the reader to lose sight of the arguments which you are trying to develop. It is here that you can help the reader, by returning periodically to the main thread of the argument. In later chapters it can be a useful strategy to refer the reader back to earlier stages of the argument. For example, you might write that 'this analysis is related to the second overall aim of the study, outlined on page 19 of chapter 1'. Alternatively, you might say that 'the context of this project, as outlined in the introduction, has had implications for this choice of research design'.

Such references help the reader to move their attention backwards and forwards through the thesis, and to better appreciate the writer's line of argument. Although emphasis has been placed here on the issue of coherence, this is not to overlook previous comments about presenting alternative viewpoints. One can allude to alternative interpretations, while still maintaining the principal line of argument.

Intellectual content of a shorter thesis

It is important that we address the particular issues in writing within the new styles of doctorate, the so-called 'taught' or 'professional' doctorates. As these doctorates usually incorporate a shorter thesis than is traditionally the case, it is important to take care to assure the intellectual content of the thesis. There may be a danger that, in keeping down the word length, there is an insufficient or too superficial discussion of issues, with the result that the case for an original contribution to knowledge is not made. This could clearly have adverse consequences at the viva.

The dilemma then is to find ways of reducing the length of the text, while at the same time maintaining the scholarly standard of the argument, and in particular establishing a strong case for an original contribution to knowledge. During the writing of a traditional PhD, you can, to some extent, slowly and systematically construct arguments, without concerning yourself too much about the number of words being used. The shorter doctoral thesis, however, demands a much more focused approach, within which there is no room for repetition, or for material which is not directly concerned with the immediate thread of the argument. We now consider several possible strategies which together could be employed to reduce the length of a thesis, while still maintaining the doctoral level of the writing.

One general strategy is to try to adopt a succinct writing style, and to reduce the amount of discussion of technical and specialist terms. In a doctoral thesis, the student is trying to achieve a number of objectives simultaneously. Quite apart from demonstrating the collection and analysis of data, you are also trying to demonstrate an understanding of methodology. In order to demonstrate this to the examiners, you may, from time to time, embark on a discussion of terminology used, in order to demonstrate this wide understanding. For example, if the term 'phenomenological' is used in a sentence, it may be necessary to discuss the nature of phenomenology in order to show that you understand the correct usage. While this may be helpful in a long thesis, it may take up valuable space in a shorter one. Examiners can usually be sure of an understanding of a term simply from its being used in a correct context. In addition, if they wish to explore this, they can decide to ask questions during the viva. In other words, it may not always be necessary to explain terms such as 'positivistic', 'empirical', 'ethnographic' and the many other terms employed in methodology. It is reasonable to assume that the examiners understand them, and your knowledge can always be explored in the oral examination. An at least partial elimination of such discussions may save valuable space in a shorter thesis.

Another area in which savings of space may be made is in relation to the data. Quantitative data can usually be presented in tabular form or as statistics embedded in the text, and usually does not take up very much space. Qualitative data, often consisting of, say, extracts from interview transcripts, may be voluminous. In a typical data presentation and analysis chapter, there may, for example, be four or five extracts from data on each page. It does not seem reasonable that, in reducing a thesis from, say, 80,000 words to, say, 50,000 words, there should not be some economies in terms of the data.

In any qualitative research study, considerable quantities of data are usually discarded for a variety of reasons. The data may not be entirely relevant to the study; it may involve rather superficial, conversational exchanges between interviewer and interviewee; or in terms of content, it may duplicate data which are actually incorporated in the study. For a shorter thesis, the researcher may simply collect less data anyway. But even assuming that approximately the same amount of data are collected, there are simple strategies which can be adopted to reduce the overall length.

When selecting an extract for inclusion in the thesis, it is often tempting to include all the other extracts which appear to be presenting the same argument. It may be possible to include fewer examples and simply indicate the overall number of respondents who have argued from the same perspective. Similarly, instead of including extracts as indented quotations, which do take up considerable space, it may be possible to include shorter extracts and to incorporate them within the main text. In addition, when selecting extracts, savings of space may be made if the number of extracts is restricted to the minimum needed to construct an argument for the research. It is worth remembering that it is rarely necessary to include all of the raw data collected within a thesis. There is an assumption that a great deal more data has been collected but that it is not bound into the thesis. It may, however, be a good idea to explain the grounds and criteria upon which selections of data were made. This makes the process transparent, and reassures the reader that, although there may be a reduced quantity of data, the mechanisms for data selection are understood.

Finally, the demands of a shorter thesis make it essential that a careful balance is created between reviewing previous research on a topic, and analysing data to generate new findings. It is normal in a doctoral thesis to include an extensive review of the relevant literature, and this chapter is very often the longest in the thesis. With shorter theses, it is important that you consider very carefully what may be regarded as 'relevant'. Where savings of space are needed, it may be preferable to concentrate on the most modern research literature, and to eliminate some of the older studies. It may also be necessary to restrict the field from which the literature is drawn. These techniques should result in savings in space, and enable you to concentrate on the later data analysis sections. The importance of the latter is that it is the analysis of the data, and the drawing of conclusions, which establishes the extent to which the thesis contributes to existing knowledge. Ultimately, this is the most important criterion by which the thesis will be judged.

Further reading

Burton, D. and Bartlett, S. (2009) *Key Issues for Education Researchers*. London: Sage.

Silverman, D. (2004) *Doing Qualitative Research: A Practical Handbook*. 2nd edn. London: Sage.

Thody, A. (2006) *Writing and Presenting Research*. London: Sage.

Thomas, G. (2007) *Education and Theory: Strangers in Paradigms*. Maidenhead: Open University Press.

Wellington, J.J., Bathmaker, A. and Hunt, C. (2005) *Succeeding with Your Doctorate*. London: Sage.

3
Organizing Your Work

In this chapter we discuss some of the practical issues involved in organizing the writing of your thesis. We explore ways of planning the structure and provisional chapter lengths, and then discuss strategies by which you can manage your own time effectively. Finally, we examine methods for recording references, and different approaches to the order of writing the thesis chapters.

Study Strategies

- Experiment with different strategies for accumulating data on academic works which you might use for references.
- Build up a data bank of quotations, classified according to various criteria.
- Develop your own annotated bibliography in different subject areas.
- The main requirement is that you are able to abstract the information you need when you want to cite books or articles in your thesis.
- Talk to people who have completed a thesis to pick up tips about how they organized their own work.

Who is the audience for your thesis?

Any writer, in any genre, needs to consider the audience for the work. The readers of a thesis, just like the readers of a novel or of a short story, have certain expectations. In the case of a thesis, however, there are two distinct categories of reader. First, there are those who are involved in the assessment of the thesis. These may be tutors within the institution where you are registered for the qualification and, importantly, the external examiner or examiners from a different university. The second category of reader comprises those people who may consult the thesis when it is finally successful and is placed upon the library shelves. Most students will quite rightly focus upon the first category of reader. Perhaps we can consider, then, some aspects of how examiners see things.

Examiners

One issue which may concern you is how much you should explain certain topics which you are confident the examiner will know about. For example, suppose that you are adopting a symbolic interactionist approach to your research. You may consider the extent to which it is necessary to summarize the basic principles of the perspective, when it is highly likely that the examiner will be familiar with these.

In response to this issue, it is probably best for you to view the thesis as an opportunity to demonstrate your knowledge and understanding. Hence, it is desirable (and perhaps in most cases essential) to present a coherent account of the underlying principles of the approach which has been adopted. This should be balanced in length and detail, of course, depending upon the scale and academic level of the thesis. In general terms, one should not omit information from the thesis on the assumption that the examiner will be familiar with it.

Sometimes, however, this principle can be taken to extremes. When writing about the choice of methodology, and explaining the basis of selecting one approach and rejecting others, there is the temptation to write what amounts to a survey of different research methods. In other words, the student writes a summary of all the research methods which might potentially have been chosen, and then indicates the reason for selecting one of these. This often results in an excessively long methodology chapter, which reads rather like a condensed textbook on research methods! It is usually adequate in this situation to discuss the methodology chosen, its basic assumptions and the reasons for selecting it, and in so doing to allude briefly to the reasons for not adopting other approaches. This is normally sufficient, without adding any more detail.

Example – Questions on methodology

Remember that your examiners will not only want to know the reasons for your choosing a particular methodology, but will also want to know the problems you encountered with it. No methodology is perfect, and during your viva they may well ask you how you might amend the methodology if you were repeating the research. This is partly to test the extent to which you are being self-reflective.

Grammar and presentation

Another area in which you can help the reader is grammar and punctuation. Good grammar and punctuation are of enormous practical help to the reader. If a comma is omitted in a crucial position, it may significantly alter the meaning of the sentence, or render it difficult to understand. This may result in the examiner needing to reread a sentence, in order to begin to grasp the meaning. If such errors are repeated throughout the thesis, then not only is it an irritation, but it can also make the reading process very tiring for the examiner. While some grammatical errors may simply be a nuisance to the reader, other errors may make it very difficult for the examiner to understand the arguments which are being proposed.

Another way in which you can help the reader is in the style of the page format. A thesis often has chapters which are fairly long, and the use of subheadings is very helpful in providing a structure for each chapter. Often, the researcher will divide the subsections, producing a hierarchy of sections. It is important that each level of subsection in the hierarchy has its own characteristic font for the title. It may be indicated using italicization, bold text or underlining, or simply by font size. The important issue is to help the reader to be aware of the type of subsection being read at any one time. This helps readers to work their way through the thesis, and to follow the arguments being made. The use of subheadings in text is discussed in Drew and Bingham (2001, p. 93).

The length of the thesis and of individual chapters

As we saw in Chapter 1, theses differ considerably in length, depending upon the type of master's degree or doctorate. It is important that you comply with the university regulations on this matter. Individual courses often have their own specific regulations. A word length may be expressed as a maximum, or as a 'normal' maximum, or as a range from a lower to a higher limit, or as a specific length with a plus or minus tolerance of say 10 per cent. Some examiners may regard it as a deficiency of a thesis if you significantly exceed the word length, because you have not been able to adequately express your analysis and arguments within the space stipulated. In the case of a thesis which is substantially shorter than required, there is the distinct possibility that there has simply not been the amount of writing to express arguments at the correct academic level. It is therefore important to try to comply as closely as possible to the length required.

Probably the best means of achieving this is to plan the structure of the thesis carefully before you start writing, and then to allocate a specific number of words to each chapter. This provides you with a series of goals. In doing this it is necessary to take decisions about the length of some chapters in relation to others. There will normally be a chapter devoted to a review of the literature of the substantive subject matter, and this chapter will usually be longer than, say, the introduction, and possibly longer than the methodology chapter. In a long chapter such as the literature review, provisional decisions should be taken about the relative lengths of any subsections. At this stage, the planned chapter lengths will necessarily be provisional. Nevertheless, an approximate set of word-length targets makes it much easier to achieve the overall thesis word length.

Example – Thesis plan showing typical chapter lengths

The following plan assumes a thesis length of 50,000 words.

Introduction	5,000 words
Literature review	8,000 words
Methodology	7,000 words
Data presentation and analysis (I)	8,000 words
Data presentation and analysis (II)	8,000 words
Data presentation and analysis (III)	8,000 words
Conclusion and recommendations	6,000 words

This is a guide to the possible apportionment of the total word length to individual chapters. However, the structure of different theses will vary considerably. For example, theses based on qualitative data may require longer data presentation and analysis chapters than theses based upon quantitative data.

Implications for writing style

The length of a thesis also has certain implications for the writing style which is adopted. For example, a doctoral thesis of 50,000 words imposes certain restrictions upon the researcher which are not present in a doctoral thesis of 80,000 words.

The fundamental issue is that, in both theses, you still have to present work which is an original contribution to knowledge, and which also demonstrates an adequate understanding of relevant research methods. Assuming that the research is of the same broad scale, then you need to adopt strategies for the shorter thesis to ensure that essentially the same sophistication of ideas can be attained within a shorter length.

It may be necessary, for example in the case of qualitative data, to select extracts from the data which are somewhat shorter than normal, or to use fewer extracts. Quotations from books or journal articles may need to be shorter, or more carefully selected. It may be necessary on occasion, when referring to a section in a text, to quote simply the author, date and page number, rather than using an actual quotation. It may also be possible to be more efficient with space in the thesis, by summarizing data in tabular form. This may be much easier with quantitative data than with qualitative data, but it is a strategy worth bearing in mind. Overall, however, the length of the thesis does mean you sometimes need to be more succinct and sometimes more discursive in your writing style.

Practical matters – typing and organizing the developing thesis

Before we start discussing these practical issues, everyone has their own distinctive style of working and it would be unfair to try to recommend one approach to the exclusion of all others. Nevertheless, some approaches to writing a thesis may well save time, and make it easier for you to make amendments and corrections.

Typing the thesis

It is preferable for you to type your own thesis, as this gives you the maximum degree of control over the final manuscript. At every stage of thesis writing you need to make amendments to the manuscript, particularly following discussions with your supervisor. These minor amendments may have a variety of other effects, such as altering the pagination or moving subheadings to the bottom of a page, and it is extremely helpful if you can make adjustments immediately where necessary.

Writing strategies

A thesis is a very large undertaking, and it is almost inevitably written small sections at a time. Usually at the beginning, you take decisions about the font size for headings and subheadings, and about the myriad other factors in ensuring a layout which meets the requirements of the university. However, as the writing proceeds, it is extremely easy to forget the decisions which have been taken about layout, and all kinds of inconsistencies start to develop in your writing. These may not become evident until the completion of the first draft of the whole thesis, when it is read in its entirety. The result is very often a great deal of tedious editing. To some extent it is possible to reduce this type of editing, by maintaining a list of the key formatting decisions as you take them. Such decisions might include the use of capitalization on certain words, the use of acronyms, hyphens and italics, and general issues concerning the layout of, for example, new chapter headings. Whenever such issues recur, this list can then be consulted. It may not eliminate inconsistencies entirely, but it will almost certainly reduce their frequency.

Some students prefer to write substantial parts of the thesis by hand, before word processing. This does have the advantage that a certain amount of editing can be conducted during the process of transferring text to your computer. Nevertheless, even after word processing, it may be necessary to print out the text, and to edit it. If possible, typing directly onto the screen may eventually save time. The editing can then be done in one process. In addition, the disadvantage of writing by hand is that one is never sure about the number of words which have been written, and about the relative lengths of different sections. Typing directly on to your computer enables you to monitor the scope and layout of the work much more easily.

It is also useful to organize the developing thesis in terms of computer files. A good general idea is to save each chapter of the thesis as a separate file. The preliminary pages, such as the title page and the contents, can all be saved as a single file. This also applies to the developing list of references and to appendices. One of the advantages of having separate files for each chapter is that when amendments are made, particularly of the order of, say, an additional paragraph, then the inevitable changes to the positioning of the remainder of the text are not excessive. Indeed, it may be desirable to divide large chapters, such as the review of the literature, into several smaller files for this very reason.

Example – Using electronic files

Saving sections of the thesis as separate files has a number of advantages.

1 If you save the thesis as a single file, even a small change in one part of the thesis could cause major disruption to the text in other parts of the file. This problem is avoided with multiple files.
2 If the thesis is saved as a number of separate files, then there is less danger of losing your work. If one file becomes corrupted or damaged, the other files may be unaffected. In any case, all files should be backed up as a matter of course.
3 With separate files, it is easier to send a portion of the thesis to someone else, for example your supervisor.

Although it is usual practice to save one chapter per file, you can choose how to subdivide your thesis into files. It is easy to amend page numbering of files as you work, and add additional material; or you can wait until the thesis is nearly completed before adding page numbers.

Self-imposed writing targets

Producing a thesis is a many faceted task. You have to conduct an extensive literature search, design the research, collect and analyse the data, and decide on the structure of the thesis. It is very easy to immerse yourself in tasks associated with the literature review and the data collection, and not give sufficient attention to planning the actual thesis. There is a slight but tangible risk that some students may continue diligently with the data collection and analysis, and never start writing the thesis. In the case of a master's degree, they may not start the writing stage until very close to the submission date. Even though all the background reading may have been completed, and the data collected and analysed, some students may experience an enormous reticence at actually starting the writing. This may be because they have very high standards and want every sentence to be perfect, or simply because they do not know quite how to start. These feelings are widespread, and experienced to a greater or lesser extent by everyone who is about to embark on a creative task.

Perhaps the most straightforward strategy for overcoming such natural uncertainties at the beginning of the thesis is simply to start writing it! This may seem over simplistic but, fortunately, computers do enable you to make additions and amendments to text very easily. The best strategy is often to start writing the first draft in the full knowledge that additional references can be added later and the style can be amended any number of times. If you remember that you are only writing a first draft, then to some extent this will help remove some of the anxiety about trying to produce high-quality text from the beginning. Once you have started the writing, the tension is broken, and your writing progresses more smoothly. It is important to have a clear plan about the content of the chapter being written, and this kind of advice is given in the second part of this book.

Schedule

In addition, it can be useful to adopt a comparable approach to planning a time schedule for your writing. When the submission date for a thesis is known, then it is relatively easy to calculate the number of words to be written on average each day. Adjustments should be made to allow a certain number of rest days. The advantage of such writing targets is that you know quite clearly whether or not you are on schedule. This assumes, of course, that your strategy is to write a certain number of words each day, rather than trying to write large sections of the thesis in a concentrated period of time.

Each person will have their own way of working. Some may prefer to write small amounts on a regular basis, while others may prefer to allocate a substantial amount of time to writing, and try to write a major part of the thesis during that period. There is no 'correct' way of working, and the main criterion is ultimately whether the method adopted results in a completed thesis. However, one of the main aspects to remember is that most theses benefit from revision. There is no need to write and rewrite each sentence as the thesis develops, in the hope of attaining perfection with the first version. There are plenty of opportunities later to refine the writing. This, in a sense, is an argument for keeping to self-imposed targets, in the knowledge that the work can be improved later.

Time management and maintaining progress

Research students often find time management difficult. The nature of the problem is different, however, for full-time and part-time students.

Full-time students

Full-time students may be able to devote all of the working week to their research and writing, and their difficulty will be maintaining progress within a largely unstructured period of time. They will have some tutorials, and perhaps research seminars, to attend. From time to time they will also attend conferences and lectures, but a typical week will include long periods when they will be expected to organize their own work patterns. Herein lies the potential problem. Assuming that you know the submission date for the thesis, then it is possible to calculate a desired rate of progress. However, it is not always easy to ensure that the tasks you complete on a daily basis reflect that rate of progress. For example, if it becomes evident that you have collected an insufficient number of references, it may be necessary to suspend writing for a period. You then have to decide the number of working days you need to spend in the library. Clearly, a literature search is an open-ended activity, and herein lies the danger in time management. You can always imagine that there is just one more crucial reference waiting to be identified. Your literature search can go on and on. In some ways activities like this are very reassuring. You have the feeling that something constructive is being done, and hence it often demands determination to cease that activity and return to the task of writing. If your thesis is to be completed within the approximate time set, then there are crucial decisions to be taken about when to cease activities such as a literature search. You are rarely satisfied with the number of references collected, or with the extent of your reading on methodological issues, but there comes a time when this must be balanced against the need to maintain progress.

To put this issue in another way, the dilemma for the full-time research student is that there is sometimes almost too much time! It certainly may not feel like this to the student; nevertheless, most people have some difficulty in organizing their time when there are relatively few extrinsically imposed targets in the week. The extent of the time available may sometimes result in students becoming almost too perfectionist in their writing. Very small matters may be checked again and again, when really it may be more important to reflect on the larger-scale research issues in the thesis.

Part-time students

Part-time research students usually have very different problems. In many cases they may have to combine their research with the pressures of a full-time job and of looking after a family. To a part-time student in this position, the life of a full-time researcher must seem idyllic! In time management terms, it is important for the part-time student to think carefully about a working strategy which can be integrated into the other demands of a busy life. One thing is evident – it will probably be very difficult to identify a significant block of time when they will be able to write a major part of the thesis. It seems much more likely that they will need to write very small sections in the short periods of time available.

It may be possible to identify such periods of time at lunch break at work, or in the late evening when, say, children have gone to bed. None of these times will be ideal for academic writing but, if progress is to be made, then it is necessary to make the most of them. However, part of the difficulty of writing a long piece of work in very small sections is that the final product may appear disjointed. Sections do not flow from one to the next. In addition, it is very easy, when sitting down at the computer, to forget what has been written in the previous section. Therefore, if this pattern of working is dictated by lifestyle demands, it is a good idea to adopt the writing slogan of 'little and often'. If a small amount of the thesis is written every day, even if it is only, say, 300 words or a single side of A4 paper, then the daily routine should help to ensure some degree of continuity. A little editing on the draft of the thesis should help to smooth out any inconsistencies or apparent discontinuities in the text.

Such strategies will rarely be as adequate as the situation of having substantial periods of time to write a thesis. Nevertheless, many people do complete master's and doctoral theses in this way, and so it is clearly possible to do so. For many there are no alternatives, and sometimes the very high level of motivation of part-time mature students is more than a compensation for the rather difficult circumstances under which the thesis is written. Different aspects of time management are discussed in Phillips and Pugh (2000, p. 85) and Turner (2002, pp. 32–43).

Accumulating your list of references

The use of quotations from academic works and citing books and articles are important features of academic writing. Referring to a leading author or researcher is a way of illustrating or supporting an argument. It is important that the entire process of referencing is conducted according to accepted academic conventions, and details of such conventions are included in Chapter 6. For the time being, it is worth reflecting on ways in which the collection of appropriate references can be organized in order to minimize time and effort, and to ensure that during the writing of the thesis all the necessary details of publications are readily available.

When undertaking the preliminary reading for research and writing, it is very important to note down the full bibliographic details of any publication which you intend to use. These can then be entered in a Word file by alphabetical order of author surname, to produce an accumulating resource of works which have been consulted: in effect, a bibliography. At the time you place a new entry in the bibliography, you may remember clearly the significance of that particular work. However, a few weeks later, that relevance may be largely forgotten. When you start to write up, you may have completely forgotten the intended reason for including that citation. The only solution at that stage is to relocate the book or article, and refresh your memory. If this process were repeated for each entry in the bibliography, then the total additional work seems very daunting indeed. Moreover, particularly in the case of a book, it may be difficult to retrieve it in a library.

One possible solution is to create an annotated bibliography when you first read the book or article. The first stage in this process is to try to decide at the reading stage whether you intend merely to cite the work, or to include a quotation from it. If the former, then it is useful to include a few notes in the bibliography to remind yourself about the reason for including that book or article. In other words, it will be helpful to note the broad content of the book or article, and the argument in the thesis which it substantiates. As long as the full bibliographic details are also noted, it should not then be necessary to relocate the book or article.

On the other hand, if the intention is to use one or more quotations from a work, you should select the extracts and type them out carefully in the bibliography. Later, when the thesis is being written, these quotations can be used at an appropriate place. There will be no need to make additional visits to the library to locate the original work. When reading a quotation on its own, removed from the original context, it is possible to forget the exact meaning suggested by the author; therefore, it is best to add a few notes in the bibliography to remind you of the context. There are many ways of accumulating a list of references, and the best strategy often depends upon the ease with which you have access to an academic library. The above strategy is useful if you cannot easily make many return visits, since it enables all the necessary information to be recorded at the first reading of source material. Maker and Lenier (1996) suggest some strategies for reading academic literature analytically, while Gash (1989, p. 70) discusses how to keep records of references. There are also a number of digital packages available which enable you to input details of articles and books, and to arrange these automatically as a list of references. These are discussed in the second part of Chapter 9.

Signpost to success – Referencing

Select your references with care and accuracy. Relevant and detailed referencing is central to a good thesis.

The order of writing the thesis

Students starting to write their thesis often assume that it must be written in the order of the chapters, starting with the title of the thesis and ending with the conclusion and references. We have already seen in the previous section that it is advantageous to accumulate a list of references over a period of time. Indeed, the collection of references can continue during the entire period of writing the thesis. This is often necessary if the final list of references is to contain the most current publications. In the case of a doctoral thesis, the writing process may take 18 months. During that time many journal articles and books may be published, some of which could be relevant to the thesis. Examiners usually expect the latest publications to be noted in the final thesis.

In fact, there are many elements in a thesis for which final decisions on content do not need to be taken until the last minute. You can accumulate potential inclusions for the appendix during the writing period, and then determine the exact contents when the bulk of the thesis has been written. It may be necessary at certain points in the thesis to refer to the appendices, but it is possible to leave many decisions about content until most of the thesis has been prepared. Although it is helpful to have a provisional title during the writing stage, it is possible to amend this at the end of the process. Certainly, it is normal for the abstract to be written when the bulk of the thesis has been completed. The principal reason for this is that, as the abstract is a synopsis of the whole thesis, it is usually necessary to have written most of the latter, in order to prepare an abstract.

In order to complete your thesis in the shortest time possible, it is useful to conduct different aspects of the research and writing process in parallel. For example, once the broad principles of the research design have been decided and you are clear about the different stages of sampling and data collection, then the latter process can start. However, data collection often proceeds over a period of time. For example, suppose that you are conducting interviews with different staff members and pupils in several high schools. It will rarely be possible to arrange interviews on consecutive days. The interview appointments may extend over several weeks or months. There will be many gaps in the data collection process, and it is often useful to use this time constructively on some other aspect of the research or writing. Periods such as this can often usefully be filled by conducting literature searches and by writing sections of the literature review chapter. Such a chapter is often divided into different sections, relating to aspects of the subject matter of the thesis. To some extent, then, the chapter can be written at separate stages.

It is also sometimes possible to write sections of other chapters whenever that fits in conveniently with the developing research process. Once the researcher is aware of the context in which the research will be conducted, it may be possible to write certain parts of the introductory chapter. The reasons for selecting the particular research subject can be described and analysed, and the context for the research, be it perhaps a school or a hospital, can be described. Similarly, once the methodology for the research has been determined, then certain elements of the methodology chapter can be written. Such a chapter usually includes a discussion of theoretical aspects of the methodology, and it may be possible to write a draft of sections of this while continuing with data collection and analysis.

Example – Continuity of the thesis

Whichever approach you select for writing the thesis, there will inevitably be a few errors with what film-makers call 'continuity'. That is, you say something in one part of the thesis, which contradicts something elsewhere. The best way to put this right, is to read and check the final manuscript in one go, or at least as close to this as possible.

Of course, some people may prefer to write their thesis in a strictly conventional manner, from beginning to end. One may argue that the major advantage of this is that the thesis is more likely to be coherent and to flow well from earlier to later chapters. However, there can never be one way of writing a thesis which suits the needs of all students. It may be necessary for some students to be very creative with their time management in order to complete their thesis in a reasonable time.

Self-motivation

When students start writing a thesis, they are usually full of enthusiasm for the task ahead. Everything is new and exciting, and studying for a master's or doctorate adds a whole new dimension to your life. However, as the work proceeds, you may become more aware of the scale of the task. It perhaps becomes more and more difficult to envisage how you will actually complete this undertaking. Other things may crop up unexpectedly in your life, which interfere with your research and writing, and it seems more and more difficult to make progress.

It is very easy to spend your time thinking about the future, and how wonderful it will be to finish your course. Actually, this can sometimes be quite demotivating, because you think continually about all the things you have to do in order to achieve your goal. Sometimes, it is more effective and reassuring just to concentrate on the small task you have to do at this moment, for example, finding a new reference, reading part of an article, and writing a new paragraph. You do need to be planning for the development of your thesis, but it is not necessarily very motivating to become preoccupied with all the jobs you have to do. If you concentrate on the present task, you can feel confident that each little job done will contribute to the whole.

Even the smallest amount of work, done regularly, will accumulate quite quickly. Most people take between four and five years to get their PhD, depending on whether they are full-time or part-time. Let us suppose that you spend very roughly half the time doing the research, and half the time writing a thesis of 80,000 words. If you were to write 100 words a day – which is very little; only five lines on a typical computer screen – you would finish the thesis in two years and two months. This would be quite enough to stay on schedule. In reality, you will probably do much more, but this is just an indication of what can be achieved with limited but regular targets!

Further reading

Gillett, A., Hammond, A. and Martala, M. (2009) *Successful Academic Writing*. Harlow: Pearson Longman.

O'Dochartaigh, N. (2007) *Internet Research Skills: How To Do Your Literature Search and Find Research Information Online*. 2nd edn. London: Sage.

Phelps, R., Fisher, K. and Ellis, A. (2007) *Organizing and Managing Your Research: A Practical Guide for Postgraduates*. London: Sage.

Walliman, N. (2005) *Your Research Project: A Step-by-Step Guide for the First-Time Researcher*. 2nd edn. London: Sage.

4
The Role of the Supervisor

In this chapter we explore the overall role of the thesis supervisor, and the ways in which you can work together to maximize chances of success. We look at how your supervisor can help with reading drafts of your work, and with advice on the structure of your thesis. If you have travelled abroad to study, and are away from your home country, we discuss ways in which your supervisor may be able to help with your research and thesis.

Study Strategies

- Try to think of ways in which you can help your supervisor to help you!
- For example, a few days before a tutorial, email your supervisor with a list of things you are uncertain about, or perhaps aspects of methodology on which you would like advice. Your supervisor will then be able to plan more effectively for the tutorial.
- When you send your supervisor a draft of your work, use a highlighting pen to indicate sections on which you would particularly appreciate some comments.
- If you know of other commitments developing in your life, make your supervisors aware of them, and then they will not have undue expectations of the amount of work you can produce.
- When you send your supervisor a sample of work, try to check the spelling and grammar as carefully as possible. Errors in this area can distract supervisors from reflecting upon important issues such as methodology and analysis.

The functions of your supervisor or supervisory team

Your supervisor is the person who will advise you on the development of your research plan, the conduct of the research and the writing of the thesis. The supervisor's role is clearly not one of doing the work for you, but of providing advice and support in order to help you produce the best thesis of which you are capable. For a master's thesis it is normal to have only one supervisor, whereas for a doctorate there will usually be a principal supervisor along with one or two second supervisors. The principal supervisor is sometimes known as the director of studies. Custom and practice in relation to supervision may differ slightly from one university to another, but this chapter describes fairly typical situations. Supervisors are expected to possess an appropriate range of knowledge and skills to supervise the different research projects with which they are involved. They are expected to have a knowledge not only of the subject matter of the research, but also of the methodology to be used. However, at doctoral level it may be that no single supervisor has an adequate depth of understanding in all of these areas. The supervisor may be an expert on the subject matter, but you may have selected a methodology with which the supervisor is only partially familiar. For this reason, it is the norm at this level for there to be more than one supervisor. It is important that, as a whole, the supervisory team possesses the knowledge and skills to advise you on all aspects of the research. In order to ensure this, the supervisory team will normally be subject to a form of vetting by the university to ensure that collectively they have the appropriate background to support your research. The system of vetting the supervisory team may be part of the approval process for your research proposal. Typically, the supervisors may have to submit details of their qualifications, research expertise and the number of theses which they have successfully supervised.

Example – Tutorials

For these reasons it is important that as often as is practical, the whole supervisory team meets the student for tutorials. There should ideally be a collaborative relationship between the supervisors, for example:

'In a perfect world, I think I would prefer to see a little more data here – just to strengthen the argument. What do you think?' (turning to another supervisor)

(Continued)

(Continued)

'Yes, I'm sure that would help. Would you (turning to the student) have any additional data; or could it be collected at this stage?'

Being party to this kind of collaboration, should give you greater confidence in the advice you are receiving.

Besides providing advice to the student throughout the development of the thesis, supervisors have an important role in nominating academics as both internal and external examiners for the viva voce examination. Supervisors do not appoint the examiners, but make suggestions to the committee whose role involves making such appointments. In addition, supervisors are involved in the administrative matters connected with your research programme. They may be involved in your annual enrolment, and may also plan a series of research training events to ensure that you develop an appropriate understanding of methodological issues. Inevitably, the supervisor is also involved in an element of your pastoral care, helping with encouragement and support through the inevitable high and low moments of a long period of research.

Summary – The role of the supervisor

The supervisor's role includes:

- Helping the student to develop a detailed research proposal.
- Providing advice on the research design, data collection and data analysis.
- Guiding the student in the writing of the thesis.
- Nominating potential examiners for the viva voce examination.
- Advising the student on preparation for the viva voce.
- Providing advice on administrative matters throughout the research programme.
- Advising the student on an appropriate research training programme.

Selecting a supervisor or being allocated one

The relationship between supervisor and student is important, and your final success depends on this relationship functioning well. It is arguably a more personal relationship than that normally between a student and their lecturer. The reason for this is that in thesis supervision the supervisor and student are to a certain extent working together, rather than being cast in the roles of teacher and taught. It is therefore important that both the supervisor and student have a sense of empathy about the research project. This can probably only be determined if there are preliminary discussions before the lecturer agrees to supervise a particular project.

In some cases students will know several potential supervisors, because they may have been taught by them on previous courses. In other cases, students may rely on a potential supervisor being identified by a university department. Either way, it seems desirable that both parties meet to discuss the proposed research, without a prior commitment on either side. It is important that both supervisor and student feel that they can work together constructively, and that they both have a feeling of empathy with the project. If either party has any doubts about the relationship, then it is probably best for these to be acknowledged openly, and for the student to explore the possibility of a different supervisor. It is also worth mentioning that there may be administrative reasons for a lecturer not being able to act as a supervisor. For example, sometimes lecturers are restricted in the number of research students that they are permitted to supervise, and hence may not be able to accept more students. Issues involved in identifying a supervisor are discussed in Leonard (2001, pp. 85–7).

Appreciating your supervisor's perspective

Although the relationship between supervisor and student can be very rewarding, it can also at times be complex and difficult. Students have never been supervisors, and usually are unaware of the pressures of the university lecturer's job. On the other hand, it may be a number of years since the lecturer has been a student, and the passing of years may have resulted in the lecturer forgetting many of the pressures upon the student. This is a situation which can easily result in misunderstandings!

Perhaps the main thing to be said about supervisors is that they really want their students to succeed. They want this first and foremost for the sake of their students, but it is also very rewarding for supervisors to help their students successfully complete their research. They often keep records of the number of students they have successfully supervised. Indeed, sometimes they may be asked by a university for such records, particularly when approval is being given for the supervisory team of a new research student. In such a case, the university may wish to know whether the team has an appropriate level of supervisory experience for the student.

Although supervisors want their students to succeed, there are limits to the amount of help which they may provide for their students. They may feel, for example, that it would be exceeding the limits of their role to proofread and correct the style of writing and expression throughout a thesis. If they find that a student is making a particular type of error, they may prefer to indicate one instance of such an error, and then leave it to the student to identify all the other examples throughout the thesis. The student may appear to have misunderstood a particular aspect of the methodology. The supervisor may explain the error, and then leave the student to identify and correct examples of that misunderstanding. Similarly the supervisor may feel that the literature review chapter should contain more recent citations. The supervisor may even suggest certain writers for the student to examine, but leave the search for actual sources to the student.

When the thesis is completed, university procedures may require the supervisor to sign a pro forma agreeing that it is of a suitable standard to be submitted for examination. The student may not be aware of this requirement, and yet it may put the supervisor under a certain degree of pressure. If a student has written a rather indifferent thesis, the supervisor may feel the need to keep returning it to the student for corrections to be made. When this has happened several times, the student may begin to feel that the supervisor is being unduly demanding. However, the explanation may be that the supervisor is trying to ensure that the thesis is as good as possible, before the form is signed authorizing the oral examination.

Finally, it is possible that the members of a student's supervisory team do not all share the same view about the thesis. One supervisor may feel that the research has been well designed with a sound methodology, while another supervisor may have reservations. Even though there may be genuine differences of opinion, it is important that an attempt is made at reconciliation, in order that the student may be given coherent guidance. As a student, there may sometimes be advantages in meeting your supervisors separately, but the danger inherent in this is that you may feel that you have received rather different guidance from each. On the other hand, if you meet the team of supervisors together, they can all listen to each other's viewpoints, and then try to synthesize these into unified advice.

Working well with your supervisor

An effective relationship between supervisor and student works to the mutual benefit of both. The student is able to draw upon the experience of the supervisor and to receive sound advice on the developing thesis. The supervisor has the professional reward of seeing a student develop academically and, hopefully, complete their qualification. However, at the heart of a good working relationship of this type is openness and honesty in communication, so each person is clear about their expectations of the other.

It is generally a good idea for supervisors to be clear and precise about the changes which they feel are necessary in a thesis. This is preferable to hinting at changes in a rather vague manner, and leaving the student to interpret what is required. Equally, students should be prepared to ask clearly for the kind of help which they feel is required. For their part, supervisors should state clearly the help they are prepared to give, and those areas in which they feel they cannot contribute. For example, a student may assume that the supervisor will help with the proofreading of the final draft of the thesis. The supervisor may say that she is more than happy to read the thesis to check on academic matters such as the validity of the arguments, but is not able to correct the thesis for typographical errors or mistakes in grammar or punctuation. The supervisor may feel that this is the province of the student. The important issue is that both supervisor and student explain their position to the other, and give reasons to justify their decisions.

Example – A written statement of suggested amendments.

When supervisors have seen a draft of several chapters, or even of the whole thesis, they will inevitably have suggestions to make concerning amendments. It is usually helpful for the student to receive a verbal explanation, and a written summary of the key suggestions. The supervisor may write, for example: 'It would be helpful to have a brief discussion of the problems of validity when data is collected from employees in the presence of their manager. This could be mentioned initially in the methodology chapter. You could return to the issue in the Conclusion, in order to explain how validity threats were minimized throughout the research.'

Supervisors would probably be prepared to discuss such an issue in tutorials, but would then expect a student to take responsibility for writing the section concerned.

Sometimes students expect to receive from supervisors very precise answers to questions concerning the content of the thesis. For example, a student might ask 'How should I relate my chosen methodology to the aims of the thesis?' The student may feel that their supervisor has a single, well-tried strategy which will guarantee success. It is rare, however, for there to be a single, straightforward answer to issues in research, and the supervisor will need to ensure that the student fully appreciates this. The supervisor may feel that the best strategy is to outline several different ways of approaching the issue, and then to ask the student to make their own choice of an approach. The student, of course, may feel that the supervisor is being rather less than helpful, and it is important that the supervisor explains clearly the philosophical reason for there not being a simple, formulaic answer.

It is also usually helpful in the relationship between student and supervisor if you explain to your supervisor about any specific pressures which are affecting your work. If your supervisor is aware of such pressures, then they will not have the same expectation in terms of your output of work. Your supervisor may also be able to direct you to a colleague in the university who can help you with any problems. It is also useful if students recognize that their supervisors also have many professional pressures, and may not be able to read drafts of work, or arrange tutorials, at exactly the time wished by students. Supervisors will typically have many other teaching, administrative and research commitments, which they try to balance.

What to do if you are unhappy with your supervisor

Most relationships between students and supervisors have their high and low points, but very occasionally a relationship may deteriorate to a point where the student feels some action must be taken. If this occurs, then most supervisors prefer that their students share their feelings with them, rather than talking to someone else. Most supervisors want nothing more than to have a good working relationship with their students, and will normally do their best to achieve this. A breakdown in the relationship can often have something to do with different unspoken expectations on the part of student and tutor.

As an example, consider a situation where you feel that you are not making sufficient progress and are floundering with the thesis, and need more frequent tutorials. You might be making slow progress, not because you need more tutorials, but because of a single, discrete problem which can be solved quickly by your supervisor. For example, you might simply need a few suggestions for suitable reading on methodology, rather than additional tutorials. If the fundamental cause of the problem can be identified, then there may well be a quick and easy solution. Your supervisor may be allocated a number of research students, on the assumption that each will require a certain number of tutorials per academic year, and might not have the time to increase your tutorial allocation. If the issue is explored openly between you and your supervisor, then any misunderstanding may be eliminated.

However, in a small number of cases, it could just be that supervisor and student are unable to work together. There may be any number of reasons for this, but if after an honest exchange of views, it appears that nothing can be salvaged from the relationship, then it is preferable if the student asks for a change of supervisor. Such a request need not be problematic for a university department, and it should be possible for the change to be made very rapidly. It is usually better if the request is made to the existing supervisor, and it may be possible for one of the supporting supervisors to assume the principal role. The advantage of this approach is that the exchange can usually be made with a minimum of administration.

However, in situations where you feel that the relationship has deteriorated to such a level that it is no longer possible to have a meaningful discussion with your supervisor, you should seek a meeting with the Head of Department or the Dean of the Faculty. This will inevitably formalize the issue, but sometimes there are situations where this is necessary. Let us assume for the sake of argument that there is some blame on both sides; the result is still likely to be that a new director of studies is appointed. The university may also have a formal published procedure by which you may apply to change supervisor.

We can sum up this issue by saying that every research student should have a supervisor to whom they feel they can relate well, and with whom they feel they can work well in a successful academic relationship. If this is not the case, for any reason, the student should seek a new supervisor and be reassured that this is not an unreasonable action.

Negotiating targets and deadlines

At the beginning of a research project, it is advisable to include a timescale for completion of key stages in the process. This is important because of the potentially open-ended nature of the task. Without a clear time schedule, it is easy for students to lack focus, which can result in taking much longer than is necessary to write the thesis. The matter is complicated by the nature of the submission process for postgraduate theses. On a master's programme, a submission date is normally stipulated for the thesis, which is submitted in much the same way as any other module or unit of work. However, the thesis for a research degree can usually be submitted at any time in the academic year. It can therefore be much easier to plan a submission strategy for a master's thesis, than for a doctoral thesis. In the latter case, there is no specific deadline, and there can be a tendency for students to be insufficiently focused on the task. In the absence of an extrinsic target, it can be very helpful to set one.

Setting targets

It is desirable to set a completion target in conjunction with the supervisor. During the progress of a research thesis, there are sometimes stages which are deceptively time-consuming. For example, each member of the supervisory team will need to read the draft thesis, and provide comments. The binding of the thesis in preparation for the viva may take some time, and the examiners may need to receive the thesis some considerable time before the date of the actual viva. Many of these potential delays are outside your influence, and should be taken into account when planning your overall writing schedule.

Signpost to success – setting targets

Set yourself a series of staged targets in order to complete the thesis on schedule. Do everything possible to meet your targets.

It can be a great help to the supervisor in some administrative aspects of the process, if you have clear writing targets, and manage to adhere to these. The supervisor often has to initiate the process for the selection of examiners for the viva, and having a fairly clear idea of the submission date for the thesis is a help in this. The examiners can be given a reliable estimate of the likely date of the oral examination.

Arranging a pattern of tutorials

Most of the actual process of teaching during the writing of the thesis takes place in tutorials. It is very helpful for both the supervisor and yourself if a pattern of tutorials can be established, in order that you receive regular advice at key stages of the writing process.

Some tutorials may be with the principal supervisor, while others may involve the whole supervisory team. In the latter case, this offers an opportunity to resolve any slight differences in advice between supervisors. Normally these will not be very great, but it can be very useful for you to listen to differences of opinion, and to try to resolve these in the thesis.

In a tutorial, you may ask a great many questions and the supervisor may give a lot of advice. If more than one supervisor is present, then there is the further dimension of differences in emphasis between them. It is very important to maintain an accurate record of each tutorial. You can then use this record as a checklist for future action on the thesis. For the supervisor, the record acts as an aide-memoire of the advice given, and enables him or her to check at the next tutorial on the action you have taken.

Some supervisors have a well-regulated system using a pro forma to summarize the discussion in a tutorial, and this pro forma is then usually signed by the supervisors present. There is usually a space to enter the actions agreed by either the supervisor or yourself before the next tutorial, and the date agreed for the next tutorial. If the supervisor does not employ a system such a this, then it may be helpful for you to replicate it in some way. This might be accomplished by keeping careful notes, or by suggesting to the supervisor that you initiate jointly a similar system. The issue of tutorial records is discussed in Sharp and Howard (1996, pp. 177–8).

Advice on methodology and design

One of the supervisor's main functions is to ensure not only that the research design is appropriate to the aims of the research, but also that the design and methodology are integrated well into the thesis. The supervisor should be familiar with the methodology used, and should help you to ensure that no significant methodological issues are omitted.

The literature on methodology is extensive, and there is always a danger that you write too extensively and exceed the allocated number of words. One of the areas in which your supervisor can help is in defining those methodological issues which it is essential to discuss. It is almost always necessary, for example, to discuss the reasons for choosing the particular methodology for the research. There is often not the space to write about all the alternative methodologies and the reasons for rejecting them for the particular study in question, but it will probably be necessary at least to allude to them.

One of the main purposes of the methodology chapter is to provide a coherent account of the chosen approach, and to clarify the nature of any specialist concepts which have been used. For example, if a thesis claims that an ethnographic approach has been used for the research, then you need to explain the philosophical and sociological underpinnings of that approach. It will also be necessary to refer to key literature in the area. When writing about methodological issues you need to be very precise in the style of writing, primarily because the concepts used can be complex, and it is easy to make unjustified assumptions.

As an example, the terms 'science' and 'scientific' require careful use, as they are susceptible to rather different interpretations. For example, you might apply the term 'scientific' to positivistic research, at the same time implying that qualitative methods are less scientific. You might suggest that 'science' implies a procedure involving the testing of hypotheses. Other students might adopt a more general interpretation of science as a process characterized by systematic enquiry. If you use terms such as 'science' in a rather imprecise manner, or in a way which makes unjustified assumptions, then the supervisor should be able to identify such cases and suggest strategies for making the text more precise.

However, it is one thing to choose a particular methodology and to write about it in a coherent, rigorous manner, and it is another to establish in the mind of the reader that the research as carried out actually used that methodology. For example, you may claim in your thesis that the research employed a grounded theory approach. It is important to establish quite clearly that the research as conducted exhibited all the characteristics of the grounded theory approach. The supervisor should be able to check that this linkage has been made satisfactorily.

Advice on structuring the thesis

Although there are broadly accepted conventions for the structure of a research thesis, often particular features of a research project suggest ways of organizing this. For example, suppose that in a study of the career histories of schoolteachers, both questionnaires and interviews were used. After analysing the data, you have to decide how to subdivide the analysis into separate chapters.

One strategy is to include all of the analysis resulting from the questionnaire data in one chapter, and that from the interview data in a separate chapter. However, as the interview data would be more extensive, it may be necessary to subdivide this into several different chapters. This method of identifying chapters rests upon the different methods of collecting data, and may therefore be seen as a rather mechanistic strategy. It is unrelated to the results of the data analysis in terms of developing concepts and ideas which have emerged from the research. Some students therefore prefer to use the emerging analysis as the basis for identifying different chapters, and indeed to name these based upon the concepts from the analysis. The supervisor will almost certainly have a contribution to make here, in terms of suggesting ways of subdividing the data into chapters.

Thinking about the examiners

It is very likely that the supervisors will have experience of examining theses as well as of supervising them. This gives them a considerable advantage in seeing the thesis from the perspective of the reader and of the examiner. Inevitably, the student gets so familiar with the thesis that it is difficult to identify any shortcomings. Supervisors, on the other hand, can distance themselves from the thesis, and identify areas for improvement.

For example, some students include a great deal of material in the appendices. Not only does this make the thesis unwieldy and bulky, but some of this material may not directly enhance the thesis. The supervisor may be able to suggest ways in which the material can be reduced in volume, while still retaining key documents. In other cases, students may not have ensured that the thesis is sufficiently cohesive. It may give the impression of consisting of a series of distinct, but unrelated, chapters. The supervisor may be able to suggest strategies for overcoming this, such as making reference in one chapter to the contents of a later chapter.

When considering the impression a thesis will have on the examiners, supervisors will often give thought to the way in which the introductory chapter sets the scene. A thesis is a very long piece of work for examiners to read, and they frequently rely on the intro-duction to give them an appreciation of the later sections. Although the introduction will not go into great detail about methodology, it will give an indication of the nature of the research design and of the type of data collected. This kind of information helps the examiner to grasp the nature of the research study from the beginning and hence perhaps better to appreciate each section as it is read. The supervisor will be able to judge whether the introduction does satisfactorily achieve this end, or whether amendments are required.

Reading sections of the thesis as it is written

It is important that your supervisor reads each chapter of the thesis as it is completed. It is very useful for you and the supervisor to agree that a specific chapter will be written by a certain date. The supervisor can then read and annotate the manuscript. The process provides your supervisor with a measure of your progress, and gives you feedback on whether your work is of the required quality. Nevertheless, it is important to acknowledge that there are limitations to the type of feedback a supervisor can provide after reading a single chapter.

Perhaps the most important issue is that the reading of a single chapter is decontextualized from the remainder of the thesis. It may be, say, two months since your supervisor read the previous chapter, and the subsequent chapter has not yet been written. Under these circumstances, it is difficult to do much more than comment on the chapter in isolation. Nevertheless, there are many useful pieces of advice which the supervisor can provide:

- when looking at the early chapters of a thesis, identifying any errors of either content or presentation, which should not be continued in later chapters;
- checking if the referencing style meets the accepted conventions, and if the layout of the chapter is consistent in terms of headings and subheadings;
- identifying any errors of punctuation or grammar which are being consistently generated, these can be identified and corrected;
- ensuring that there are no conceptual misunderstandings, and no instances of specialist terms being used in an incorrect manner.

Commenting on drafts

Supervisors do differ in their approach to providing feedback on drafts of a thesis. Some may provide detailed annotations on the manuscript, identifying very minor issues, while others may only address very broad issues and leave you with the actual implementation. Equally, students may differ in their expectations. Some may be happy to receive general advice, while others may expect their supervisors to indicate to them every error to be corrected. This highlights an almost philosophical issue about the nature of supervision. It could be argued that supervision is concerned with providing overarching support and guidance, trying to ensure that you do not stray too far from the standards which are expected. In order to achieve this, it will be necessary to identify examples from your writing where amendments are required. However, supervision arguably does not involve the detailed amendment of your work by the supervisor. There is no doubt a debate to be had here about the acceptable extent of intervention by the supervisor on the one hand, and the need to preserve the integrity of the thesis as your own work on the other.

> ## Example – When is the thesis finished?
>
> It is very common for students to ask their supervisors, 'Have I done all the amendments I need to do? Is the thesis finished now?' The assumption is that there is a clear, fixed point at which a thesis is completed! It will always be possible to add something, or amend something, in a thesis. What the supervisor can say is whether or not there are any key errors which remain to be corrected.

Selecting the team of examiners for the viva voce

In the case of research degrees, universities normally have a formal mechanism by which individuals are approved to act as examiners for a particular thesis. The approval mechanism may consist of a committee of academics who are experienced as supervisors and examiners. They consider the academic background of the examiners who are proposed and their suitability for examining the particular thesis subject. Among the factors taken into account are the publication record of the people proposed, in so far as this indicates an expertise in the subject matter of the thesis. They also ensure that the examiners have sufficient experience of examining at the required level. There are usually two or three examiners, and at least one of them, the external examiner, will be from an institution other than the one at which the thesis has been completed. Supervisors are not normally involved in the approval process; thereby maintaining their objectivity in the sense that they are not involved in the appointment of examiners for their own students. However, the supervisory team is normally involved in the preparation of nominees to be submitted for approval as examiners.

Proposing examiners

As you near completion of your thesis, the supervisory team usually meets to discuss possible examiners. In arriving at a list of nominees for examiners, the supervisors will have to take into account any relevant university regulations. Such regulations may stipulate, for example, that the examining team has a certain level of experience of examining candidates at the relevant level. Regulations may also stipulate the balance between external and internal examiners, and the total number of examiners permitted. A fairly typical combination would be three examiners, of whom one is external to the institution at which you are registered.

In nominating examiners, supervisors take account of the need for the examiners to be able to demonstrate a record of expertise in the subject area and methodology of the thesis. On the one hand, this is important from the viewpoint of the university in appointing examiners who are able to uphold the quality of the awards made by the university. On the other hand, it is important that you are examined by academics who understand the content of your thesis and the methodology used. Once the examiners have been appointed, you usually are informed of their names, and the supervisors make arrangements for the oral examination. Although it has often been left to the principal supervisor to make these arrangements, there is a growing trend for the viva to be arranged by the appointed internal examiner. This arguably increases the objectivity of the process in that it further separates the functions of the supervisors and the examiners. Delamont et al. (1997, p. 140) discuss the process of selecting examiners.

The needs of overseas students

When overseas students are researching and writing a thesis, they will often experience a number of difficulties which will not apply to 'home' students. For the sake of this discussion, we define overseas students as those studying in a country which is not their country of birth, in a language which is not their first language. If you are an overseas student, there are therefore two main types of difficulty you may experience; one deriving from cultural issues and the other from language issues.

In terms of culture, you may be studying in an educational system which is different from that in your home country. The terminology used may be different, and the teaching style might be very different. In the UK and, for example, in the USA and Australia, there tends to be a tradition of encouraging students to become autonomous learners and researchers. Lecturers try to avoid telling students what they should be thinking about an issue. They may decide to explain several different ways of considering a problem, and then ask students to reflect on the perspective or viewpoint which they prefer. This may be different to the situation in some countries where lecturers may advocate one particular viewpoint, and expect their students to adopt that perspective. If you are more familiar with receiving a strong sense of direction from your lecturers, being asked to take more decisions by yourself could give you some concerns.

Example – Being an autonomous researcher

You may ask your supervisors to advise you on selecting a methodological approach for your research. Their response may be: 'Please think about what you consider to be the most appropriate approach, and write a summary of the reasons. We will then discuss this at our next tutorial.'

They will be encouraging you to take an active approach to your research, before they give their opinion.

With regard to language issues, you will undoubtedly have some concerns about whether you will be able to express yourself adequately in your new language. However, you should feel reassured that your university would not have accepted you unless they thought you had sufficient linguistic competence. You will still probably find it much slower to write in your new language, and there will probably remain a number of minor errors in your writing. Your supervisors may be happy to correct some of these when they read your draft work, but this will depend on the time they have available. They will probably not want to be involved in extensive grammatical corrections. First, it would be too time-consuming and, second, it could involve them in rewriting some of your work. There is a fine line between supervisors correcting grammatical errors, and in effect rewriting your thesis. They may be willing to do the former, but not the latter. With regard to help with language, most universities employ staff whose job it is to help students with language issues. You should therefore be able to obtain help with improving your writing style. Your supervisors will usually be happy to explain to you the sort of errors you are making, and then leave you to correct these in your manuscript. They will certainly help you with issues arising from the academic content of your thesis. To sum up, supervisors will be sympathetic to your position, and will help you as much as they feel able, as long as the thesis remains your work and not theirs!

A checklist for supervisors

To conclude this chapter, here is a list of practical ideas to help the relationship between supervisor and researcher to function smoothly. It is worth remembering, though, that researching and writing a thesis should be a collaborative venture between supervisor and researcher. It is in that spirit that the following list is suggested.

1 At the beginning of the research, supervisors and students develop a modus operandi for tutorials. Decide on the frequency of tutorials, and perhaps work out a schedule of dates for the year. Decide who will maintain a record of the tutorials, and how this will be disseminated to the others.
2 Set some targets for the research and for the thesis writing. Reach an agreement on how and when drafts of written work will be submitted.
3 Agree on the length of tutorials.
4 Supervisors discuss with students, the latter's needs in terms of additional study, for example of research methods. Overseas students may need language support. Students will probably need help and guidance in arranging such additional study.
5 Develop a system whereby students can be informed of appropriate seminars and conferences to attend. Discuss any possible financial support.

6 Discuss long-term targets for the completion of the thesis. Develop a list of provisional target dates, even though these may be amended later.

7 Make sure students understand the main stages in the development of the study. For example, there may be a transfer stage between MPhil and PhD. Supervisors should ensure students fully understand what will be required, and the process involved.

8 While students are involved in collecting data, supervisors should take all reasonable steps to ensure their safety and provide them with relevant advice. They should also advise students on ethical procedures to ensure the well-being of those who are providing data.

9 Supervisors should explain carefully to students, the limits of the help they can provide during the supervision process.

10 Supervisors should ensure that students fully understand the assessment procedures for the thesis. They should do everything reasonable to assist students in reaching a successful conclusion to their studies. However, students should be clear that the ultimate responsibility for the quality of their work and for their performance in the examination process lies with themselves.

Further reading

Churchill, H. and Sanders, T. (2007) *Getting Your PhD: A Practical Insider's Guide*. London: Sage.

Denscombe, M. (2010) *The Good Research Guide: For Small-scale Social Research Projects*. 4th edn. Maidenhead: Open University Press.

Morss, K. and Murray, R. (2005) *Teaching at University: A Guide for Postgraduates and Researchers*. London: Sage.

Mounsey, C. (2002) *One Step Ahead: Essays and Dissertations*. Oxford: Oxford University Press.

Silverman, D. (2004) *Doing Qualitative Research: A Practical Handbook*. 2nd edn. London: Sage.

5
Your Role as a Student

In this chapter we look at some of the ways in which you can prepare yourself for work on your thesis. We consider the things you can learn from talking to other research students, and from reading successful theses. You will need to continue your own education in, for example, research methods, while you are working on your thesis, and we look at ways in which you can achieve this. We also reflect upon ways in which you can work well with your supervisors, and help them to support you.

Study Strategies

- Make a special effort to cultivate contacts, both among other research students, and among experienced researchers and academics.
- Look at a number of other research theses, particularly in your subject area, in order to get ideas for the structure and presentation of your own thesis.
- Agree a timetable of tutorials and submission dates with your supervisors, so that they will know when to expect samples of work.
- Search out as many opportunities as possible to disseminate your work.

Initial worries and concerns

Starting any new university course is a very exciting prospect. You meet new lecturers and fellow students. Many new opportunities open up and, as you look forward to gaining a new qualification, you quite naturally think of new career possibilities. When you are being taught in groups with other students, it is often reassuring because you are all studying the same subject and the same course materials. You have the same essay or examination to do, and if you have some anxieties, you can always discuss these with fellow students. Your tutor will usually give you a set of target dates by which you have to submit your work. Although you will have a lot of studying to do, much of the organization of your studies is taken out of your hands. You just have to make sure that you meet your deadlines.

When you start work on a thesis, however, things are often completely different. First, there is no set topic to study. You are expected to identify your own research subject. Your friends will all have their own subjects, and hence direct comparisons will not be easy. You will, of course, be able to share general experiences of working on a thesis, but none of you will be researching exactly the same topic. Although one or two of you may share the same supervisor, generally you will each have a different supervisory team. Your tutorials will be individually arranged, and therefore you will not be taught at the same time. As you and your friends work on your theses, inevitably some will move ahead faster than others, which will make it less and less easy for you to gain mutual support. All of these factors may combine to give you a slight feeling of isolation. Certainly you will have the support of your supervisor or supervisors, who will do their best to ensure you feel comfortable with your studies, but it is almost inevitable that from time to time, you will feel rather alone.

When you are taught in a class, you usually all meet at least once a week, and your tutor will remind you of submission dates, and where approximately you should be with your studies. However, when you are starting research for a thesis, there is usually no organizational plan. Your supervisor will probably provide general advice on how to plan your work, but will normally expect you to develop your own schedule. When you are used to being told what to do by your lecturer, this can prove quite a challenge. Initially, you will probably feel anxious about whether you are making sufficient progress, although this feeling may fade as you start to develop a pattern of work with your supervisor.

Researching and writing a thesis occupies such a long period of time, that it is sometimes difficult to know when you are ready to start writing. As you start to explore the literature on the subject you are researching, you realize there is an almost infinite amount of material to read. It is a natural feeling to wonder when you will have acquired sufficient understanding of your subject, to start drafting part of the thesis – the introduction, for example. There is always a temptation to keep reading and taking notes, and not to start work on the thesis. There is a similar problem with the collection of data. It is always easy to think that you will need to collect just a little more data before starting to analyse it and begin writing. These anxieties probably affect everyone who is doing some kind of creative work. It is always tempting to continue the preparatory phase, rather than to start on the actual task. Of course, the preparatory phase is very important, but there comes a point when you need to produce some actual work. This worry almost certainly stems from the fact that you are concerned about the quality of your work.

This is where your supervisor can help. You do not necessarily need to have collected all of your data before you start to draft parts of the introductory chapter of your thesis. You could write one or two pages explaining the significance of the research subject, or why you have selected this topic to investigate. Type these pages in a formal style, as you would expect them to appear in the final thesis, and then ask a few questions of your supervisor.

Example – Asking for reassurance

When submitting an initial sample of work, these are some questions you could put to your supervisor:

1 Is the writing style too formal, too informal, or just about right?
2 Are there places where I could have changed from a formal, academic style to the first person singular?
3 Have I included an appropriate number of references?
4 Are the academic arguments sound?
5 Overall, is the standard of the work at the appropriate academic level?

Constructive feedback from your supervisor should help to overcome some of your initial worries. Remember, too, that you are not unique in having initial doubts about your work. Everyone feels like this to some extent. The main thing is to keep going! There are, however, several other sources of reassurance.

Talking to current and former research students

Researching and writing a thesis can be a solitary activity. It is not always easy to engage others in a discussion about what you are studying. Unless they have done something similar, it will not be easy for them to understand either your subject matter, or the nature of the task of research. It can therefore be very pleasant and reassuring to talk to other research students. They will probably be just as happy to discuss their research, as you will be to talk about your thesis.

Having discussions with other research students is potentially a wonderful learning opportunity for you. Particularly if they have completed their thesis, it enables you to glean ideas on such aspects as how they organized their work and how they prepared for the oral examination. For people who have worked on a thesis, it has usually been such an important feature of their lives that it lives with them for a long time. They will often give you insights into the difficulties they experienced, and this can help you put your own anxieties into context. The tips they give you can often be enormously useful.

Example – Questions to put to other research students

Here are some ideas for questions to raise with other thesis students.

1 How often did you have tutorials?
2 How did your supervisor give you feedback on your work?
3 Could you always find enough references for the literature review?
4 Did you exceed the word limit for your thesis? If so, did it matter?
5 How did you organize your work on your computer?
6 How long did it take from handing in your thesis, to having it examined?
7 How have you used your thesis to develop your career?

The last question is useful to put to students who have finished their thesis. When you are either choosing your thesis subject, or planning the data to collect, most students tend to be influenced solely by the topics which interest them. This is no bad thing, but it is also worth considering how you might use your thesis or qualification in the future. You might use it for entry to a new course, or to gain access to further training, or for applying for a particular type of job.

Example – Practical use of a thesis

You might be interested in researching some aspects of management. This is such a wide subject, however, that it would make sense to select a context in which you ultimately hope to develop your career. For example, if you anticipated trying to get a job in health service management, other things being equal, it would be sensible to conduct research in this type of context.

It is definitely worth talking to other research students about the practical ways in which they have used their new qualification.

Reading research theses

Reading other master's and doctoral theses can be one of the best preparations both for your research and for your academic writing. Although there are broadly agreed conventions for the structure of academic theses, you will probably notice fairly quickly that each thesis is different. One, for example, may have a single very long literature review chapter, while another may subdivide this into two or more smaller chapters. One thesis may have a single chapter for the discussion of methodological issues, while another may integrate the discussion of such matters within other chapters. Generally speaking all theses should contain a discussion of the same issues, but the emphasis given to each will differ, and the overall structure will vary.

These variations will depend on the personal preferences of the student and the advice given by the supervisory team. The thesis structure may also depend to a certain extent upon the nature of the methodology employed. If you are using a quantitative approach your supervisor may advise you to adopt a fairly conventional structure. On the other hand, people using action research as their methodology have often experimented with non-conventional approaches to their writing. As qualitative research often generates a considerable volume of data, the data chapters in such theses are frequently very long. The reverse may be true of quantitative theses. In the second part of this book, the advice given on thesis structure adopts a 'middle-of-the-road' approach. The structure described is fairly conventional, and would enable you to include all of the important aspects of an academic thesis. However, depending upon some of the issues mentioned above, you might wish to amend this structure to suit your own needs.

It can also be informative to look at the way in which data is recorded. Qualitative studies often include a great deal of data, sometimes in long sections. In other cases, the data is in small sections, or even parts of sentences. You will probably note many different styles here. It may be helpful for you to reflect on the reasons for selecting a specific approach. Overall, it is a useful idea to look at a range of theses, and to collect ideas for structuring your own. When doing so, it is sensible to remember that while you do not have to be a slave to convention, it is wise to adopt a structure which provides the space to discuss the essential academic issues.

Understanding your supervisors

When most students meet their supervisors, they tend naturally to concentrate on the advice which they are given. They probably assume that their supervisors know precisely how the research should be conducted, and how this should be described in the thesis. However, this is not quite an accurate assumption. It may be useful for you, if we dispel one or two of the common myths about supervisors. This is not to undermine your confidence, but simply to give you a more accurate impression of how supervisors can and cannot be of help.

The first thing to be clear about, is that your supervisors want you to be successful with your thesis and your qualification. In a perfect world, they would like you to pass your thesis, and not to have to make any amendments or revisions. In the real world, they know that some students will be asked to revise their theses, but ideally they are trying to reduce this number to a minimum. To this extent, you can have confidence that your supervisors will do their best to help you succeed. However, there are some common-sense limits to the help which supervisors can give you. Do remember that all supervisors are human, and may take a different view of their role. The comments in this section are typical of many supervisors, but may not apply to all.

Supervisors will advise you on the academic content of your thesis. This advice will, of necessity, sometimes be fairly general. They are clearly not going to tell you exactly what should go in to each sentence you write. However, they may, for example, advise you on certain key arguments to make sure that you include them in your discussion. They will probably be quite happy to provide general advice before you write a chapter, and certainly to read a draft once you have written it. They will normally advise you on any key omissions, but will not normally tell you exactly what to put into the thesis. While they are reading the draft chapter, they may do some proofreading for you, and note minor corrections, although most supervisors would not see this as being officially their job. If your writing style is awkward, and this is making it difficult to understand your arguments, they may offer advice on style, and perhaps rewrite a few sentences. However, from then on, they would expect you to put this advice into practice yourself. The point here is that supervisors want to give you as much help as they can, but want to ensure also that the thesis remains primarily *your* work.

You should also remember that supervisors cannot give you an exact and precise answer to every question. If you were to put the same question to a number of different supervisors, you would probably get a variety of slightly different responses.

Example – Different answers to the same question

Let us suppose that you were to describe your intended research to several different supervisors, and then ask their advice about the size of the sample to use. If they were asked independently, there would probably be slight differences in their advice. They might suggest selecting different categories of people. It is not that any

(Continued)

(Continued)

of the advice may be 'wrong', but merely that different supervisors may focus on different aspects of the research.

You would need to go back to your research aims, and then take a decision within the broad parameters of the advice received. When finally you have your oral examination, you would need to defend the reasons for *your* decision.

As supervisors have a fairly close involvement in the evolution of a thesis, they are not always permitted to assess the work of their own students. In the case of a 'taught' master's degree, the supervisor may well be the initial examiner, but the thesis will also usually be read by either an internal or external examiner, to provide a second opinion on the quality of the work. In the case of a master's degree by research, such as an MPhil, the supervisor will not normally be involved in the examination. The same usually applies to all doctoral theses.

This situation with regard to examination of the thesis makes it very difficult for the supervisor to answer the question most favoured by students when they have completed the first draft of their thesis: 'Will it pass?' From the student's point of view, this is a perfectly reasonable question. Supervisors are people of experience, who have been through the same academic system. Surely they should know whether a thesis is up to standard! Even though your supervisors may have given you the very best advice of which they are capable, there is unfortunately no guarantee that your examiners will view the thesis in exactly the same way. Normally, in the vast majority of cases, if your supervisor thinks the thesis is fine, then your examiners will take a broadly similar view, even though they may require some amendments here and there. However, there are no absolute guarantees about anything in life, and in the final analysis, you, as the student, have to take responsibility for your own work. When, or if, you put that question to your supervisor – 'Will it pass?' – he or she will probably reply along the following lines.

Example – Will it pass?

In response to this question, your supervisor may say something like this: 'Well, now that you have made those amendments, I think it is a good thesis. If I were the examiner I would certainly pass it. However, not everyone takes exactly the same view of theses, so you must be aware that your examiners might want you to make further amendments. There is no way of predicting this. During the viva, you also will have the opportunity to clarify issues which they raise. The way that you do this may have an effect upon the extent of the revisions they ask for. In the days before you finally submit the thesis, you need to consider carefully whether it needs any further amendments. Ultimately this is your work, and you need to convince the examiners that you have achieved what you set out to do.'

Helping your supervisor to help you

You probably will not see all the many other things which your supervisor does in the week. It is easy to imagine that you are their most important student, and their main priority! In fact, supervisors have many other responsibilities. They will probably teach classes of undergraduate and master's students, be involved in developing new courses, be engaged in research and writing research papers, and be attending conferences and giving lectures. The list could go on and on. As your supervisors have this wide range of commitments, it will be very helpful to them if your work is well organized. They will probably find it very useful to be able to identify time slots in their diaries for meetings with you, and for reading samples of your work. This enables them to organize time for their other responsibilities, and build their commitment to you.

Just before the end of each tutorial, make sure there is an agreement about the work you will produce for the next tutorial. Ensure you both know the date when it will be submitted, and when your supervisor will have commented on it and returned it to you. Try to avoid leaving this to chance. If any issues occur in your life which may prevent your sticking to your schedule, then do mention these to your supervisors, unless they are too confidential. This will help them understand the pressures you are trying to overcome. You may have some specific areas in your research which are causing you difficulty. Make sure you mention these to your supervisors. This may, for example, be a specialist aspect of methodology. Even if they are not too sure about it themselves, they will probably be able to arrange for you to talk to one of their colleagues.

In relation to this, some students imagine that their supervisors are all-knowing, and can easily draw upon a limitless supply of knowledge about research! I suspect most supervisors would not want to claim omniscience. If you come across a term or concept in your reading which is giving you difficulty, then one strategy is to email your supervisor and ask them if you can discuss it at the next tutorial. This will enable them to work out a strategy for explaining it to you and, if necessary, to enlist the help of a colleague.

Developing a pattern of work

When it comes to writing essays or assignments, the stereotype is that students leave it until the very last minute before the submission date, and then work through the night to finish it in one go! Even though this may not be a particularly good idea for an essay, the approach will just not work with a thesis. An essay is much shorter, and to some extent it is possible to write it all at once. The thesis, however, demands a much more cumulative approach. Even if you decide to have a major effort and write a whole chapter, you will be brought to a halt every so often by the need to check some information, or to look up a reference. The whole exercise lends itself to a gradual and progressive approach.

In broad terms there are probably two main strategies you could adopt. You could write the thesis bit by bit, assembling the information, data or references as the need arises. On the other hand you could adopt a more thematic approach. This would involve collecting all the references you could imagine needing, having all of the data ready, and all of the information and discussion you intend to use about methodology. You can then draw upon this resource as and when it is required for writing the thesis. I tend to favour the latter approach because, once you have assembled all of the information you require, you will be able to proceed more smoothly with the writing.

There is then the question of motivation and having the inspiration to write. Some writers feel that they have to wait for inspiration to come, before they can make progress. The other approach is that you establish a pattern of writing, for example one hour every morning, and then stick to that. Sometimes you may find that you have little inspiration, and do not write very much. However, the argument is that by sticking to the self-imposed pattern, you will find that inspiration comes more frequently and regularly! Everyone has to find their own pattern of work, and the same system will not work for everyone.

One advantage of a regular working pattern is that it is much easier for you to judge the progress of your work. You will begin to be able to predict the number of words you will write each week. When you are then discussing handing in your next chapter to your supervisor, you will be able to estimate the date of submission more easily.

Attending conferences, courses and seminars

A final aspect of your life is 'networking'. As a research student, it may seem that you are often working in solitude, without much contact with other students. While this is true in one sense, you are in fact part of a very large community of researchers and academics, all linked by virtue of the aim to add to human knowledge. However esoteric your subject may be, it is almost certain that scattered across the country and the world, there will be many others working on similar issues. Maintaining regular contact with such people is not only a pleasure and a support, but also brings a number of very practical advantages for your work. Conferences and seminars are one of the major ways in which academics report their work to the wider research community. This is often quicker and more direct than writing a long journal article. The researcher may present a short paper at a conference and provide a summary of their provisional findings. They will receive feedback from the audience, and may use that in preparing a more detailed version of their findings for an article. You will also be able to add conference papers to your list of references. By attending conferences you will be able to keep much more up to date with the latest research, for inclusion in your thesis.

Many conferences also provide opportunities for research students to present brief summaries of their own work, perhaps by contributing either an abbreviated paper or a poster. These are very useful to help your research reach a wider audience, and to provide a focus for discussions with other academics. It is also very useful for young researchers to make as many contacts as they can with senior academics from other institutions. Generally speaking, experienced researchers and academics are very happy to help younger researchers. As you develop your range of contacts, people may be willing to act as referees for you or invite you to join them on research projects. There may be invitations to speak at forthcoming conferences, or to contribute to books or journals. You may also hear informally about future job possibilities, and many other opportunities in the academic world.

In summary, although your thesis and the accompanying qualification will be your principal concern, you will naturally want to use this to help develop your career, and networking at conferences and similar events is one of the major ways to help achieve this.

Further reading

Cottrell, S. (2005) *Critical Thinking Skills: Developing Effective Analysis and Argument*. Basingstoke: Palgrave Macmillan.

Kamler, B. and Thomson, P. (2006) *Helping Doctoral Students Write: Pedagogies for Supervision*. Abingdon: Routledge.

Kitchin, R. and Fuller, D. (2005) *The Academic's Guide to Publishing*. London: Sage.

Phillips, E. and Pugh, D.S. (2010) *How to get a PhD*, 5th edn. Maidenhead: Open University Press.

Wallace, M. and Wray, A. (2006) *Critical Reading and Writing for Postgraduates*. London: Sage.

6

Grammar, Punctuation and Conventions of Academic Writing

In this chapter we examine the style of academic writing required in order for you to be successful with your thesis. We look at gender-neutral language, and at some of the conventions of grammar and punctuation. We also discuss how you can use digital-based methods for quotations and referencing.

Study Strategies

- When reading academic books or theses, make a list of the non-English expressions you encounter. If you do not know the meaning, then consult a dictionary. If you are not familiar with the phrase, then the chances are that many other readers were in the same position. For each term or expression, try to develop a straightforward English alternative. Which do you prefer, and why?
- When you read an academic book or thesis which employs footnotes, analyse whether it would have been clearer to include some of the material in the main text.
- When you come across abbreviations, ask yourself whether some of them are ambiguous; that is, they could have been used for other terms.

First person or third person?

One of the issues which concerns most students when writing theses is whether they should employ the first person or the rather more formal third person. For example, is it more appropriate to write in the first person 'I started this research because I became interested in the subject of student achievement', or to say 'The researcher decided to start this research because of an interest in the subject of student achievement'? Another formal style sometimes used in academic writing is the passive voice as in 'It was decided to start this research because of an interest in the subject of student achievement'.

The traditional way of writing about research is to use the third person or passive voice, and it may be useful initially to explore the reasons for this. Most educational and social science research was originally influenced by the model of research employed in the physical sciences. It tended to be positivist and quantitative in its orientation, and to adopt the perspective of the apparently objective researcher who was distanced from the research. Phrases such as 'a survey was conducted', or 'the experimental data supported the assertion', tended to be used. This style of expression seemed to be appropriate for a positivist approach to research. It suggested that the decisions taken in research were fairly precise, and that research was an impartial, objective activity. The writing style also implied that researchers were people who followed procedures and protocols, and who tried to distance their own value systems from the activity of research.

Developing use of the first person

As educational research gradually became more influenced by philosophical approaches, such as phenomenology, there was a growing awareness of the importance of individual interpretation by the researcher, who interacted with the data rather than analysed it in an impersonal way. Research was seen as an activity which continually involved choices. There were choices to be made about research design, about methodology, about data collection and many other aspects of the research process. Such choices almost inevitably involved the researcher in taking subjective decisions. Such decisions were subjective because, although it was possible to assemble evidence to support either one decision or another, in the final analysis researchers often needed to take personal decisions about the direction in which their research would progress. Research came to be viewed less as a neat, linear process, and more as a complex activity in which there could be frequent changes of direction and emphasis. Given this change of orientation for some educational research, it was perhaps natural that the use of the first person became more accepted in certain circumstances. This was particularly true of action research studies, and research influenced by phenomenological and interpretative perspectives.

A position has now been reached in writing about research, where although the third person is generally favoured in most cases, it is acknowledged that the first person is appropriate in a number of different contexts, and is favoured in some. We now explore the use of the first and third persons in different situations.

Use in specific circumstances

There are many contexts in research writing where decisions are reported. For example, we may write 'The researcher decided to adopt a case study design for this piece of research because of the distinctive character of the research problem and the need to collect in-depth data'. What is important here is that the grounds for this decision have been articulated. If this has been done thoroughly, then it does not appear to make any difference whether one uses the third person or the first person. The crucial factor is that the decision was carefully considered. However, it is important that you do not stray into using the first person to indicate a form of bias in decision-making. For example, it would not be appropriate to say 'I believe that a case study design would be the best to adopt' since it implies an element of value judgement, rather than a reliance upon the available evidence.

In some situations in research it is necessary to discuss the complexities of the interactions between researcher and respondents. For example, in ethnographic studies, researchers may try to adopt strategies which help them to blend into the research context and hence to preserve the ecological validity of the setting. The manner in which this is accomplished may involve a number of subtle aspects in the behaviour of the researcher. For example, in an ethnographic study of a college, researchers may adopt an informal dress code, and may try to avoid situations where they would be noticed. It may be much easier to discuss this issue in the first person, since this writing style would enable researchers to discuss the many ways in which they try to move through a research setting, causing as little disruption as possible to the social organization.

Example – Collecting data

In your methodology chapter, when you are writing about the collection of data, it may sometimes be more natural to write in the first person. For example, if you are describing how you informed potential respondents about your research, it might be easier to say: 'I explained to each group of respondents that nothing they said would be reported to anyone else. I emphasized that I would not keep any records of their names, so that there was no way I could link them with their interview data.'

Writing reflexive accounts is another area in which it is likely to be much easier and more natural to write in the first person. If you are discussing your own academic and intellectual development, your own preferred ways of conducting research and the theoretical perspectives which you feel shed most light on the nature of the world, then it may seem much more natural to write in the first person. After all, a reflexive account is about you as a person. It is a form of intellectual autobiography. To start every sentence with a phrase such as 'The researcher considers that . . .' or 'The researcher has formed the view that . . .' does seem rather artificial.

Signpost to success – Writing style

Write in a style which communicates your ideas clearly and accurately, and which is appropriate for your methodology.

In summary, although the use of the third person may be more widely accepted, there are a number of occasions when the first person is not only acceptable, but may be more desirable. There may also be a number of other occasions when for stylistic reasons, such as to introduce variety into the prose, it may be a good idea to introduce the first person. The issue of more fundamental importance, however, is that, irrespective of the first or third person being used, the assertions made or decisions reached should be based upon clearly adduced evidence. Writing in the first or third person is discussed in Fairbairn and Winch (1991, pp. 75–82).

Gender-neutral language

It is very important to select terminology which treats both genders equally, and does not make assumptions about one gender as opposed to the other. To select language which does unfairly distinguish the genders may be sexist and may encourage existing gender stereotypes.

For example, in a thesis concerning school management, the student may write in the introduction that 'the headteacher has an increasingly complex role; his duties, for instance, may involve complicated financial issues'. If this was written about the headteacher role in general, then there is no justification for associating the role with the male gender. This is sexist and reinforces the stereotype of men being associated with management roles. There is no need to include 'his' in the above sentence. It can easily be rewritten as 'the headteacher has an increasingly complex role, involving complicated financial issues'.

Another simple strategy in general statements is to employ the plural. For example, 'Headteachers have an increasingly complex role; their duties, for instance, may involve complicated financial issues'. The plural form avoids any specification of gender.

When reporting empirical data, however, there may often be instances where it is necessary to refer to the gender of a respondent. In such instances, the use of the relevant pronoun, he or she, may be appropriate and even necessary for reporting the research. It may have been made clear earlier in the thesis that some respondents were male and some female, and therefore it will seem natural to refer to some as 'he' and some as 'she'.

Sometimes, of course, research treats gender as a variable in its own right. The purpose of such research may be to identify any differences between respondents which may have a connection with gender. In such cases it is acceptable to refer to the two genders.

Example – Research and gender

An example of this is the extensive work which has been carried out on the relative performance of boys and girls in certain school subjects. This is important because it may shed light on the relationship between academic performance and social processes in the classroom.

In discussion of general research issues, writers and researchers employ a number of strategies to avoid the use of a single gender pronoun. Sometimes, the use of a pronoun will be alternated, using 'he' in one chapter or section, 'she' in the next section, followed by reversion to 'he'. However, this strategy can sometimes be confusing for the reader. In addition, the use of a particular pronoun may be unsuitable in one section or chapter, and yet the predetermined scheme requires its use. Another strategy is to use the forms 'she or he', s/he or s(he). All of these may appear a little clumsy and distracting. The most natural way of avoiding the specification of a gender is to adopt the plural form, or to restructure the sentence in some way so that pronouns are avoided.

It is still fairly common for male-orientated expressions to be used, particularly when referring to occupations. An enquiry desk may be described as being 'manned', when it could be better described as being staffed. It is sexist to speak of 'manpower' issues when terms such as personnel issues or human resource issues could be used. It is inappropriate to write 'workmen' when the non-sexist alternative of workers is available. Alternative terms are usually readily available, and with a little care and thought sexist language can be avoided.

Layout for quotations

It is frequently necessary to include extracts from books, journal articles or research reports. These extracts or quotations are used to support arguments, for illustrative purposes, and to help to set the context for the research. It is of fundamental importance that the reader can recognize a quotation as being distinct from the main text written by the student. If the extracts taken directly from another source are merged in with the main text, then the student may be accused of plagiarism. The plagiarism may not be intentional, nevertheless the responsibility to make it clear when material from other sources has been used rests with the student.

The normal strategy for longer quotations is to type the quotation in italics, to use a narrower line spacing and to indent the quotation from the left. It is also normal to leave an additional line space at the beginning and end of the quotation. Thus, the following quotation (which is fictional) could be set out as follows:

Smith and Jones, in their work on the teaching of French in secondary schools, pointed out that:

Resources tended to be limited to conventional textbooks which concentrated on the finer and more abstract concepts in French grammar. The books had few illustrations and did not appear designed to convey a feeling for contemporary French life. (1962: 27)

The numbers in brackets at the end of the quotation refer respectively to the year of publication and the page number of the quotation. The layout of quotations in this form clearly separates the quotation from the remainder of the text, and helps the reader of the thesis to differentiate between the two types of material. It should be noted that in the above example of an indented, longer quotation there are no quotation marks at the beginning and end of the extract.

Sometimes, however, it is useful to insert a shorter extract, perhaps only part of a sentence, within the main text. In order to do this, it is normal to use quotation marks, but to leave the size, format and spacing of the text as it is. In the following example, such an extract might be set out as follows:

When exploring the use of conversational practice in the teaching of French, two writers have argued that 'the emphasis should be upon the pupils enjoying the use of the language, rather than upon an exaggerated concern with grammatical accuracy' (Smith and Jones, 1962: 51).

Care is needed with this form of quotation. It is not uncommon for students to type the first quotation mark but to omit the second. This is very confusing for the reader as it is unclear when the extract ends and the main text begins.

Digital-based referencing and citation packages

One of the characteristic features of academic writing is citing authors and works within the text, and the inclusion of a list of references to these citations at the end. This process requires the management of a great deal of information. You will need to insert the details of authors, texts and extracts in a suitable place, so that there is minimum disruption to the flow of the writing. In addition, citations need to be added where they are relevant and make sense in the context of the issue being discussed. Extracts need to be added where they illustrate or support an argument you are making. In other words, this is a very complex task, and to help you achieve it, you need your information and resources arranged in as systematic a way as possible.

A further difficulty is that you do not always find references or quotations at the time when you are writing. You need to be able to note down all the relevant details, and to add these later to the appropriate place in your electronic filing system. It is important that your filing system corresponds to the anticipated structure of your thesis. For example, if you know that your methodology chapter will have a section which discusses action research, then you need to accumulate references to action research in a separate file from which you can draw items as necessary. All of this can be achieved in an electronic filing system which you devise yourself.

There are also a number of electronic research management tools available, which enable you to collect and file the references which you identify as potentially useful. Examples of these systems include EndNote® (Thomson Reuters, 2012) and RefWorks© (RefWorks©, 2009). These types of information management systems will typically perform a range of useful tasks for you. They can carry out searches of a range of academic sources available online, and then arrange these materials in a way which suits your needs. You can then manipulate these articles and books into lists of references, using one of a selection of different format styles. If you wish to use a referencing style which employs footnotes, then you can arrange for the insertion of the latter where appropriate. As with all types of academic software, you have to invest time in learning how to use the system. The time investment needed may be a factor in your decision about how to manage your research reference materials.

The Harvard system of referencing

Two principal systems of referencing are used for academic writing and theses. One system employs superscript numbers in the text to refer the reader to a list of references at the end of either the chapter or the thesis. Here, the full bibliographic details of the citation are provided. Sometimes, the superscript numbers are used to refer to the same details, but these are provided as a footnote on the page on which they occur. The advantage of this system is that the superscript numbers constitute a minimal interruption to the reading of the text. However, if it is necessary to add further references during the writing of the thesis, then it is important to check that all the subsequent numbers have been altered appropriately.

The alternative system, and the one which was used for illustrative purposes in the 'Layout for quotations' section, is usually termed the Harvard system, and has grown in popularity in academic writing in education and the social sciences. In the main text, a quotation is annotated with the surname of the author, the date of publication of the work and the page number from which the quotation was taken. The full bibliographic details are then provided in a list of references at the end of the work (see Figure 6.1). The disadvantage of the Harvard system is that the insertion of author details in the text does sometimes make the reading of the thesis a little awkward. On the other hand, it is useful to note the name of the author of a text while reading the thesis. With the Harvard system there is also no difficulty in adding new references within the text.

It is sometimes necessary to refer several times to the same work. This may be because that book is a seminal work which is of central importance to the arguments being developed. In general, unless there are pressing reasons to do so, avoid citing the same work too many times. It may give the examiners the impression, rightly or wrongly, that you have not surveyed the available literature thoroughly. Where there are multiple references to the same work, some writers tend to use phrases such as 'ibid.' or 'op. cit.'. Unless these are used with great precision, and the reader is completely familiar with their use, they may be confusing. It is normal simply to repeat the full citation, repeating author, year and providing the new page number. Although repetitious, it is completely unambiguous.

Sometimes an author may have published more than one work in a single year, and you wish to cite all of them. In such cases, the citations in the main text may be distinguished by using the form 1962a, 1962b, 1962c, and so on. The full bibliographic details are then provided as normal at the end of the thesis.

It is common to wish to indicate in a thesis the writers who have made a particular contribution to a field. In such a case it may not be necessary to include quotations, but merely to mention the authors as key figures in the field. For instance, you might write:

> A number of writers have investigated the impact of teaching contemporary European philosophy alongside the teaching of a European language (Smith, 1961; Jones, 1983; and Dixon, 2001).

In this example, the student is simply indicating that the works by Smith, Jones and Dixon are a useful source of material on the issue in question. Referencing such as this is useful where you wish to indicate the broad span of the field of the literature, without at this stage going into detail about specific quotations.

At the end of the thesis it is normal to list the full bibliographic details of all the works which have been cited in the text. These are listed by alphabetical order of author surname. Slightly different conventions apply to the referencing of books, academic journal articles and other types of publication. The principal variations are indicated below using fictional examples.

A book is referenced in the following way:

Smith, J. (1963) *The Theory of European Culture*. Birmingham: Language Press.

The key features are that the book title is printed in italics, and that this is followed by the place of publication and the name of the publisher.

A chapter in an edited volume is referenced as follows:

Jones, S. (2000) 'Contemporary existentialist thought', in M. Bradley (ed.), *A History of Modern Philosophy*. London: Thames Publications. pp. 39–57.

It should be noted here that again it is the title of the book which is printed in italics. The chapter title is printed in quotation marks. It is also the convention that the initial of the editor's name precedes the surname. The pages at the end indicate the extent of the chapter within the book.

One of the most common forms of reference used is the academic journal article, and this is referenced as follows:

Jones, P. (2002) 'Phenomenology in sociological theory', *Journal of Interpretative Studies*, 28(3): 202–30.

The title of the journal is placed in italics rather than the title of the journal article. The latter is identified with quotation marks. The numbers at the end are respectively the volume number, the issue number and the page span of the article within the journal. The total number of copies or issues of a journal published in a specific year constitutes a 'volume'. Hence, Volume 1, is the total number of issues published in the first year of publication of the journal, Volume 2 in the second year, and so on. In the above example, the *Journal of Interpretative Studies* is in its twenty-eighth year of publication. The issue concerned is the third issue of the journal during that year.

If you wish to quote from another thesis which is in a library, then this can be referenced as follows:

Collin, J. (2001) 'The origins of the German university system'. PhD thesis, University of Northtown, England.

academic tradition and is an inherited part of educational thinking in the western world (Gonczi, 1999). This divide can result in tensions within the assessment strategies in professional courses such as midwifery. An assessment strategy is necessary that places an emphasis on competent performance in a clinical context and is part of an education designed to render students safe to practise. At the same time there is an equally important need to examine students' knowledge base for the profession into which they are being socialised and inducted (Edwards and Knight, 1995). Managing practice assessment and theoretical assessment produces tensions for students. So within the pre-registration midwifery curriculum there is clearly a need to have an assessment strategy that is student-focused and promotes understanding on a variety of dimensions in order to foster in students the development of transferable contextualised skills.

The assessment of attitudes and values

The assessment of attitudes and values is notoriously difficult to achieve yet it is recognised that these professional attributes are very important (Bedford et al, 1993; Eraut, 1993; Hager et al, 1994). This challenge to assessment practices has sometimes been avoided with the emphasis being placed on knowledge and skills. Limiting the assessment of practice in this way has the potential to deny students the opportunity to learn from their experience and develop the requisite professional attitudes and values (Bedford et al, 1993; Boud et al, 1993; Bradshaw, 1997). Not only does the student midwife need to develop a professional attitude towards those in her care but also the appropriate attitudes for critical thinking. These include intellectual humility and the courage to contemplate change based on sound evidence, integrity, perseverance and empathy (Miller et al, 1998; Taylor, 2000a). Hager et al (1994) conclude that the most reliable way of assessing attitudes and values is in the

30

Duffy, M. E. (1985) 'Designing Nursing Research: The qualitative-quantitative debate', *Journal of Advanced Nursing* 10: 225-231.

Dux, C. M. (1989) 'An investigation into whether nurse teachers take into account the individual learning styles of their students when formulating teaching strategies', *Nurse Education Today* 9: 186-191.

Edwards, A. and Knight, P (1995) 'The Assessment of Competence in Higher Education' in Edwards, A. and Knight, P. (eds.) *Assessing Competence in Higher Education*. London: Kogan Page.

Ellis, R. (ed.) (1988) 'Competence in the Caring Professions' in *Professional Competence and Quality Assurance in the Caring Professions*. London: Croom Helm.

English National Board (1995) *Creating Life Long Learners: partnerships for care*. London: English National Board.

English National Board (1996) *Learning From Each Other: The Involvement of People Who Use Services And Their Carers in Education and Training*. London: English National Board.

English National Board (2001) *Education in Focus. Strengthening Pre-registration Nursing and Midwifery Education. Section 3:Guidelines for Pre-registration Midwifery Programmes*. London: English National Board.

English National Board and Department of Health (2001a) *Developments in multiprofessional education. Placements in Focus. Guidance for education in practice for health care professionals*. London: ENB and DOH.

English National Board and Department of Health (2001b) *Preparation of Mentors and Teachers. A new framework of guidance*. London: ENB and DOH.

English National Board and Open University (2001) *Assessing Practice in Nursing and Midwifery*.

Entwistle, N. (1988) *Styles of Learning And Teaching*. London: David Fulton Publishers.

Eraut, M. (1993) *Assessing Competence in the Professions*. Sheffield: Methods Strategy Unit, Educational Department.

Erickson, F. (1990) 'Qualitative methods', *Research in Teaching and Learning* 2: 77-94.

Evans, N. (1987) *Assessing Experiential Learning. A Review of Progress and Practice*. Longman for Further Education Unit Productions.

234

Figure 6.1   Sample pages from a thesis to illustrate referencing

There are many other types of publications by, for example, government departments. There may be no self-evident author, and the body which has actually published the document may be far from clear. Rather than trying to deal with every possible permutation of form of publication, the most sensible course of action may well be for you to consult reference works such as Turabian (1996) or British Standards Institution (1990).

Although conventions are important, it is worth remembering the principal reason for referencing systems. It is to help you to identify the source of a quotation and, if necessary, to locate the original publication as easily as possible. An important principle in the use of any referencing system is to be consistent. Particularly, where you are referencing publications which are not easily subsumed under the main categories of publication, it is important that having devised a referencing system, you adhere to it throughout the thesis.

Referencing websites

Students are increasingly using the Internet for reference materials, and hence there is a need to be able to cite these sources. There are, however, several difficulties in using such materials. An author of a web page is not always indicated. In addition, there may be no indication of the academic source of the text, or whether the author is affiliated with an academic institution. Many web pages on academic subjects derive from authoritative sources, but you should always exercise caution when using and citing such sources if the author and associated institution are unclear. As a general rule, web pages are amended and updated much more frequently than printed material published in a conventional way. Hence it is important, when citing such material, to provide the date when the site was accessed.

It is also worth remembering that printed publications are subjected to a range of thorough quality control measures prior to publication. Web pages, even those deriving from reputable academic sources, may not have been subject to the same degree of quality control.

The general method for citing a web page is illustrated by the following fictional example:

Jennings, P. (2003) An annotated bibliography of contemporary psychology. (Online) Available: http://www.bup.ac.uk/humlit/socialscience/psych.htm (accessed 2 January 2003)

It should be remembered, however, that the systems of referencing and protocols for electronic sources are still developing, and some variability may be encountered.

Use of notes and footnotes

It is sometimes necessary to include additional material which is felt to be inappropriate to place in the main text. This kind of material may be information which is supplementary to the principal arguments of the text, or it may consist of additional specialist references. Such material may be included in footnotes at the bottom of the relevant page, or in notes at the end of each chapter or at the end of the thesis. The selection of the system to be used for notes or footnotes is to some extent a matter of individual taste, and may also depend upon the accepted conventions for the particular university.

All the systems utilize superscript numbers which are placed in the text alongside the issue to which the note refers. Numbering proceeds sequentially throughout a chapter, and then recommences for the next chapter. For footnotes, the additional material is placed at the bottom of the relevant page. Alternatively, notes may be collated in numerical order at the end of each chapter, or all of the notes for the thesis may be collected together at the end and arranged in chapter order. In the latter case, the notes are usually typed immediately prior to the final list of references for the thesis. The superscript numbers included in the main text may be a distraction for readers, and it is often better to add them at the end of the sentence to which they refer, rather than attaching them above a word in the middle of a sentence.

However, notes of any kind inevitably take the reader's attention away from the main text. In the case of notes at the end of chapters or the main thesis, the reader needs regularly to move backwards and forwards through the thesis, and this may be distracting. It can be argued that much of the material sometimes included in notes would be better placed in the main text.

Non-English terms and expressions

Generally speaking, care should be taken with the inclusion of such terms. It is important that you reflect carefully upon the reasons for their use, and do not employ the term when there is an acceptable English alternative. Where non-English terms are used, however, there are some considerations to take into account.

There are a number of expressions from other languages which are now used regularly in English. If that is the case, and if the word normally carries an accent mark in the original language, then this is omitted in English use. An example is 'denouement', from French, where the original acute accent above the first vowel is omitted. If it is necessary to refer to an overseas location, the English version of the name, rather than the indigenous version, is used. Thus, you should use 'Florence' rather than 'Firenze'.

There are some differences in the manner in which the titles of books and other works are typed in English compared to other languages. In English it is normal for the first word of the title and also for the other key words to start with a capital letter, for example, Functionalism in Modern Sociological Thought. In other languages, however, it is normally only the first word and all proper nouns which are capitalized, for example, Dans deux semaines.

Non-English terms which are used regularly in English are not italicized, for example, 'in situ' or 'status quo'. However, an expression such as 'suigeneris' would probably be italicized. When contemplating the use of an expression from another language it is worth considering whether it is likely to be understood by most readers. If not, then it is probably worth trying to express the ideas in English, even if it is necessary to employ rather more words.

Example – Some non-English terms and their meanings

The following are some non-English terms (in this case Latin) which are found with some frequency in academic writing. There are of course others, from a variety of languages. However, it must be said that, in the case of all terms listed below, it would be perfectly possible to express the same idea using straightforward English.

a fortiori	with greater reason
ceteris paribus	other things being equal
ex post facto	after the event has occurred
ipso facto	by the very fact
magnum opus	great work, or most significant work
non sequitur	does not follow
prima facie	at first sight
sine qua non	a necessary condition
ultra vires	beyond legal rights

English and American spellings

The issue which occurs most commonly in academic writing is the selection of the form of verbs which can end in either 'ise' or 'ize'. In English theses, the latter form is the norm. Examples of words which are used fairly commonly in an academic context, and where this issue arises, include 'hypothesize', 'synthesize' and 'socialize'. However, there are words which do take the 'ise' form including 'supervise' and 'supervisor', and note also the spelling of 'analyse'.

Remember that in computer software programmes originating in America, the 'ize' form of verbs is often highlighted as a spelling error.

Abbreviations

Abbreviations should be used sparingly. When inserted in the text to any great extent, they have the effect of breaking up the text, and making it more difficult to read. The reader may forget the meaning of some of the abbreviations and need to turn back regularly to consult the glossary.

Sometimes a thesis is concerned with an issue or issues which have fairly long names. It may also be necessary to repeat these names with great frequency. An example of such a term might be 'computer-based education and training'. If this term was repeated many times in a thesis, it could result in the text becoming rather boring to read, and make the structure of sentences appear rather awkward. Under those circumstances it might be preferable to develop an acronym such as CBET. When an abbreviation is used for the first time, then the full form of the term should be given first, followed by the abbreviation in brackets afterwards. From that point onwards, the abbreviation may be used on its own. It is a good idea also to include a list of abbreviations near the beginning of the thesis, usually just before the beginning of the first chapter.

Acronyms for official organizations normally have no full stops. Examples include SOAS, UMIST and OUP. Some abbreviations such as Dr, carry no full stop. Others such as C.E., B.C.E., Ph.D., e.g. and i.e. do carry full stops.

Italicizing and capitalization

The titles of all books, journals and other academic works are italicized. However, the titles of chapters in books or of articles in journals are not italicized. You should be cautious about using italics to emphasize a word or term. The reason for the italicization or the intended nuance of meaning may not be self-evident to the reader. Such a use of italics demands a degree of interpretation on the part of the reader, and the latter may interpret the word in a different way from that intended.

Capitals should be used for the names of academic organizations such as the University of Oxford or the British Library. If one is referring repeatedly to a specific institution, for example the University of London, then after the first use one may simply refer to the institution as 'the University', but an initial capital should be used to indicate that it is the particular university being discussed. When referring to the present incumbent of a post, and not to the post in general, capitals are used, for example the Vice-Chancellor. Adjectives which are derived from the name of a person, for example Kantian or Aristotelian, have an initial capital letter.

The use of hyphens, dashes, numerals and the apostrophe

When two words are treated as a single concept, they are normally hyphenated. Examples include 'post-structuralist' and 'hypothetico-deductive'. However, if each word carries its own significance, then no hyphen is used. Examples could be 'symbolic interactionism' and 'labelling theory'. However, there may be considerable variation in practice.

Dashes are of two main kinds. The short dash is equivalent in length to a double hyphen and has no spaces at beginning or end. It is used to show a connection between two terms as in 'the ethnographic–interactionist approach to research'. The long dash is used to indicate an additional inclusion in a sentence such as: 'The positivist approach to research – relying as it does upon quantitative data – may be suitable where the researcher feels able to define the precisely measurable concepts within the research.' However, the use of either commas or brackets may be a more appropriate technique. The long dash has the same length as the short dash, but has a space at the beginning and end.

When indicating a span between two numbers, for example page numbers, only the second two digits need be provided, for example 432–53. The dash used is a short dash. Dates are normally printed in the format 16 January 1932. Centuries are normally written in the form 'the nineteenth century'. If a number relates to precise statistical data, it is normally written in numerals. On the other hand, if it is part of the text, or at the beginning of a sentence, then it is normally written in words. Larger numbers in the text, which would be long and awkward in words, may be written in numerals.

The most common use of the apostrophe is in indicating possession. An element of confusion may arise when you are trying to indicate the possessive for a person whose name ends in an 's'. In such cases, the possessive is indicated by adding an apostrophe and a second 's', for example Keynes's or Morris's. Sometimes an apostrophe is erroneously added to a date, when the purpose is to indicate a decade as a span of time. The correct style is to omit the apostrophe, as in the 1960s. The use of the apostrophe is discussed in Creme and Lea (1997, pp. 136–7).

Consistency, consistency and, above all, consistency!

For both master's and doctoral theses, there is a reasonable amount of flexibility in the conventions of academic writing. For example, some students indicate indented quotations by using a smaller font and narrower line spacing, while others will employ italics. In terms of the referencing system used, there are many publications which are unconventional in one form or another, and hence you may have to devise your own system for providing the bibliographic details. It is certainly difficult to formulate precise and invariable rules for italicizing and capitalization. Similarly, there is considerable variation in the use of hyphens and dashes.

It is often only when you actually start to write that the needs of the language of that particular thesis are identified. For example, it may become apparent that it will be absolutely necessary to employ certain non-English expressions with regularity. It may be necessary to include quotations from other languages. As the typing of the thesis develops, the specific needs will become apparent. Clearly you will wish to abide by accepted academic conventions wherever possible, but there may be some cases where you will need to develop conventions which are unique to your thesis.

Example: Referring to literature from other countries

If you are researching a subject which involves data from texts written originally in a different language, you will need to make a decision about the system to be used for transposition. This issue may confront students of literature or of comparative religion. In some cases, there may be several different systems available and your choice will need to be explained to the reader.

When this is the case, it is important that such conventions are fully explained, and that they are used consistently. In addition, in all other cases where there may be a choice of conventions, it is important to make a selection of format, and then to abide by that choice throughout the thesis. Even slight variations in practice can be an irritant for the reader. Consistency is perhaps more important than the choice of convention which has been made.

Example – Key issues in academic writing

It is perhaps worth summarizing the key issues which you should normally try to keep in mind when writing in an academic context:

- Try to write in a style which is objective, balanced and does not contain bias.
- If you need to be more subjective, and use the first person, then approach this cautiously.
- Select terms and expressions which are gender-neutral.
- Decide on an accepted referencing style, and then adhere to it.
- Give careful attention to spelling and grammar.
- Be consistent in all matters of academic style, in order to give coherence to your thesis.

Further reading

Jackson, H. (2005) *Good Grammar for Students*. London: Sage.

Redman, P. (2005) *Good Essay Writing: A Social Sciences Guide*. 3rd edn. London: Sage.

Rudestam, K.E. and Newton, R.R. (2007) *Surviving Your Dissertation: A Comprehensive Guide to Content and Process*. 3rd edn. Los Angeles, CA: Sage.

Swales, J. and Feak, C.B. (2004) *Academic Writing for Graduate Students: Essential Tasks and Skills*. 2nd edn. Ann Arbor, MI: University of Michigan Press.

Wyse, D. (2007) *The Good Writing Guide for Education Students*. London: Sage.

7

Layout of the Thesis

In this chapter we consider the presentation of the thesis. We look at different aspects of page layout, formatting and the use of titles and subtitles. We also examine the use of tables and figures, and the content of the appendices. Every thesis should be presented in a clear and straightforward style, in order to assist the reader. This chapter will help you to do this.

Study Strategies

- Before you start typing, look at examples of theses, academic journals and academic books, for ideas on page layout, headings and general formatting. Make notes on the various ways in which the pages, tables and illustrations are designed, and then type up some sample pages on your computer.
- Think about the various requirements of your subject matter and thesis, and then decide on a plan for the formatting and layout.
- Work out a hierarchy of headings, subheadings and sub-subheadings, and type up a sample sheet, noting the size and style of font. Keep this beside you as a guide, when working on the thesis.

Page layout

Theses are intended to be serious documents and, generally speaking, are presented in a fairly formal manner. If, for example, a thesis were to contain a number of brightly coloured illustrations and a great deal of decorative formatting, then it might be considered to have too informal an appearance to satisfy the expectations of examiners. In fact, the extent of the decorative work might detract from the seriousness and academic content of the arguments. This is just one example of why it is important to present your thesis in such a way that it meets the expectations of people in terms of appearance. The importance of layout is discussed in Berger (1993, p. 63).

Font size and style

When starting to type your thesis, or arranging the typing, it helps to decide as soon as possible on a variety of layout issues. The font size for the main text will probably be 11 or 12 point, and it is best to use double-spacing. Most students opt for one of the most commonly used font styles in academic writing, such as Times New Roman or Arial. It may sound rather conventional to say so, but it is probably best to avoid the more decorative or unusual fonts available. This approach is again consonant with the philosophy of presenting the thesis in a fairly formal style.

Page layout

Pages should be numbered throughout using arabic numerals starting on the first page of the first chapter. The preliminary pages such as the contents, acknowledgements or glossary are numbered using lower-case roman numerals. Once the typing has been finalized, the appropriate page numbers may be added to the contents pages. The space around the edge of a typical page is probably adequate as determined by the default page margins on your computer. The only exception is the left-hand or binding edge of the paper. The margin here should be increased by about one centimetre, to allow additional space when the thesis is permanently bound. If the space is not left, then when pages are turned it will be difficult to read the left-hand text. Examination of an existing permanently bound thesis will provide guidance on the exact amount of additional margin you need to leave. Care should be taken not to make the left-hand margin too wide, as this may make the page layout seem disproportionate in shape. Some students prefer to justify the right-hand edge of the text, while others prefer to leave this unjustified. To some extent this is a matter of taste. Again, an examination of existing theses may help you decide on the system you prefer.

Use of headings, subheadings and titles

Apart from the basic size of font used throughout the thesis, decisions need to be taken about the font size for the title page, the headings to pages such as the abstract or contents, chapter headings and subheadings throughout chapters. It is natural to associate the size of the font, and whether or not it is printed in bold, with the importance of that title or heading. Thus, on the title page the title should probably be in a larger font size than anything else in the thesis. Your name should be commensurately smaller. Ideas for the actual sizes and layout can be obtained from other theses.

All the text should be typed on one side of the paper only. Each chapter should begin on a new page. Each chapter should be numbered in arabic numerals, as in 'Chapter 1', followed lower down the page by the title of the chapter. These titles could be in 14 or 16 point, depending upon taste, and will probably be in bold. It is also a good idea to print the titles of all the preliminary pages in bold and in the same font size as for the chapter headings. This will establish consistency for main headings throughout the thesis. Headings and subheadings are not normally underlined, but distinguished by either size of font, or the use of bold or italics.

Subheadings are a very useful device. They enable you to structure each chapter in a more meaningful way, and to subdivide the subject matter so that it can be better understood. However, if not used in a logical way, subheadings can confuse the reader. Subheadings constitute a form of hierarchy. At the top of the hierarchy are the chapter titles, followed by the first level of subheadings and then, if necessary, a second level of subheadings. The principal layout requirement is that throughout the thesis the same level of subheading should be identified by the same type of formatting. For example, level one may be indicated by 12 point bold, and level two by 12 point bold italics.

The next requirement for subheadings is to try to use them in a consistent way in different chapters. This is not always easy to achieve because of the different subject matter of each chapter. However, there are some straightforward precautions which can be taken to try to avoid confusion. Sometimes chapters begin with a few paragraphs of an introductory nature, and you identify these with a subheading 'Introduction' at the beginning of the chapter. However, subsequent chapters may either start with no subheading at all or with a different subheading. If one chapter is to start with a subheading 'Introduction', then it is desirable that all do. It is also helpful if all chapters have approximately the same number of subheadings at each level. It is not necessary to have exactly the same number, but there should at least be some similarity in number. All these strategies are designed to give a sense of structure to the thesis and inspire in the reader the feeling that there is rationality to its layout.

Some writers attach a numerical system to the subheadings. For example, the first subheading of chapter 1 would be numbered 1.1, and the first second-level subheading would be numbered 1.1.1. In the second chapter, the numbering would be 2.1 and 2.1.1 respectively. This does give a precision to the subheadings, but is more characteristic of the style of a report than of a thesis.

Layout of contents pages

The table of contents sets out the structure of the thesis, with all of the main sections and subsections, along with the page numbers on which they commence. Although the table of contents is placed very near the beginning of the thesis, there are several sections which come before it. The title page is followed by an abstract of the thesis. This summarizes in about one side of A4, all of the key features of the thesis, including the data, the analysis, and the conclusions drawn. It is usually obligatory to include an abstract. After this, there are one or two sections which may be included, depending upon your wishes as the writer. You may decide to include a 'Dedication' page, on which you mention the names of important people in your life, who have inspired you to work on this thesis. Some students, for example, dedicate their thesis to members of their family. After this, you may have an 'Acknowledgements' page on which you include the names of those who have been of significant help. These may include your supervisors, or those academics whom you have consulted. These preliminary pages are usually numbered with lower-case Roman numerals starting from the title page. However, although the title page and abstract are included in the counting of page numbers, the actual numerals are usually excluded from those pages.

We now come to the table of contents. This does not mention any of the previous preliminary pages. Only the sections which come after the Table of Contents are included. A typical table of contents is set out below, although it should be noted that individual universities have their own regulations on the layout of theses.

Example – Table of contents

Table of contents

The tables page should list all tabular presentations in the order in which they appear in the thesis. Each entry should state the number of the table, the title and the page number on which it appears. The same system is used for the figures page. Further details of the use of tables and figures are provided later in this chapter. A page listing abbreviations used in the thesis is often useful. This may include acronyms or other forms of abbreviation. If you decide to use an abbreviation throughout the thesis, it is normal to only provide the full version on the first occasion you use it. The page which lists appendices, should provide the names and the page numbers of the different sections of supplementary material included. Further details of the use of appendices are provided later in this chapter. Depending upon the subject matter, some theses may require you to transpose words from one language into English. This may be necessary particularly where you refer to literature in a different language. Where such transliteration takes place, you may need to use diacritical marks above or below letters, in order to indicate the pronunciation. In such a case, an explanatory list is very useful.

After these pages, you can list the chapter numbers, their titles and the page numbers on which they start. It is important to note that the page numbering system changes with the start of the chapters. The first page of chapter 1, is numbered as page 1 using arabic numerals. For the remainder of the thesis, all pages are numbered in sequence using arabic numerals. Under each chapter heading, you could also list the subheadings and their page numbers included in that chapter. Subheadings would usually be indented, in order to distinguish them from the chapter headings.

After the list of chapters, will be included a list of the references of all works cited in the thesis. If necessary, there may then be a glossary, providing short definitions of key terms which you have used. Finally, there will be a list of appendices. The main thing to remember when preparing the table of contents, is that it is primarily a guide to give readers an overview of the structure of your thesis, and to help them navigate from one section to another.

Signpost to success – Headings and subheadings

Give careful thought to the use of headings, in order to help your reader understand the structure of the thesis.

Frequency of quotations

The selection of quotations and the manner in which they are integrated into the text, and into the emerging arguments, are academic issues. On the assumption that you have selected appropriate quotations from relevant sources, and have used the correct bibliographic details, there still remain some important issues of layout. You often find an extremely interesting book or article which contains a great deal of relevance to the thesis. It becomes very tempting to include long extracts from such a work. However, if you succumb to this temptation, then there are several results, none of which enhance the thesis. The repeated use of one reference gives the impression, rightly or wrongly, that only a limited number of sources have been consulted. In addition, the use of long extracts gives the impression that you have relied upon other writers to formulate the arguments, rather than preparing and structuring your own original arguments. Finally, from the viewpoint of the layout of the page it is evident to the examiner from a glance at each page that the text consists predominantly of quotations rather than original text.

Example – Analysing texts

There is one situation where it may be permissible, or even necessary, to include long quotations from the same text. This is where the text is a seminal work, central to the thesis, and you are analysing the ideas which it contains. If you are definitely analysing and critiquing the text, rather than just including extracts for illustrative purposes, then it may be justifiable to include a number of lengthy quotations.

As long quotations are both indented and placed in italics it is very easy, scanning through the thesis, to form an idea of the proportion of quotations to original text. An excessive use of quotations is easily discernible. The question arises, however, about what counts as 'excessive'. As a supervisor, I have often been asked by students about the number of quotations they should include in the text, and about the length of those quotations. There cannot be, of course, a precise formulaic answer to this question. The number and frequency of quotations may be greater in the introduction, the literature review and methodology chapters. In the later chapters of the thesis, there will be a greater emphasis upon presenting and analysing the data, rather than reviewing the writing of notable people in the field. However, even in areas of the thesis where there is a legitimate dependence upon quotations, the latter should not assume a disproportionate importance in comparison to the original text. As a very approximate rule of thumb, the quotations on a typical page should not exceed about one-third of the total lines. Of course some pages may have slightly more space devoted to quotations, and others less. Overall, however, this kind of balance should be achieved. If the frequency of quotations tends to exceed this balance, then the impression may be given that you have been relying too much on the selective use of the ideas of others.

Use of bullet points and formatting

One of the advantages of word processing packages is that they enable people to produce documents which look as professional as a published product. However, a disadvantage has been that such technology has encouraged people to present their ideas in an abbreviated form, typified by the use of bullet points and similar techniques. Ideas are summarized and presented almost as notes. Similarly, access to the presentation of graphics has encouraged people to present information in visually pleasing ways, but in a form which does not encourage the discussion of ideas to the extent that they may merit and require. Such technology has brought many advantages for academics, but it should be employed with great caution.

A thesis is primarily a work devoted to academic analysis and discussion. The ideas involved are invariably complex, and by their very nature require extensive discussion. Many of the concepts cannot be employed satisfactorily without analysing their use and discussing the nuances of the various meanings which may be attributed to them. The use of bullet points to express such ideas sometimes results in an oversimplification. There may be a use for bullet points or enumeration in a conclusion or at the end of chapters, but even there they should be used with caution. Occasionally there are places where bullet points may be profitably used. An example is in the presentation of the aims of the thesis. Rather than discussing the aims in a general way and embedding them within an ordinary paragraph, they can be listed in a precise way using numbers or bullet points. This helps to identify them clearly, and to make it easier for you to refer back to them from a later point in the thesis. To that extent, numbers may be preferable to bullet points, since you can refer to a specific numbered aim.

Example – Differences between types of theses

It is worth qualifying this argument when comparing theses in the humanities with those in mathematics, science or engineering. The former may require a more discursive use of language, while the latter may well lend themselves to the use of summaries and succinct statements of results.

It is now extremely easy to make documents appear very decorative, using, for example, Gothic lettering and ornate borders and boxes. While these may be suitable for business cards and invitations, they are less suitable for theses. Contrary to the apparent expectations of a minority of students, examiners do not award additional merit points for the exotic presentation of theses! Quite the contrary. A thesis is evaluated in terms of the quality of the intellectual content. The style of presentation should be simple and straightforward, and should not detract from the academic content. An elaborate or extravagant style of presentation will not be viewed as an asset.

Including tables and figures in the thesis

A 'table' consists of the presentation of data or information in a combination of horizontal rows and vertical columns. Horizontal and vertical lines are normally reduced to a minimum, and therefore the table does not usually consist of cells, as in a spreadsheet. The information included in tables is often of a numerical nature, although this need not be the case. A figure, on the other hand, consists of a drawing, diagram, statistical display such as a histogram, or illustration. Tables and figures are distinguished both by the title and by a separate numbering system.

The decision to incorporate information in a table or figure should be considered carefully. It may be more appropriate to include the information in the normal text of the thesis. For example, if you wish to support an argument by quoting three separate percentage figures, these could quite easily be included in the text and do not require a separate table. If they were presented as a table, then the latter may seem rather inconsequential. Both tables and figures should be used to improve the clarity of the presentation of the thesis. They should enable the reader to understand the thesis more easily, to grasp the significance of the data more easily, and to appreciate the arguments and theoretical content of the thesis more readily. If they are unlikely to achieve these aims, then you should consider omitting them and including the information in the text in the normal way.

Tables

A table might be employed if there is a substantial amount of numerical data to be discussed, and to set this out in a logical, tabular form might help the reader. A table can help to make comparisons between data, to understand statistical relationships better and to appreciate the way in which data may be subdivided into smaller groups. Tables can often be used to advantage for the presentation of qualitative data, or for the systematic presentation of verbal comparisons or contrasts. For example, if the advantages and disadvantages of an educational initiative are being discussed, then to present these in discursive form may involve a lengthy written discussion. By the end of the discussion, the reader may have difficulty in recollecting all the arguments. It is more useful if these are presented in summary form, showing the advantages on one side of a table, and the disadvantages on the other. Thus tables should not be employed in an attempt to improve the appearance of a thesis, but should have a specific function. That function should be to enhance the ease with which the content of the thesis may be understood.

Figures

Much the same applies to the use of figures. The explanation of a theoretical model may be aided considerably by its presentation in diagrammatic form, illustrating the connections between the different theoretical constructs. An algorithm may be very helpful in explaining the sequence in which a research project was conducted. A pie chart may be useful to explain quickly the different proportions in a group of data. However, as with tables, an inappropriate or excessive use of presentations such as pie charts may be perceived as over-simplistic.

Example – Use of diagrams

A thesis, particularly at doctoral level, is characterized by the sophistication, complexity and nuancing of the concepts used. In order to demonstrate that the intellectual content is at the appropriate level, concepts have to be discussed in a very detailed way. The excessive use of charts and diagrams may give the impression that ideas have not been treated at a sufficient level of sophistication.

Numbering

Tables and figures are numbered separately throughout the thesis, according to the number of the chapter and to their sequence in that particular chapter. For example, the third table in Chapter 7 would be designated 'Table 7.3', and the fifth figure in Chapter 1 would be entitled 'Figure 1.5'. Numbering of both tables and figures starts afresh in each new chapter. The numbering system provides you with a precise method for referring to a table or figure from the text. If you use a phrase such as 'in the table above' or 'in the figure on the previous page', there is always the danger that this may prove to be less than accurate. When amendments and additions are made to the thesis, a certain amount of text often flows from one page to another, and such instructions may no longer be relevant. However, if you refer to a numbered table as 'in Table 2.7', then there is no ambiguity.

A table should be numbered as above, and should also carry a title which is an accurate description of the content of the table. A variety of computerized tabular formats are available, some very decorative. A simple design as shown in the table below is preferred.

Table 7.1   Example of table format

Table 3.4   Numbers of students at Southtown University by category of subject

	Undergraduates	Postgraduates	Research	All
Technology	3.27	0.27	0.20	3.74
Humanities	1.11	0.07	0.03	1.21
Fine Arts	0.56	0.06	0.02	0.64
Sciences	2.93	0.39	0.13	3.45
Social Sciences	1.89	0.15	0.09	2.13
Total	9.76	0.94	0.47	11.17

Notes: 1 Numbers are × 1000.
2 Numbers refer to students registered by the 3rd week in October.

Listing references and including a bibliography

Within the Harvard system, all the references cited in the main text should be listed at the end of the thesis, immediately prior to the appendices. The works are listed by alphabetical order of the surname of the author. The list should be headed 'References'. Normally such a list is not subdivided into sections of any kind. Having one list makes it easier for the reader to locate the full bibliographical details of any work cited.

The alternative system is to have a list at the end which includes all the works cited, but also includes any works which you consider to be of particular interest or significance to the thesis. The criteria for selecting such works varies. These may be books which you have consulted in writing the thesis, but perhaps have not needed to cite in the text. They may be important works, but are only of peripheral significance to the subject or methodology of the thesis. Such works, when selected, should be incorporated in the list of references, also by alphabetical order of surname. A list which includes both cited and non-cited works should be entitled 'Bibliography'.

Both systems are accepted as legitimate, although the list of references rather than the bibliography is the most common approach. One could argue that if a work is sufficiently significant to be included in a bibliography, then one might wonder why it has not been cited in the main thesis. However, this is only one view, and if it is felt that a bibliography should be compiled, then there is no reason for not doing so. The distinction between references and bibliography is discussed in Preece (1994, p. 226).

When formatting the list of references, the general style should be as indicated in Chapter 6. However, there are a number of inconsistencies or errors which are commonly made. The first is to make the list rather more ornate by using bold, capitals or underlining. The only formatting which is required is the use of italicization. In books, the title of the book should be in italics; in edited books it is the title of the book and not the titles of individual chapters which should be italicized; and, finally, in relation to journal articles, it is the name of the journal which should be italicized, and not the title of the article.

Sometimes students try to create a series of vertical columns, with the name of the author in one column, the name of the book title in another, and so on. This is not necessary and, in any case, it is very difficult to ensure a uniform approach, given the great variety of written materials which are usually included in a list of references. It is simpler and easier to type in full lines, starting a fresh line for each new author.

At the end of each book reference there should be, in order, the place of publication followed by the name of the publisher. Sometimes students will put these in one order for one publication, and then reverse the order further down the list. Another common inconsistency is to use only initials for the first name(s) of the author – which is the normal system – and then sometimes to revert to quoting the full name or names. The initial has a full stop afterwards, and there should be consistency in using this.

The use of appendices

Generally speaking, items should not be included in the appendix unless absolutely necessary to a proper understanding of the thesis. It is tempting to imagine that a great deal of material included in the appendix adds in some way to the quality of the thesis. This is not necessarily so. In fact, it can be an unwelcome distraction. If some of the material is patently peripheral to the thesis, then a large appendix may be a distinct inconvenience to read. If some material is central to a proper appreciation of the thesis, then there may be a strong argument for including it in the main body of the thesis. Only if material is important for a sound understanding of the thesis can it properly be included in the appendix. The latter should not, however, be regarded as an extending file into which one puts anything and everything which may be loosely connected with the thesis!

Example – The issue of binding

It is worth remembering that if the appendix grows and grows, you may have to bind the thesis in two separate parts. This will not only be more costly for you, but is also much more awkward (and expensive) when it comes to posting the thesis to examiners.

Questionnaires and schedules

One of the elements which is traditionally, and quite correctly, included in an appendix is an example of a questionnaire which has been used in the data collection. It is not normal to include examples of completed questionnaires in the appendix. They would be very bulky and would not serve any particularly useful purpose. Occasionally, specific questions in a questionnaire have been poorly or inaccurately answered, and you may wish to include these to demonstrate a particular issue about the completion of the questionnaire. However, usually, a single good copy of an uncompleted questionnaire is quite adequate. When the data are being described and analysed in the thesis chapters, readers can consult the appendix to examine the nature of the original questionnaire question and can appreciate the original instructions which were given to respondents. Along with the questionnaire it is often a good idea to include any explanatory letters which were sent to the respondents, and any letters or circulars to respondents which discussed ethical issues in the research. These are relevant to include in the appendix because they enable readers to appreciate the practical measures which were taken in the research in relation to the discussion of such issues in the text. The same principle also applies to the inclusion of interview schedules. A blank copy of an interview schedule should be included along with any preliminary advice given to interviewees in relation to the proposed conduct of the interviews or interview ethics. All these items enable a better understanding of the discussions in the text concerning such matters as sampling or the collection of data.

Official documents

The inclusion of official documents should be treated carefully. These may be bulky, and it may be more suitable to include them in the references. A relevant quotation can be included in the text, and this then precludes the need to include the entire document in the appendix. A compromise might be to include copies of one or two pages in the appendix. At the beginning of the appendices, there should be a clear contents page, indicating the documents which have been included.

Summary – Appendices

- Only include essential documents in the appendix.
- Consider placing items in the main thesis rather than in the appendix.
- Raw data should only exceptionally be included.
- A blank copy of a questionnaire or interview schedule may be included.
- The inclusion of long official documents should be avoided.

Consistency, consistency and starting as you mean to go on

When reading a thesis, it is not so much the system of formatting or layout which strikes you, as the inconsistencies in whichever system has been used. The same kind of data should always be presented in the same way. It is easy to set out data in one way in one chapter, and then to change the system slightly in a later chapter. Every effort should be made to adhere to a single system. If the same kind of data is set out differently, then it can be misunderstood. Readers are no longer comparing the same things.

Hence, layout and formatting are not simply matters of aesthetics. They are important because they can help readers to understand the thesis.

Further reading

Burnett, J. (2009) *Doing Your Social Science Dissertation*. London: Sage.
Hart, C. (2004) *Doing Your Masters Dissertation*. London: Sage.
Thody, A. (2006) *Writing and Presenting Research*. London: Sage.
Thomas, G. (2009) *How To Do Your Research Project*. London: Sage.
Wellington, J.J., Bathmaker, A. and Hunt, C. (2005) *Succeeding with Your Doctorate*. London: Sage.

Part 2

Writing Your Thesis

8

The Preliminary Pages and the Introduction

In this chapter we examine the ways in which you can structure the early pages of your thesis, prior to the first chapter. We then consider the different elements which you should include in the introductory chapter. In particular we discuss the explanation of the choice of topic, and the writing of research aims.

Study Strategies

The kind of verbs which are often used at the beginning of aims are very useful not only for that purpose, but also in general throughout a thesis. It is a good idea to maintain a list of such verbs. They may be characterized as verbs which describe an academic process, yet which imply that the process is continuing without reaching a definite conclusion. As you read theses and academic books, make a note of such verbs. Here are some examples:

- To discuss (an idea).
- To examine (a proposal).
- To analyse (some data).
- To synthesize (several ideas or propositions).
- To explore (an issue).
- To reflect on (a theoretical model).

(Continued)

(Continued)

- To investigate (a range of concepts).
- To propose (a possible explanation).
- To systematize (some initial data).
- To test (a hypothesis).

Title page, abstract and contents

The title page is important because it carries the key information about the thesis including the full and definitive title, and the name of the student. The title page also carries the name of the award for which the thesis is being submitted, and the date of submission. The significance of the title page is reflected in the fact that universities usually have a specified form of words which you are asked to include on the title page. See the example opposite of the typical wording for a title page.

Example – Length of the title

A very long title is usually inappropriate for a thesis. A title should be sufficiently detailed to inform the potential reader about the key aspects of the thesis – and no more. Generally, the two key points to be included are the subject matter of the study, and the research method used. Thus we might have:

A philosophical enquiry into the ethics of decision-making in business.

or

An ethnographic study of working patterns among junior doctors.

In laying out the title page it is important to type the title itself sufficiently prominently. Ideas for the relative sizes of the different parts of the text can be obtained easily from other theses or from books. The reason for using the phrase 'in partial fulfilment of' is that this accurately describes the function of the thesis. In the case of master's degrees and professional doctorates, there are other components besides the thesis which comprise the work for the award. Even in the case of the PhD there is still the viva voce examination. This is regarded as an integral part of the examination process, and the assessment of your performance in the oral examination is combined with the assessment of the thesis in an overall judgement. The layout of the title page is discussed in Silbergh (2001, p. 179).

> ## Example – Wording for a thesis title page
>
> - The influence of Plato on contemporary curriculum development.
> - Antonia J. Smith.
> - A thesis submitted in partial fulfilment of the requirements for the degree of Doctor of Philosophy awarded by the University of Southbridge.
> - March, 2003.

The abstract

An abstract of the thesis is placed on the page immediately following the title page. The abstract is a synopsis of the entire thesis, including the analysis of the results and the conclusion. For this reason, it is difficult to write the abstract at an early stage of the thesis. It is normally one of the last sections of the thesis to be written. Hence strategies for writing the abstract are discussed at the end of Chapter 11. The abstract is an essential part of the thesis, and will probably be the first part which is read by the examiners. It is therefore important that it is written clearly. It is an opportunity to provide the examiners with a clear and precise statement of the nature of the thesis. They will use the abstract to gain their initial impressions of the thesis, its subject matter and methodology. The usual convention is that the abstract is restricted to a single side. Using double-line spacing, there may not be sufficient space to summarize the thesis adequately, and some students use a narrower line spacing for the abstract. It is a very good idea to read several examples of abstracts before starting to write one yourself. Précis-writing is a difficult art, and a number of drafts may be required. The abstract is discussed in Wolcott (2001, pp. 150–1).

Contents pages

The contents pages are next in order in the thesis. These are again very important from the perspective of the examiners. They will read the contents pages very carefully to gain a preliminary picture of the structure of the thesis. The examiners will probably return again and again to the contents pages, to remind themselves of the prior and forthcoming sections. When the thesis is first being written you may only have the broadest idea of its structure. This may be restricted to draft titles for the main chapters.

As your writing proceeds, however, sections and subsections will be added, and these will need to be added to the contents pages. If a system of numbers and sub-numbers related to chapters has been used, then these will also be added to the contents pages. It is important that the structure as reflected in the contents is not so complex that it is difficult to grasp the overall structure. Perhaps the most important aspect of the structure, and of the contents, is that it should be evident to examiners that the thesis is logically organized. It is a great help if examiners can look at the contents and immediately grasp a rationale for the structure of the thesis. Although the contents pages can be compiled gradually, the page numbers can only be added at the final stage, when these become determined for the thesis as a whole.

Tables, figures, abbreviations, key terms and acknowledgements

The tables and figures in the thesis should be listed separately, and clearly numbered using the numbering system adopted in the main text. Once the page numbers have been finalized, these should also be added to the lists of tables and figures. Each table and figure should have a clear, unique title.

Abbreviations

It is sometimes useful to include in the preliminary pages a list of the main abbreviations or acronyms used in the thesis. This can act as a point of reference for readers, and provide preliminary notice of abbreviations which may be commonly used. There is no need to include in the list those abbreviations which are very commonly understood, for example PhD. On the first occasion that an abbreviation is used, it should be written in full, in order to provide an explanation. However, where a thesis contains a variety of abbreviations, then the list at the beginning can provide a useful reference point.

Key terms

Sometimes a thesis may employ one or two key concepts or ideas, which are subject to different interpretations. If the concepts are philosophically problematic and require a thorough analysis, then it will be more appropriate to place this discussion in the body of the thesis. The discussion will probably require some considerable space, and it would be inappropriate to try to include this in the preliminary pages. However, if it is simply a matter of identifying a particular usage of a term, then it may be possible to summarize this in the form, 'For the purposes of this thesis, the term X is used in the context of . . .'. Much depends on the nature of the thesis and the terms to be included, but this may be one strategy which could be used.

The alternative to this approach, particularly if there are a number of terms which require explanation, is to include a glossary at the end of the thesis. This is normally placed after the list of references. The glossary can include any specialist terms which are used, and provide a brief definition of the term. The terms should be arranged in alphabetical order.

Acknowledgements

Many students like to acknowledge the help they have received and, if so, a list of acknowledgements is often included near the beginning of the thesis. Such acknowledgements might be to library staff or to lecturers who have acted as their supervisors. Students also sometimes wish to acknowledge the support of their family. The text on the acknowledgements page should normally be brief.

Before leaving the subject of the preliminary pages it is worth noting that these pages are numbered with roman numerals. The first page of the first chapter of the thesis marks the beginning of the use of arabic numerals. These are then continued throughout the thesis.

Why is this particular topic being researched?

We now consider the main elements which should be included in the first chapter – the introduction. This is a very significant chapter as it is the first to be read by the examiners, and it inevitably creates an impression in their minds about your writing style and of the broad nature of the thesis. The main purpose of the introduction is to provide an overview of the research study, and of the key factors which were influential in its inception. It sets the scene, providing a glimpse of the setting for the research and of the methodology. It should also state the aims of the thesis.

The introductory chapter should normally commence with a few paragraphs which summarize briefly the nature of the thesis. The subject of the research, the nature of the methodology, and the research setting are briefly described. These early paragraphs should enable readers to grasp the essentials of the thesis, and provide an early framework around which to understand the remainder. The rest of the chapter should expand on this early description and lead further into the nature of the study.

It is always interesting in the introduction to read about the origin of the idea for the research. Students get ideas for their research from a variety of sources. Sometimes they take an initial idea to their supervisor, and after a series of discussions a more focused idea emerges. In other cases, they may have read about a piece of previous research and feel that there is an opportunity to take this further. This usually is dependent upon there being a suitable context available in which to collect data. For example, you may read some research involving a survey of the management of high schools nationally, and decide that it would be interesting to explore whether the findings appear to be relevant to several local schools.

Alternatively, a research idea may derive from a practical problem within the educational system. This is particularly the case with action research designs. For example, a practising teacher enrolled for a research degree may be interested in the ways in which field trips and overseas trips for students are arranged. The teacher may feel that there is scope to improve the planning mechanisms for such trips. This then could form the basis for an action research study.

What is important in this chapter is that readers gain a sense of the way in which the research started. It helps them to understand the motivation behind the thesis if they can appreciate the starting point for the research idea, and see the way in which this has been followed through to a conclusion.

What is the significance of the topic?

A discussion of the origin of the idea can lead on to an exploration of the wider significance of the research. For example, let us suppose that the topic selected is a study of the recruitment of young people who have a history of low achievement at school, to courses in further and higher education. The specific setting for the research might be a local university and several nearby colleges. However, although the research is being conducted in a fairly localized setting, it has implications for the wider debate about widening participation in education.

Unless a research project consists of a large-scale survey, the likelihood is that most social science research will take place in a setting which is restricted in some way. Social science research is often time-consuming, in part because it involves collecting data from human participants. This usually results in the need to place parameters around the conduct of the research, in order, among other reasons, to make the project manageable. It is therefore always useful for you to try to look at the broader picture, and to try to explain how your research is located in a wider framework. Such a framework might involve such factors as current government policies or initiatives, or demonstrated social trends which have become evident from other research.

> ### Example – The social purpose of research
>
> In a discussion of the significance of your research, it is always useful to try to think of its social purpose. Some research has more direct and clear social benefits than others. However, it would be unusual for a research study not to have some potential benefit to society, and it is useful to analyse this in your introduction.

Explaining the context of the research

It is extremely rare for research to break completely new ground. In many cases, there will have been similar research studies where the data was collected in a comparable context. It is very helpful in the introductory chapter if the research project can be set within a context, which outlines the nature of the related studies which have been carried out in the past. It is often useful if the areas of research which are related to the subject of the thesis can be identified. This helps to establish a research framework within which the present study can be located.

For example, in relation to a study of the problems faced by mature students in higher education, there are a number of distinct subject areas where there may have been related research studies. These areas include adult education, student motivation, assessment in education, study skills, psychology and sociology of education, and distance education. It is important to view a research study within the context of a network of other research. If these relationships between research areas can be outlined here, then they form a basis for the structuring of the literature review chapter. The studies which have been conducted within each area can be revisited in much more detail, providing a firm research basis for the current study.

This is just one example of a strategy which is very important in writing a thesis, and that is to provide linkages between its different sections. Even a master's thesis is a long document, and it is not always easy to gain a sense of its cohesion. In this instance, you have the opportunity to indicate the broad areas which will be addressed in the second chapter, and this inevitably helps readers adjust to the way in which the thesis is developing.

The background of the researcher

Social science research increasingly recognizes that the definition of a research question, and the subsequent collection and analysis of data, is very much an activity which involves interpretative processes on the part of the researcher. Research questions do not arise in a vacuum. They are developed by a researcher during a process of interaction with the social context in which they are working. The research question which evolves may depend upon many factors including the interests of the researcher, the reading which they have done on previous research, and the environmental influences to which they have been subject, for example in the workplace. From these various factors and influences, the researcher develops a research idea which will ultimately become the subject matter for the thesis.

A great deal of research in education and the social sciences derives from practical issues and problems which are located in the related professions. For example, a teacher who is concerned about issues of pupil discipline in schools, may well be interested in researching a specific aspect of the improvement of pupil behaviour. A social worker who spends a good deal of time involved with the issue of drug taking, may well be interested in strategies for providing better drugs education for young people. However, perhaps one significant aspect of this process is that it is the researcher who at some point makes a choice of the research subject. The choice is very much subjective and influenced by the interests and background of the researcher.

It is important to acknowledge the complexity of this process, since it is easy to treat the selection of thesis subject and methodology as if they are rather more simple and straightforward decisions. In fact, the choice of research subject depends upon the complex interplay of factors, and the manner in which the researcher interprets them. Having acknowledged this, it becomes important that the researcher documents some of these influences in the thesis. Not only does this documentation explain something of the background to what are complex decisions, but it also provides useful contextual information for the reader to begin to appreciate decisions taken later in data analysis. If the subject is connected with the workplace of the researcher, then it is important to describe the researcher's role, and relevant aspects of the functioning of that workplace. Here again, there are interpretative decisions to be taken to describe one aspect of the workplace, and to omit another.

It is important that the researcher takes the opportunity in the introduction to explain some of these issues which may be relevant to the choice of research subject. The researcher's previous academic background may be relevant, in that it may be used to explain how an interest in the research subject arose. If the research is connected with the researcher's current employment role, then it may be very relevant for the researcher to describe that role, and to analyse the relationship between that and the research subject. Again, if the research subject has evolved from previous research in which the researcher was involved, then it may be relevant to describe some of this research in the introduction. In summary, the personal background of the researcher, in so far as it provides the context for the selection of subject matter for the thesis, should be explained and analysed carefully in the introduction.

Where is the research being conducted and why?

Perhaps the principal aim of the introduction is to describe the broad nature and subject of the research, so that the reader can appreciate more easily the details supplied later. In the methodology chapter there will normally be a detailed discussion of the data collection process, and the location in which that took place. However, it is very useful to indicate in the introduction some of the main features of the location of the data collection, and the reasons for planning the research in that way. In effect, this may involve a discussion of some aspects of the sampling process.

The question of a location in which to conduct research often arises in professionally orientated research where the researcher is investigating some aspect of life at their workplace. Teachers may be investigating a new approach to pupil learning in their own school; community workers may be exploring new ways of motivating young people to become involved in community projects; and social workers may be investigating new strategies for protecting vulnerable children. Where the workplace of the researcher is also the location for the research, there are two main areas which should be addressed in the introduction. The first is to describe the relevant features of the workplace, and the second is to justify the research being conducted there.

Let us imagine that a thesis is based upon case study research into an innovative programme of pastoral care for students in a further education college. The researcher is involved in the pastoral care system, and decides to investigate its effectiveness. Readers of the thesis will be interested in the features of the college which are relevant to an understanding of the new pastoral care system. This description of the college might begin with a brief review of its location in terms of the characteristics of the catchment area, and the type of town or city in which it is located. It will also probably include such elements as the number of staff and students, a description of the immediate geographical vicinity of the college, and its recent history. The account may then move on to describe the departmental structure of the college, and the range of courses which it offers. It will be important in terms of research ethics to ensure that the college retains its anonymity in the thesis. Therefore, this descriptive account will not include the actual name of the town in which it is located, nor any other descriptive features which might help to identify the college.

Having provided a broad description of the college, it may be necessary to highlight some of the features which relate specifically to the pastoral care system. These features might include the recent academic performance of students in the college, their pattern of attendance at the college, and trends in terms of finding future employment. There will be more detailed discussion of these issues in the methodology chapter, but these broad details will enable readers to gain an initial understanding of the context of the research.

However, there remains an important question for the researcher to answer in the introduction, and that is the reason for selecting this college as the subject for the case study. As the researcher is a lecturer in the college, the principal reason for selecting the college may seem to be that the researcher is familiar with the environment, and that data collection would be convenient. However, this may not be the case at all. It may be that the pastoral care system in this college is genuinely new and innovative, and that it provides a model for other colleges. The systematic investigation of this system may be helpful to other colleges in developing their own systems. In addition, the researcher may want to make out a case that this college is typical, in many ways, of a number of other further education colleges, and hence that the data can legitimately be generalized to other colleges. There may be a number of reasons for selecting this college, but it is important that these are articulated here, to make clear the rationale for the research.

Example – Choice of research location

When describing, and perhaps justifying, the choice of a location in which to conduct the research, it is very important that you provide reasons which are related to the actual research and its aims. The reasons should not be related to factors which concern the convenience of the researcher in any way. It may be that the location is near the researcher's home, or that it is easy to visit the location during work time. However, these would not be perceived as justifiable reasons in research terms.

The research aims

The aims are one of the most important aspects of any thesis. They should express clearly and precisely the anticipated achievements of the research study. They are an expression of the things which you hope you will know and understand at the end of the study, which you do not know now. In the case of a doctoral study they set out the original contribution to knowledge which it is anticipated will be achieved.

Signpost to success – Aims

Your research aims are at the very heart of your thesis. They should be the thread which links it together.

Aims provide a measure of success for the research study. As they express the things you hope you will achieve, they provide a yardstick by which to judge the study. In the conclusion of the thesis, you should revisit the aims, and comment upon the extent to which they have been achieved. It is not necessarily a criticism of the research or of the thesis if some of the aims have not been achieved. The most important issue is that there is an analysis of the possible reasons for not meeting the aims. It follows that the aims should be expressed in such a manner that it is evident how they could be achieved. Good research aims are expressed in a clear, precise and logical manner.

When writing the thesis, you should never lose sight of the aims. The aims should directly or indirectly determine a great deal of the structure of the thesis. For example, it is likely that the aims will contain certain terms or concepts which are central to the research study. These concepts will also be, for example, a central element in the review of the literature. In addition, when the data is being analysed, it will be important to indicate the ways in which the analysis appears to shed light on the key ideas embedded in the aims. In other words, it is difficult to imagine any aspect of the thesis which is not affected to some extent by the content of the aims.

Example – Typical research aims

The following aims are based upon a study to investigate the experiences of teacher training students during teaching practice in further education colleges.

1 To explore the perceptions of teacher training students of the effectiveness of their practical teaching experience.
2 To investigate the nature of the resources provided for them by the college.
3 To examine the level of support provided by the college mentor.
4 To analyse the validity of the practical teaching as a learning experience.

The aims outlined in the example have several characteristics worth noting. They all begin with a verb in the infinitive which indicates an active process of investigation or analysis. It can be useful to begin a list of aims with a phrase such as: 'The principal aims of this research study are:' This enables each aim to be read as if following from this introduction. The choice of introductory verb is important. It should be such as to suggest an ongoing process. To start an aim with 'to discover' would be inappropriate because it would suggest a finality to the research process. It would imply that if this research project was successful then it would have the final word to say on this particular subject.

Aims should be expressed in such a manner that the nature of the evidence required to meet them is clear. For example, in terms of the second aim, one can imagine visiting the college, and asking the college mentor about the nature of the teaching resources provided to help the student teacher. We do not know where such investigations might lead, but from the aim we are reasonably clear about where we might begin our search for data.

Example – The sophistication of aims

It is important that aims should reflect the level of award for which the thesis is being prepared. For example, the previous aim discussed might be suitable for a master's-level thesis. However, at doctoral level, the aim should be worded in such a way that it stimulates a more sophisticated investigation. At doctoral level, the aim could be worded as: 'To analyse the factors which appear to influence the distribution of resources by the college.' This aim is more sophisticated because it sets out to examine the underlying social processes which may be operating in the college.

Finally, aims should not be phrased in such a way to imply any value judgements, or to implicitly prejudge the outcome of the research. It would be inappropriate, for example, to write an aim in the form 'To investigate the innovative nature of the resources provided . . .', because we might assume that the writer is saying that the resources are to some extent innovative. In other words, aims should be expressed in a neutral manner, without any implicit assumptions about the findings of the research. It is often a good idea to phrase the aims in a brief and succinct manner, and to enumerate them for ease of reference.

The research objectives

Many theses rely upon a list of aims to indicate the purpose of the research. The aims are intended to provide a broad indication of the purpose of the research. However, some students prefer to subdivide those aims into objectives. These are rather more precise statements of intent. They may describe the actual activities which the researcher intends to undertake. For example, the first aim in the 'Typical research aims' example could be divided into the following objectives:

1 To conduct semi-structured interviews with a sample of 25 students who have completed their teaching practice.
2 To distribute a self-completion questionnaire to a cohort of 210 students.
3 To analyse the key expected outcomes of the period of teaching practice.

Objectives may often, although not exclusively, be characterized by verbs which imply activities such as 'distribute' or 'calculate'. In that sense, they may be more task-orientated than aims. It is not essential to break down the aims into objectives, although it can provide a preliminary idea of the key features of the research design and methodology.

Further reading

Burton, D. and Bartlett, S. (2009) *Key Issues for Education Researchers*. London: Sage.
Lichtman, M. (2010) *Understanding and Evaluating Qualitative Educational Research*. London: Sage.
Silverman, D. (2004) *Doing Qualitative Research: A Practical Handbook*. 2nd edn. London: Sage.
Thody, A. (2006) *Writing and Presenting Research*. London: Sage.
Walliman, N. (2005) *Your Research Project: A Step-by-Step Guide for the First-Time Researcher*. 2nd edn. London: Sage.

9

The Literature Review

In this chapter we consider different approaches to the writing of the literature review. We examine strategies for subdividing the literature, and for coping with an apparent lack of relevant studies. We also discuss the use of a variety of research sources, including material from the Internet, and the different ways in which you can carry out an online search.

Study Strategies

- Conduct a literature search on the Internet, on a subject which is of interest to you in research. Decide which items you might cite in a thesis and which you would consider unsuitable. Make a list of the criteria you use for acceptance or rejection.

(i) General issues concerning the literature review

The purpose of the literature review

The chapter which deals with literature that is relevant to the subject matter of the thesis, is often one of the longest. It is usually placed near the beginning of the thesis, often the second chapter. The literature review is usually concerned primarily with the research and writing connected with the main subject matter of the research study. It does not usually concern the literature connected with the research methodology. For example, in an action research study, the literature on the history, theory and practice of action research would be dealt with primarily in the methodology chapter, rather than in the literature review chapter.

The use of the word 'review' is interesting. This does not mean that you provide a detailed analysis and discussion of a book or of a research article. There would not be the space to achieve this and, at the same time, to provide a reasonable coverage of the subject field. The word 'review' indicates that you should summarize the broad content of the research article or study, and indicate clearly any linkages with other studies in the field, thus conveying something of the academic relationships within the subject area. If possible the commentary on each piece of literature should explain succinctly the key findings of the study, and indicate the potential or actual significance of the study within a national or international framework.

Example – Review or analysis

Presenting a chronological list of research in a subject field, with a brief summary of the nature and findings of each, is not suitable for a literature 'review'. Perhaps the problem here is with the word 'review'. A literature review should involve 'analysis' above all else. The analytic process can involve many different facets, but, for example, you should try to categorize the literature; show how research in the area has evolved and is related to that in other subjects. Try to show how your research integrates with that mentioned in the analysis, and indicate something of the impact which research in the subject has had in society at large.

The principal purpose of the literature review is to establish the academic and research areas which are of relevance to the subject of the research. Consider a thesis with the following title: 'Quality assurance issues in distance learning in higher education'. Ideally, there would be sufficient literature devoted to the exact subject matter of the title. However, this may not be entirely so, and it may be necessary to consider some of the concepts included in the title. There are three key concepts in this title: 'quality assurance', 'distance learning' and 'higher education'. It may well be that there are available research studies on the subject of distance learning which also mention some quality assurance issues. Equally there may be articles on higher education in general which also mention the impact of distance learning. The primary function of the literature review is to try to establish those academic areas in which are located the previous studies and research which are of most relevance to the current study.

Leading on from that, the literature review seeks to lay a foundation for the current research. It sets the thesis within a research context consisting of relevant research studies and other analyses of related ideas. The new thesis should not be seen as an isolated study, but as a study which exists in an academic tradition, and the purpose of the literature review is to try to establish the nature of that tradition.

The type of literature to be discussed in this chapter should be largely reports of research relevant to the subject matter of the thesis. The main location of such research will be articles in academic journals. Another useful source may be reports of research which are published as booklets and pamphlets. Government agencies and official organizations frequently commission small-scale research studies, and then publish them themselves for distribution within the profession. Such publications can be a very useful source of relevant literature.

You may be unsure about the types of books which are suitable for discussion in a literature review chapter. For convenience, we can divide academic books into four categories, for the purposes of this discussion. Textbooks, whether for school, college or university students, are generally unsuitable for discussion in the literature review chapter. A textbook is primarily concerned with the transmission of established knowledge. Textbooks can be extremely useful in helping you understand issues which you will discuss in your thesis, but they are usually less appropriate for evaluation in a literature review. Having said that, some textbooks do rather more than simply convey current knowledge. Through their discussion of concepts and ideas, they may go beyond the mere transmission of understanding. They do, to a degree, extend our current understanding. The books which come into this category are often a matter of personal academic opinion. Hence, you cannot say that textbooks must be permanently excluded from a literature review chapter, but their inclusion should certainly be treated with caution.

Some books, while not being based upon empirical research, do appear to set out to extend the barriers of understanding. They typically take a subject, and review the main contributions to understanding in that field. They then take this further, by analysing these concepts and ideas, such that there develops a contribution to understanding. Such books may bear some of the characteristics of textbooks, and the barrier between the two categories may be debatable. Nevertheless, books which you feel fall into this category are generally suitable for inclusion in the literature review chapter.

Then there are edited books, which consist of a series of individual chapters, usually each written by a separate academic. The chapters are all connected by means of a common theme, and the book edited by a noted academic in that field. In books of this type each chapter is usually authoritative, and frequently based upon empirical research. Some chapters may, however, be philosophical in nature, consisting of a conceptual analysis of various key ideas in the field. Chapters from edited books such as this are generally appropriate for inclusion in the literature review.

> ### Example – Limitations of literature
>
> It is perfectly possible to employ types of literature which are unconventional or which do not comply with accepted academic norms. However, in such cases, you should always explain the reasons for selecting the material, and also its limitations. In this way, you demonstrate that you are thinking analytically about it, and not just using it because it is convenient, or for some other non-academic reason.

Finally, there are books which are based upon empirical studies. In a sense these are longer versions of academic journal articles. They often report on major research studies, and are suitable for inclusion in the literature review.

Besides these main categories of source materials, there are other ways in which research studies are reported. You may find reports in academic newspapers such as the *Times Educational Supplement*, on radio and television programmes, and in professional journals. Frequently, however, such reports represent distilled versions of the full report, and wherever possible the original version of the research report should be evaluated. Aspects of the literature review are discussed in Arksey and Knight (1999, pp. 47–9).

Style of writing for the literature review

The literature review may be a very long chapter and usually requires some form of structure. It can be extremely confusing to read a discussion of the literature where the books and articles are not presented in a particular order. The simplest means of organizing the works is to discuss them in chronological order. This, however, may not always be the most appropriate system. Works on different subjects may be grouped together and, with date of publication as the only criterion of order, the discussion may still be very confusing. Another strategy would be to base the structure on different types of publications. Chapters in books, journal articles and single-author books could be grouped separately. This, however, would still result in works on different subjects being discussed together. Strategies for subdividing the literature based on subject matter are discussed in the next section. What is important, however, is that there is some kind of structure to the chapter, since without this it is difficult to discuss the links and similarities which occur between different cited works.

For the present discussion of writing style, let us assume that an overall structure has been established for the chapter, and that you are beginning to discuss a new research article. The example shows how a section of a literature review might be written. It relates to the previously mentioned thesis title of 'Quality assurance issues in distance learning in higher education'.

The general style of writing and structure represented in this example is repeated throughout the literature review. The key feature of the approach is that each work or piece of research which is cited is summarized and discussed briefly. This discussion may be only about one paragraph in length. At the beginning and end of the discussion, linkages with the previous and later works cited are established. In addition, you can also comment on links with works cited in other parts of the chapter. It is usual to provide a quotation to illustrate the summary which you have provided, or to support an argument which you are developing. In many places, the literature review chapter may be descriptive in nature. That is, it may summarize the key features of previous research. However, wherever the opportunity arises, you should try to identify trends in the literature, or areas in which separate research studies, directly or indirectly, appear to be supporting a shared argument or viewpoint. Moreover, the literature review should look back at the aims in the previous chapter, and seek to set each individual aim within a context of previous research studies.

Example – Sample from a literature review

The previous study suggests that an important factor in the perceived success of distance learning strategies is the degree of intervention of the tutor. The students in the sample appeared to want a considerable level of interaction with their tutors, rather than a situation in which they were expected to learn in isolation from computer-based learning materials.

These findings appear to have been reflected in the study by Smith and Jones (2003). They conducted semi-structured interviews with a sample of 85 sociology students, who were each taught three modules through a distance-learning mechanism. In addition, each student had a single, one-hour tutorial per module. The students were asked how much they valued the different elements in the teaching and learning process. The researchers reported that a majority of the students felt the learning materials were well designed, but that they particularly looked forward to their tutorials. As the researchers commented:

When students were deprived of face-to-face contact with their teachers, it appeared to focus their minds on the value of tutorials. They commented on the opportunity to receive immediate feedback on their ideas; on the amount of discussion which could be conducted in a very short time; on the supportive comments received from tutors; and on the way in which the meetings with

> their tutors often resulted in greater enthusiasm and motivation for their studies. (Smith and Jones, 2003: 57)
>
> The students did not appear to be at all antagonistic to distance learning, but to have reflected upon the relative advantages of person-to-person and distance tuition.

Subdividing the available literature

The literature review chapter is much easier to read if it is divided into sections. In this form, it is also much easier to write. However, it is not always easy to determine a strategy for dividing up the chapter. The first step in the process is to conduct a preliminary survey of the literature which is relevant to the title. For the purposes of this discussion, let us consider a thesis entitled 'Multiculturalism in the secondary school curriculum'. A preliminary survey will reveal a considerable number of publications on multiculturalism, although many of these books or articles will entail a discussion of multiculturalism within a particular context. These areas might involve multiculturalism in society in general, in various sectors of the educational system, or in a variety of professions. Equally there will be many publications on different aspects of the secondary curriculum. There will certainly be separate publications on the different subject areas of the secondary curriculum. In addition to this body of literature, there are many publications on ethnicity, ethnic relations, comparative culture, comparative religion, and the different religious groups within the educational system. There are probably far too many potential categories here, and hence it would be necessary to try to define the larger, broad categories which are relevant to the subject matter of the thesis.

This is where it is useful to return to the aims of the thesis, because these provide a provisional structure within which you can begin to organize the literature review. For example, suppose one of the first aims is to explore the educational achievement of different cultural groups. This aim might suggest that one relevant area would be a body of literature which discussed the nature of culture and ethnicity, and attempted to clarify something of the conceptual issues surrounding these terms. Another relevant area could be that of educational achievement, and particularly achievement related to any aspect of culture, religion or ethnicity.

In other words, although it is relatively easy to think of possible subdivisions for the literature review chapter, it is important that those subdivisions have some relevance to the remainder of the thesis. It is not always possible to write in a purely linear fashion. The aims, the literature review, the methodology and the data are all intertwined as a coherent whole, and it is important to ensure that there is some correspondence between different sections. Here is a summary of some of the strategies which may be used to develop categories for the literature review chapter:

Summary – Subdividing the topic of a literature review

This is a summary of some strategies which can be used to determine the sections or subject areas for the literature review chapter.

- Conduct a brief survey of the literature in possibly relevant areas in order to obtain a feeling of the available literature.
- Analyse the title of the thesis and of the provisional aims, in order to determine the key words and terms which are important in the research study.
- Examine and analyse any preliminary data or pilot studies which have been conducted, and place that data in provisional categories.
- Compare the title, aims, any preliminary data, and the literature which appears to be available, and determine the categories for the chapter.
- Be prepared to amend or combine some of these categories as the literature review process evolves.

Dealing with an apparent lack of relevant literature

As a supervisor, one of the most common issues raised with me is that of locating suitable literature to review, when the student can find very little of apparent relevance to the thesis. I suspect that other supervisors are in the same position. The question of finding suitable literature is usually based on searching for books or articles which are very close in subject area to the thesis title. However, it is often extremely difficult to locate a large number of such references. For example, in the case of a research study entitled 'Community colleges in the USA and England – a comparative study', it may be relatively difficult to identify a body of literature which is specifically devoted to such comparative studies of community colleges. If you have made a thorough search of all likely sources, and have only identified relatively few references, then you should widen the field of search.

Among the topics you may wish to search are community colleges in general, community colleges in the USA, community colleges in England, and comparative studies of the English and American educational systems. Each of these searches may reveal a number of other subject areas which would be suitable to explore. Some subject searches may reveal a large number of references, others very few. This may affect your decision about which source materials to include in the chapter. When you look at some references, they may appear to have moved a relatively long way from your subject matter, and so you may wish to reject them. The other very significant factor which will affect your choice of areas to explore is the length of the thesis. A PhD thesis is a different matter from a short master's thesis. For a doctorate you may need to move some considerable way from the original title in searching for literature, in order to locate a sufficient number of references. With a master's thesis, the opposite may be the case. There are thus pragmatic considerations in terms of selecting the breadth of material to be reviewed.

One final consideration is that some students take into account the amount of literature which is potentially available when selecting the title for their research. This is an example of the argument that you cannot treat a research project or thesis in an entirely linear fashion. If you choose a title or research subject without any concern for the literature which might be available, or for the data you might be in a position to collect, then it may later prove difficult to complete the research.

Example – Research as a planned sequence

Research is often assumed to be a logical, planned process, with one stage leading to the next only when the previous stage has been completed. In many ways this is an accurate picture, but it is not the whole truth. You will often find it necessary to rethink previous decisions, as your research develops. The research process, including the literature review, is often too complex to be completely evaluated in one go.

In some ways, it is better to see research as a network of connected processes, with each process depending for its success on several others. When selecting a subject matter for the research, as a precaution, think ahead to the extent of the literature which may be available to review. If a preliminary search reveals relatively little relevant research, then a slight change in the focus of the title may open up new avenues to explore.

Making a selection from a wide variety of literature

Sometimes, although rarer, a student may be faced with such a surplus of possible literature to review that it is difficult to make a selection of those items to include. If this situation arises, then the first possibility is that the title which has been chosen is really too broad. For example, if you are planning to write a thesis on the subject of 'Curriculum development in further education', then you would almost certainly find an enormous quantity of literature. With such a title for the research, there may be no rational grounds on which one could reduce the literature to be surveyed. In order to make things more manageable you would need to change the title.

One strategy would be to limit the subject to a specific time span. The title might become 'Curriculum development in further education in the 1980s'. This would be an interesting historical study which would include many developments in vocational education and training. There would still be a lot of literature to review, but at least the subject would be more focused. Another possibility would be to examine a particular influence on curriculum development, as in the title 'Central government influence on curriculum development in further education'. Again, this would, in effect, limit the extent of the literature which needed to be surveyed. A rather different focus would be provided by the title 'Financial support for curriculum development in further education'. With a little ingenuity, it would be possible to think of many more possible titles constructed around the same central theme. Each title might make rather different demands in terms of methodology and data, and would certainly indicate a different type of research literature to be reviewed.

A broad title is not always desirable for a research study and for a thesis, because it is often very difficult to meet the resulting aims within the scope of the study. The wide range of literature to be reviewed is another complication. However, let us assume that you have narrowed your subject matter and title, but you are still faced with an extensive body of literature; other strategies have to be used. One possibility is to use only a particular type of research study. You might decide that in the example of curriculum development, you would only use research studies conducted by existing further education lecturers. You might justify this on the grounds that they are the professionals involved in the processes they are researching. As another possibility, you could restrict the literature to a certain type of course or academic programme. You might decide to use literature exclusively concerning vocational programmes, or with academic programmes. Finally, you might select studies to review which involved surveys of a number of colleges, or which explored case studies of individual colleges. Again the scope is very wide.

In the thesis, however, it is very important to explain and justify the strategy you have used. It may well be feasible to use any of the approaches mentioned above under suitable circumstances. However, the strategy used to reduce the volume of literature to be surveyed is less important than the reasons for selecting that strategy. You might wish to argue that the selection strategy results in a range of literature which is more relevant to the specific aims of the study. Alternatively, you may suggest that a particular approach to the literature selection results in more small-scale empirical studies which are relevant to the thesis subject. As with most aspects of research design and of structuring a thesis, it is very important to indicate the planning which has preceded decisions, and to explain the basis for that planning.

Employing a range of literature

When compiling works for your literature review, and indeed when citing works generally in your thesis, it is a good idea to draw upon as wide a range of types of literature as possible. This introduces variety into the thesis, and hence can make it more interesting for the reader. Also, as some academics tend to write in a restricted range of genres, it may help to ensure that you cite a wide range of writers.

In order to help you achieve this it is a good idea to enlist the help of the university library staff. There is usually an academic librarian responsible for each major subject area in a university library. That person is well informed about the many different types of publications relevant to your subject and, because information retrieval and management is at the heart of their job, is often better informed on such matters than lecturers. New electronic resources, periodicals and journals become available all the time, and lecturers may simply not have the time or information to keep up to date on them all. The academic librarian not only may indicate existing sources of which you were unaware, but may be willing to notify you of new publications as they appear.

It is important, however, to issue a word of warning about types of literature. We have commented earlier about the need to use as much research-based literature as possible. Sometimes, however, you may feel that you would like to mention articles from newspapers or from, say, weekly serious periodicals. You may wish to refer to one or two of these in either the literature review or somewhere else in the thesis. Whether or not this is appropriate depends to a large extent on the nature of your research study. For example, newspaper articles reporting current events, or serious periodicals analysing and discussing such events, may be relevant to a historical or political study. In a thesis on, say, the history of the financing of university education, such material may be valuable. It may contain extracts from ministerial speeches, and comments by vice-chancellors. However, the same type of material may not be relevant to other theses, and could seem rather populist, non-academic and insufficiently rigorous. Unfortunately, it is difficult to set down strict guidelines, and much depends on the context. Nevertheless, it is important to be cautious. In general, if the material is used, then you should feel confident that it is a reliable source in a reputable publication. If you have any concerns about its use, but still decide to use it, then it would be desirable to mention these concerns in the thesis. In addition, if your thesis lends itself to the use of a number of such sources, then it may be better to list these separately at the end of the thesis, to distinguish them from more conventional academic sources.

Signpost to success – Range of literature

Draw upon as many sources of relevant literature as possible, while at the same time ensuring that they are academically credible and relevant to your study.

Literature from the Internet

The Internet offers enormous advantages to the researcher seeking literature to review, but at the same time there are a number of areas where considerable caution should be exercised.

The Internet is very useful for providing access to original writings by noted academics, or access to sources which are otherwise difficult to locate. In many cases materials are available via your computer, when otherwise you might have to visit an archive in a distant library. You will often find an explanation of where to locate rare source material, and information on the background to that source material. There is also very useful information on academic journals (whether electronic or otherwise) which are relevant to a particular subject area.

Internet sites often provide very useful bibliographies related to a particular subject or writer. There are often links to other sites which are very useful. A brief search on the Internet will usually also reveal relevant professional societies and academic associations which exist to support studies in a specific area. Sometimes such organizations also publish collections of papers or periodicals around their specific academic interest. You will have to make a judgement whether such organizations and their publications are sufficiently scholarly to quote in your literature review. One guide is to examine the list of contributors and officers of the organization. If they are associated with colleges and universities, then you are likely to be reasonably safe in citing them.

Notwithstanding these many advantages, you should also exercise caution in using Internet sites. When you first look at a web page it is a good idea to try to ascertain the reason for establishing it. Some are set up by academic organizations, often indicated by 'edu' or 'ac' in the Internet address. On the other hand, some are set up by commercial organizations, or by organizations which exist to publicize their own ideology. The articles on the site may be about academic matters, but may be written from a particular ideological perspective. If this is the case, then you should think carefully before citing it.

Many web pages do not record the author's name or the name of any academic affiliation, and sometimes the author's name has been withheld. In such cases it is impossible to establish the academic credibility of the site, or to provide the requisite bibliographical details for inclusion in a thesis. In other cases the author of the site does record his or her name but there is no apparent academic affiliation, so the impression is given that the author has established the web pages as an expression of their own interest rather than as part of a formal academic undertaking linked to an established institution. You cannot always rely upon such material to be accurate or to be academically valid, and you should consider carefully before citing it in a thesis.

Some Internet sites include articles extracted from encyclopedias. These can be very helpful and informative as background reading on a topic, but are normally unsuitable for citing in a thesis. Some publishers put extracts from recently published books on the Internet, and these can be a valuable resource for researchers. In keeping with previous advice it would be necessary to establish that it was a research-based book before citing it in a thesis. It is not uncommon to find academic essays and papers on the Internet, written by people who have an affiliation with a university or other academic body. However, sometimes the status of the author is not established, even though they are connected with a university. The author could be a professor or a student. When the status of the author is uncertain, you should think carefully before citing the article or essay. Fortunately, some authors are extremely open and honest in explaining the status of their web pages. Sometimes an author will offer a disclaimer, stating that the written material is for background reading only, and as it has not been checked or refereed, should not be relied upon as authoritative. Such balanced and open statements are very helpful.

How old may the literature be?

The direct answer to this question is that it can, in principle, be of any age. We can easily imagine a thesis on ancient history citing the works of Roman historians. In former times historians had the distinct advantage of writing about events which were much closer to them than they are to us. However, they were not subject to the same kind of academic discipline as contemporary historians, and this has to be taken into account when reading their works. When reading older works in particular, one has to be aware of the particular perspective from which the book might have been written, or the social or political influences which impinged upon the writer.

Academic research is very much a cumulative activity. Each generation learns from the previous one, and current research inevitably builds upon the work and insights of previous academics. Contemporary research and publications are subject to the increasingly rigorous demands of modern scholarship, and for this reason it is preferable to cite publications which are as recent as possible.

Nevertheless, in most fields of enquiry there are a number of so-called seminal works which, although of varying age, have become so important in the development of the discipline that they are still referred to in academic works. There are a variety of reasons for a piece of research or book coming to be regarded as a seminal work. In some fields, the first translation of a major cultural work may still be cited. It may have been superseded by later translations, but it still retains importance as the first work of its type. In most fields, the original works by the founders of a perspective or approach are still cited. No doubt their original ideas will have been extended and amplified over the years by other writers, but the original work still retains a good deal of value. Again, all academic fields have key writers whose reputations have grown over the years, and inevitably their works become held in considerable esteem. Very often, current academics have come to realize that early research in their field had limitations, but nevertheless such research is still cited simply because it was the first attempt to explore that academic area. It was epoch-making at the time, and hence may retain its importance long into the future. However, you should always be cautious about quoting or citing older works, unless you are confident that there are academic justifications for doing so.

(ii) Online literature searching

Searching for research articles

It is relatively rare now for researchers and academics to search paper copies of academic journals on library shelves, except for specialized purposes, such as a historical study. When you are looking for academic articles, you are likely to be using a number of electronic databases, which are relevant to your subject area. A widely used bibliographic database is Google Scholar (2012). Through its search engine, it enables you to locate a wide variety of materials on a subject. It will enable you to identify theses, books, monographs and, in particular, journal articles. When articles are listed, they are ranked according to a number of characteristics such as the author, the content of the article, and the journal in which it has been published. The number of times the article has been cited is another criterion employed in the order of listing of articles. Google Scholar enables you to access articles from a very wide range of journals, thus providing a broad spread of subjects. If you prefer to consult a more specialist database, then there are a number available. PsycINFO® (American Psychological Association, 2012), for example, enables you to search for articles in the behavioural sciences area. The database currently provides access to over 2,500 journals. It should be noted that this and many other such databases do not provide full-text copies of articles. They may provide you with the bibliographic details and an abstract, but it will be your responsibility to locate a full-text version. You may be able to do this through your university academic library.

Some databases do provide the complete text of articles. One example is SocINDEX™ with Full Text (EBSCO, 2012). This database provides over 2 million items covering the principal sub-disciplines of sociology. It contains the full text of over 16,800 conference papers, and the full text of articles in 890 academic journals. Another full text database is JSTOR® (2012). This organization electronically archives the full texts of academic journals, and then enables people to search them. It currently has back copies of more than 1,400 journals archived electronically. In order to do this JSTOR® usually has agreements with publishers concerning the most recent copies of their journals which can be archived.

Finally, it is worth mentioning SciVerse®Scopus® (Elsevier B.V., 2012), which contains a database of abstracts and citations, drawn from a large library of peer-reviewed literature. It identifies articles from approximately 18,500 academic journals, and draws upon material from a total of approximately 500 different publishers. If required, it provides links to full-text articles. These are just some of a large number of search engines and databases which can be used to identify research articles. So comprehensive is the scale of these databases, that you may find your main difficulty is not identifying articles, but selecting and reading those you will include in your thesis. You will need to make your selection, and then integrate them into a thoughtful analysis for your literature review.

Searching for theses

It is now normal for academic libraries to store postgraduate theses electronically. Such libraries may still retain bound paper copies of older theses, but many of these are in the process of being digitized to increase availability. There are a number of electronic databases of theses which you can search to find studies relevant to your own research. Examples include OpenThesis (2009) and the Networked Digital Library of Theses and Dissertations (NDLTD, 2012). You may not automatically be able to access a full-text version of a thesis from such databases, and may need to access links to other organizations for this. The British Library (2012) supports EThOS (Electronic Theses Online Service), which stores copies of all theses produced within the UK higher education system. It is also actively involved in digitizing older, paper-based theses.

Another way of approaching the search for a thesis, is to examine the content of university repositories. The development of repositories has been closely linked with the trend towards the open access of research data and writing. Generally speaking, repositories support the philosophy of open access, and you should therefore be able to consult repositories in a variety of institutions, not just in your own university. Repositories are used by institutions to store electronically the research and knowledge output of their students, staff and researchers. One of the easiest ways to conduct a search is to use one of their databases of repositories, such as the Directory of Open Access Repositories (OpenDOAR, 2010). Within this database, you can access a list of the repositories in the Directory. OpenDOAR is administered from the Centre for Research Communications, at the University of Nottingham. One of the benefits of citing theses, and indeed the other types of material typically found in repositories, is that they are likely to be relatively recent, and therefore a source of up-to-date analysis on specialized topics.

Using 'grey' literature

Depending upon the nature of your research, you may want to include some less formal material in your literature review. Examples might include minutes of meetings, unpublished essays, leaflets, emails or circulars. This type of material is usually known as 'grey literature', and includes any form of document which has not been formally produced by a publishing company. At times there may be a fine dividing line between published literature and grey literature. Potentially, there is a wide range of material which you might decide to cite.

Example – Categories of grey literature

- Electronic communications, for example, emails, electronic attachments and presentations.
- Organization documents, for example, publicity materials, reports, circulars, statistical summaries, agendas, minutes of meetings and conference proceedings.
- Study materials, for example, course summaries, reading lists, bibliographies and transcripts of lectures.
- Student records, for example, essays, dissertations, coursework, notes, assignments and translations.

You will probably be able to think of many other examples – just consider the types of material you see pinned to university noticeboards or scattered around university teaching rooms.

There are some kinds of study for which grey literature may be particularly relevant. If your research involves political issues, there may well be leaflets and pamphlets which have a political content which would be very useful. The same may be true of a study involving religion. If you are conducting any kind of ethnographic study, then you may identify different kinds of documents which shed light on the social background of your study. In these types of research one of the main advantages of grey literature is that it is often relatively recent when compared with some published material. If you want to carry out a more systematic search for grey literature, you could use the OpenGrey database (Institut de l'Information Scientifique et Technique, 2011), a European-wide database of grey literature which covers a large number of different disciplines and uses English as its main language.

It is important, however, that we consider briefly some of the disadvantages of grey literature. One of the principal problems is trying to cite it accurately. There are many documents such as leaflets, pamphlets and circulars which, although containing very useful information, do not list the author or the date of publication. When it comes to referencing them, you will often have to compromise, and simply put down as much bibliographic information as you have available, even if this means that you cannot comply exactly with some of the normal referencing conventions. If there is no author listed for a document, then it may be difficult to authenticate the contents. One of the purposes of using references is to support your arguments, or to note others who have reached the same broad conclusions. If you are unable to cite an author or at least the organization which has produced the document, then the value of the citation may be limited. However, if you are using grey literature in your literature review, it may be a good idea to discuss briefly the limitations, in order to demonstrate to the reader that you are familiar with these. Sometimes the content of a document can outweigh the disadvantage of a lack of author's name.

Online library catalogues

One of the biggest developments in literature searching in recent years, has been the capacity to make the databases of numerous libraries available through one centralized search. WorldCat® (OCLC, 2012) is one of the largest of such combined library catalogues. A variety of different media are available, but clearly books and scholarly articles will be of most interest to researchers. Once you have located materials through WorldCat, the latter will identify the nearest library where you should be able to access them. However, whether or not you are able to gain access to a full document will depend on the particular library which owns the document, and whether or not you are a member of that library. There are over 70,000 libraries across the world, which are affiliated to WorldCat, and each has its own conditions for making materials available. WorldCat is essentially a very large bibliographic database which will enable you to identify an item, but may or may not furnish a link to the complete book or document. As perhaps may be expected from a combination of libraries worldwide, there are items on WorldCat in many different languages.

Copac (Copac®, 2012) is a smaller consortium of libraries which focuses upon academic and scholarly libraries in the UK and Ireland. It includes such libraries as the British Library, the university libraries of Oxford and Cambridge, the National Trust libraries, the National Library of Scotland, the library of the Natural History Museum, and York Minster Library. Copac is not in itself a library, and hence does not possess academic materials. Once you have identified an item, you may then need to obtain a copy through inter-library loans. Like WorldCat it has access to materials in many languages.

Electronic databases which integrate the catalogues from a number of national libraries can be very useful if you are researching some aspect of the culture of that country.

An example of such a national catalogue is AMICUS, the Canadian National Library Catalogue (AMICUS, 2012). AMICUS combines the contents of over 1,300 different libraries in Canada, and makes them available through a single search process. It is also bilingual in French and English.

These are just a few of the many online library catalogues which are available, and which are an invaluable resource for researchers and students.

Further reading

Gilbert, N. (2001) *Researching Social Life*. London: Sage.

Hart, C. (1998) *Doing a Literature Review: Releasing the Social Science Research Imagination*. London: Sage.

Jesson, J., Matheson, L. and Lacey, F.M. (2011) *Doing Your Literature Review: Traditional and Systematic Techniques*. London: Sage.

Machi, L.A. and McEvoy, B.T. (2009) *The Literature Review: Six Steps to Success*. Thousand Oaks, CA: Corwin Press.

Ridley, D. (2008) *The Literature Review: A Step-by-Step Guide for Students*. London: Sage.

10

Methodology

In this chapter we discuss strategies for writing an account of the methodology of the research. We explain how the definition of the sample and the collection of data follow from the specification of the aims. You examine some of the terminology used in writing about methodology, and explore ways of discussing the strengths and limitations of research methods. Finally, there is an evaluation of methods of discussing research ethics.

Study Strategies

Imagine that you have been approached to be an interviewee for a research study. Try to think of some of the things you would like to know before you agreed to take part. Here are some initial questions which you might ask:

- Have the researchers provided me with any form of identification?
- Do I know if they are affiliated with a university or reputable research organization?
- How long will my involvement take?
- Where will the interview take place?
- What is the purpose of the research?

There will probably be many other questions you would want to ask. When you have compiled your list, you should have a detailed view of many of the ethical issues which are important in social science research.

The relationship between epistemology and methodology

So far in the thesis, you have introduced the reader to the subject matter, explained the broad context of the research and outlined briefly the essentials of the research design. You have also enumerated clearly the aims of the research. In the second chapter, you have analysed in detail the previous research which has been conducted in your subject area. In this third chapter, devoted to methodology, you expand on the brief account provided in the introduction, and then explain the research design in detail.

Concept of methodology

It is worth saying a brief word here about the different terms which are associated with the concept of methodology. This chapter in a thesis is usually entitled 'methodology' and tends to include a discussion of both theoretical issues and the practical matters of data collection. The term 'methodology', however, is also used in a more specific sense, as almost a synonym for research design. In this sense it indicates the practical way in which the whole research project has been organized.

Unfortunately, terms such as 'methodology' and 'research design' are used in slightly different senses by different writers, and a precise conceptual clarification based on usage is difficult. In this chapter the term 'methodology' is used in a general sense to refer to both theoretical and practical aspects of the conduct of the research.

Methodological issues

It is very important that this chapter is not simply a descriptive account of the way in which the data is to be collected. It should be far more than that. The discussion should start with the aims, and explain how the epistemological stance which has been adopted provides a link between the aims and the practical methodological issue of collecting data. There should be an analysis of the way in which it is intended to select the sample for the research, and to analyse the data. It is important in this chapter to evaluate the ethical issues inherent in the research, and to explain the practical strategies which will be undertaken to ensure that the research complies with these ethical principles. You should also demonstrate a balanced appreciation of the methodology which you have chosen, and indicate some of the anticipated strengths and weaknesses. This debate can then be revisited in the concluding chapter, when, with the benefit of hindsight, you will be able to conduct an informed debate about the advantages and disadvantages of the whole methodology. The issue of methodology is discussed in Clough and Nutbrown (2002, pp. 21–40).

Writing tense

Before starting on the main content of this chapter, it is useful to discuss the tense in which the chapter should be written. There are two main ways of thinking about this issue. One is to imagine that the thesis is written chapter by chapter, as each stage of the practical research is conducted. In this case, we would assume that the data has not yet been collected, and hence the methodology chapter would be largely written in the future tense. We might write that 'within the interpretative perspective adopted, the majority of the data will be collected by means of semi-structured interviews'. On the other hand, we might assume that the majority of the thesis has been written after the data has been collected, in which case, we would probably write in the past tense, that 'within the interpretative perspective adopted, the majority of the data was collected by means of semi-structured interviews'. In my experience, most students tend to adopt the latter approach, writing as if they were literally producing a report of the research conducted, after the event. This tends to make the writing more straightforward, because you can always easily position yourself in time, writing about events which have already occurred.

However, even if you write largely in the past tense, there will be occasions when you may wish to write in a different tense, such as the future conditional. For example, you might wish to write that 'although interviews were the primary data collection method, there was discussion that we should employ observational techniques if they seemed appropriate'. The best strategy is to decide on the overall approach, and then vary the tense whenever the sentence appears to demand it.

Epistemology and data collection

It is important then to explain carefully in this chapter the way in which the selection of data collection strategies relates to an overall theoretical and epistemological stance for the research. It would be insufficient to say that a case study approach was being used, or that a survey was being conducted, without relating this to your epistemological position with regard to the subject of the thesis. Your epistemological approach consists of the assumptions you make, whether these are implicit or explicit, concerning the nature of the knowledge which you regard as valid in order to resolve the research question. If your research question involves investigating large-scale trends in society, then you would probably not regard in-depth, unstructured interviews with a very small sample of respondents as being epistemologically valid. However, in the case of many research questions, there are likely to be a number of different epistemological positions which you could adopt. Each of these would reflect a different approach to the research question.

In a study of the working lives of female headteachers, a positivist epistemology may employ a questionnaire with ranking scales to measure the attitudes of pupils and staff to a female headteacher. This would tend to treat knowledge as objective, verifiable and replicable. On the other hand, an interpretative epistemology might explore the different understandings of the role of the female headteacher. This would tend to treat knowledge as created and negotiated between human beings. Finally, a feminist epistemology might explore the female headteacher role as understood within the terms of a male-dominated, traditional epistemology, and wish to break free from this, examining the way feminine values may alter the atmosphere of the school. Such an epistemology may involve a value position that gender is a key factor in understanding the role of the female headteacher and the emancipation from male preconceptions. This will involve an appreciation of the gendered nature of knowledge.

It is equally important to point out that the same method of data collection can be used within the framework of different epistemologies. For example, the interview method could be used within both an interpretative and a feminist epistemology. Therefore you should clarify the reasons for using the particular data collection method in the context of a specific epistemology.

Relating choice of methodology to the aims of the thesis

In the process of writing the methodology chapter you should try to relate both the epistemology and the data collection method back to the aims established in the introduction. To a very large extent the thesis will be judged on the basis of the aims. When the examiners have read the thesis, they will look back at the aims and evaluate the extent to which you have been able to meet them. If they have not been met in any regard, they will expect to read a discussion of the reasons for this.

The discussion of the methodology should establish clearly that it will generate the type of knowledge which can reasonably be expected to satisfy the aims. This is why the aims must be very carefully worded. A slight change of nuance in the aims can easily suggest that a different methodological orientation would have been more appropriate. Let us look at the wording of three different aims, which each relate to research on the role of a female headteacher:

1 To measure the attitudes of staff and pupils to a female headteacher.
2 To explore the ways in which the attitudes of staff and pupils evolve in relation to a female headteacher.
3 To analyse the attitudes of staff and pupils towards a woman as headteacher.

In a superficial sense these three aims are not very different, and yet certain key words do transform the implicit meanings inherent in them. In the first aim, the verb 'measure' suggests the existence of precise attitudes which are susceptible to quantification. The manner in which the aim is expressed suggests a positivist epistemology which in turn may lead to the use of measurement scales within a questionnaire.

The second aim is expressed differently. The use of the verb 'evolve' suggests the assumption that attitudes do not exist as fixed entities, but develop with changing social relationships. The aim appears to suggest that this developmental process will be a feature of the research, and that the methods by which this process operates will be subject to scrutiny. The examination of these processes will entail interpretative work on the part of the researcher, and hence an interpretative epistemology supported by data collected through interviews would be appropriate.

In the third aim, the expression 'woman as headteacher' does perhaps tend to emphasize gender as an issue rather more than in the case of the phrase 'female head-teacher'. Hence the aim suggests that a feminist epistemology would be appropriate, and although various data collection strategies could be used, a qualitative approach may well be appropriate.

We can see from this that even slight changes to the wording of an aim alter the impression it gives about an appropriate epistemology and methodology. Examiners read aims very carefully for the slightest nuances of meaning. They expect the entire methodological orientation of the thesis to be consonant with those aims, and to see evidence of a coherent approach throughout.

The overall research design

By the time you have worked your way through some of the complexities of the issues in the previous section, you will have taken the key decisions about the research. The theoretical aspects of the research will have been determined, and you will now need to describe the actual mechanics of the research. The term 'research design' is often used to refer to the pragmatic aspects of the way the research was conducted. You need to explain these matters to the reader. Some of your writing will be descriptive, but at each stage it is important to offer clear reasons and arguments for the manner in which you conducted the research. When you are starting to write about the research design, think back to the beginning of the research and describe it in chronological order, working your way systematically through the different stages. Here are some of the questions you could ask yourself in order to refresh your memory and to make sure that you provide an adequate justification for the way in which the design was conducted.

> ## Example – Writing about the research design
>
> In order to write about the design, these are some of the questions you could ask yourself:
>
> 1 Where did I decide to collect the data? Why?
> 2 What kind of data did I decide to collect? Why?
> 3 Who did I ask to provide the data? Why?
> 4 How did I go about asking them? Why did I use that approach?
> 5 What arrangements did I use to collect the data? Why did I choose those arrangements?
> 6 Did I ask people for formal permission to conduct the research?
> 7 Did I offer anyone guarantees about the way the research would be conducted or reported?
> 8 How did I analyse the data? Why that method?
> 9 How did I disseminate the findings? Why?
>
> These are just some of the questions you will need to ask yourself. Many others will almost certainly occur to you.

Strategy

In later sections of this chapter, we shall examine key aspects of the research design, namely, sampling, data collection, data analysis and ethics. Prior to that, however, there are several general points which are worth making about the manner in which you write about the design. Perhaps the most important is that the reader should sense that the design process has been driven by an overall strategy. A simple example involves the way in which you discuss the location for the research. Many professionals, including educationalists, locate their research either in their own institution, or in a neighbouring school or college which is easily accessible. It is important when justifying this choice to provide a range of research-based reasons. For example, the institution may have certain unique features which will result in interesting research findings, or that it is typical of a large number of other similar institutions and hence one would be justified in generalizing any results obtained. Alternatively, some prior research may have been conducted at the institution and it would be useful to conduct more research which builds upon the earlier work. Such explanations are important and either part of, or a precursor to, discussions about sampling strategy.

Gaining access

It is not always easy for researchers to gain access to the research field, and it is often necessary to obtain permission. It is usually interesting and relevant for you to describe the process of obtaining access, and to explain the strategies which you used. Such an account will not only demonstrate the care which you took in making the early arrangements to collect data, but may also provide an indication of the nature of the context in which you were researching. If the relevant 'gatekeeper' of the institution in which you wished to research sought to place a number of conditions on your work, then this might be indicative of the general atmosphere of that institution. In turn, that might be relevant to your research.

Before collecting your data, you will have approached potential respondents to ask them for their help, or if they wished to take part in the research. You might have written to them first, or used email, or perhaps made a person-to-person approach. You almost certainly had reasons for using the particular method you chose, and it would be interesting to explain the background to this in the thesis.

Example – Making contact with respondents

The process of contacting potential respondents can be a complex experience, particularly in qualitative research studies. You will need to interest them in what you are doing, explain the nature of your research in everyday language, make them feel they would like to help you, encourage them to see the research as useful for society, and suggest the importance of their own contribution.

These processes involve a complex interaction with your respondents, and it is worthwhile documenting this in your thesis.

It is also very useful here if you can provide references which either justify the kind of decisions you took or illustrate the issue in some way. You may cite a journal article where the same issue of access was addressed in a rather different way. Alternatively, you might cite some research which used the same strategy as yourself, but for different reasons. The need to supply supporting references applies throughout the methodology chapter. Wherever possible you should provide evidence of having read around the subject, and of having reflected critically upon the methodological issue being discussed.

Pilot studies

Even though you give a lot of thought to the selection of potential respondents, it is still difficult to be sure that the data collection process will proceed smoothly. Many researchers therefore prefer to try out their data collection strategy, usually on a small sample of people, in order to see if the process functions well. A small study such as this, in advance of the main research, is known as a pilot study. It is not usually the intention to make use of the data gathered. Rather, the main purpose is to explore the effectiveness of the research process. For this reason, it is normal to select a small group of respondents who will not be part of the sample for the main study. You then go through the data collection process with them, looking carefully for any positive or negative features of the process which might come to light in the main study.

In the case of a quantitative study you give them a copy of the draft questionnaire to complete. You need to monitor the time it takes them to complete the questionnaire, which gives you an idea of whether you have included too many questions. Once they have completed the questionnaire, you could ask respondents about their experience. These are some of the issues you might want to raise with them:

- Did you understand the instructions at the beginning of the questionnaire?
- Did you manage to answer all of the questions?
- If not, why not?
- Was the questionnaire interesting and enjoyable to complete?
- Were you puzzled by any of the questions?
- Was the language used clear and easily understandable?
- Was the layout of the questionnaire clear?

On the basis of the responses to these questions you can revise the questionnaire, and hopefully improve both the response rate and the data validity, in the main study.

In the case of qualitative research, the overall purpose of the pilot study remains the same, but the procedure is slightly different. If you are using an interview method, then you might have designed an interview schedule with a series of questions. You go through the proposed interview process, and when completed, ask the respondents about their reaction to the interview. You might want to raise some of the following issues with them:

- Did you find the interview interesting?
- Did it help you clarify your own ideas about the subject?
- Did you feel at ease throughout the process?
- Were you happy to have your responses tape recorded?
- Were there any questions you would have preferred not to be asked?
- Was the interview too long or too short to explore the subject?

When you have obtained the feedback, you can revise the schedule of questions, or the structure of the interview. Alternatively, you might decide to opt for a less structured form of interview.

In other forms of qualitative research, such as ethnography, a conventional pilot study may be less relevant. In ethnographic research you would probably start by carrying out a small-scale investigation in the planned research situation. The data collected, would probably then inform the next stage of the research. This trial process would then be repeated a number of times. In this case though, each study would be part of a coherent whole, normally conducted in the selected research setting.

The selection of the sample

Most research in education and the social sciences involves the collection of data from human beings. One of the most difficult aspects of research design is deciding from whom you will collect your data. It should be stressed here that in this book we are not straying into the area of methodological processes, but of making sure you are clear about the kinds of issues you should write about in your thesis.

Population

The two basic concepts which you should discuss in your thesis are 'research population' and 'sample'. For example, in a study of the academic qualifications of high-school teachers, you should explain whether this is all high-school teachers in the state of Nevada, or high-school teachers throughout Western Australia, or teachers in England and Wales, and to whom the research applies. The total number of individuals to whom the results of the research are intended to apply constitute the research population. This is a simple, yet profoundly important, issue which is overlooked by many students. It is important to discuss this clearly, and to explain the nature of the population. Both the title of the thesis and the wording of the aims should provide a strong indication of the nature of the research population.

Sample

It is sometimes possible to collect data from every member of the population, but sometimes this is simply not feasible. It is difficult to accomplish when the population is very large, or is geographically dispersed, or when we simply do not know the number of people who are in the population. For example, you could in theory find out the names of all the high-school teachers in a particular local education authority in England and send them each a questionnaire. However, it would be practically impossible to identify all of those people in an English county who could not swim. In cases where it is difficult or impossible to collect data from the whole research population, select a subsection or sample of that population. The intention is normally that the sample is representative of the population, and that the data from the sample can also be applied to the rest of the population.

149

Probability sample

If you are adopting a positivistic approach to your research, you will probably seek a probability sample. This is a sample in which each member of the research population has a known probability of being included in the sample. The best known example of a probability sample is the simple random sample, exemplified in everyday terms by the process of 'taking names from a hat'. If you decide to employ a random sample, then you will need to describe the actual mechanism (for example, random number tables) by which the individuals were selected. You should also discuss the process by which you determined the size of the sample. There are several different statistical procedures which can be used for this. If you are not a well-informed statistician, then you should seek help with this calculation. However, it is advisable not to treat this issue superficially in the thesis, but to be quite clear about the way in which the sample size was determined.

In some forms of research you will want to ensure that respondents who meet certain criteria are included in your sample. For example, in a study of educational management systems and hierarchies, you may wish to ensure that your final sample includes people from each of a number of work role categories. You may divide your population into certain sections, and then take a random sample from each. This is a technique known as stratified random sampling. In a case such as this, it is important to explain the justification for the strata which you select. These strata should relate in some way to the key purposes of the aims of the research. Again, we are returning here to the general theme of coherence in the thesis. Each element should have a logical connection with the other elements.

Non-probability sample

In many forms of research, and particularly those which employ largely qualitative data, there is usually no attempt to employ a probability sample. The so-called non-probability samples typical of research within an interpretative perspective are usually much smaller, but the data collected is more detailed than in the case of a probability sample. Even though the sampling system may be different with this type of approach, it is still important for you to justify the type of sample, the number of people in the sample and the process by which those people were selected.

There are a number of different ways in which non-probability samples are generated. A purposive sample is one in which the researcher identifies certain respondents as being potentially able to provide useful data on the research subject. There is an element of subjectivity here, since the researcher is forming a view as to the preferred characteristics of respondents. It may simply be that the researcher is seeking respondents who are both articulate and who wish to help with the research. On the other hand, the purposive sampling process may seek to identify people who, because of their experience or contacts, have special insights into the research question. For example, in a research study into assessment procedures for public examinations in high schools, most high-school teachers would have useful data to provide. However, those teachers who, in addition, worked as examiners for an examination board would normally have additional and special insights. In a situation involving the subjective selection of respondents, it is particularly important that you describe carefully the process involved, and the kind of criteria used to select sample members. In this type of research, it will not be possible to extend the findings to a research population in the same way as with positivistic research. However, it is still important to reflect upon the extent to which findings may be generalizable in some way, and to discuss this coherently in the thesis.

In some forms of qualitative research, it is very difficult to locate appropriate people for the sample. This may be because they do not wish to be associated as respondents with the subject of the research. In a study of employees who are in disagreement with the prevalent management ideology in a large organization, many may not wish to volunteer as respondents through fear of antagonizing their managers and even, ultimately, of losing their jobs. However, if you are able to identify one such respondent, and if that respondent is able and willing to suggest one or two others who may have similar views, then you may be able to accumulate a reasonable sample of respondents. This type of sampling process is often referred to as snowball sampling. If you were to use such a technique, it is important that you describe in a straightforward and transparent manner the process by which you identified the individual members of the sample. In all sampling procedures, and perhaps particularly with snowball sampling, there are important ethical issues, and these are discussed later in the chapter. Overall, the process of sampling can raise a number of complex issues, and you should try to discuss these thoroughly in your thesis. Aspects of sampling are discussed in Denscombe (2002, pp. 142–6) and in Erickson and Nosanchuk (1992, pp. 117–33). A summary of the questions you should ask yourself before writing about your sampling strategy are listed here.

Summary – Writing about your research sample

Some of the key questions you should address are:

- How would you define your research population?
- How did you create your sample from the research population?
- Will the sample provide appropriate data to address the research aims?
- Is the sample of an adequate size?
- If your sample is a non-probability sample, have you described the criteria which exclude some people and include others?
- Have you discussed the extent to which you hope to generalize from the sample to the research population?

The process by which the data is collected

When you write this section of the methodology chapter, you may have collected most, if not all, of your data. You will therefore be describing a process which you have undertaken, and to that extent this section may be reasonably straightforward to write. However, it is still important that the topic is not treated in a perfunctory or superficial way. The key requirements of the account are that sufficient detail is provided, and that reasons and justifications are given for the strategies used.

Before you started the main process of data collection, you may have conducted a pilot study, to explore the planned research design. If you employed this strategy then it is worthwhile explaining if you gained any benefit from this, and whether it enabled you to refine your overall data collection method. In order to write a good account of the pilot study it is useful to go back in your mind to the initial decision to conduct it. Try to remember your line of reasoning, and describe that in a logical, systematic way. Try to explain the reasons for conducting the pilot study, the concerns you had about the research design and collection of data, and the way in which these were resolved by the pilot. In particular, describe carefully any changes made to the research strategy.

The same technique can be used for writing about almost any aspect of the methodology you have conducted and completed. Try to think back to the step-by-step process whereby you planned the research and reconstruct in your mind the reasons for the way you did things. You may have forgotten many of these reasons, but with careful thought you can often remember the steps that you took in the early days of the research. Ideally, it would be very useful to write these down in a notebook at the time, but in reality the early days of a research project are so busy that this may not be feasible.

It is worth noting that, as there are so many different strategies for collecting data, it is necessary to consider how best to approach the task of describing them. Within a positivistic research perspective the data collection process is very often carefully defined and circumscribed. For example, the distribution of the questionnaire is carefully planned, and the nature of the sample precisely defined. It is therefore a relatively unproblematic task to work through the procedure and to describe it in logical stages. We are not saying here that the whole process was perfect, but merely that it is fairly easy to define. Indeed, at the end of the thesis you will probably wish to review the design and indicate various ways in which the process could have been improved.

Qualitative data

In other types of research design, notably those using either a mixed-method approach or exclusively qualitative data, the process of data collection may not proceed in such a systematic manner. A prime example is in the case of the technique of theoretical sampling within grounded theory. This type of research relies upon the process of collecting and analysing data in stages, and gradually developing a theory inductively, which is based on or 'grounded' in the data. There is usually only the most general idea at the beginning of the way in which the research might proceed. There will initially be a research problem or idea, and this will stimulate the collection of some data. The data will be analysed to try to identify some concepts or themes which are relevant to the main research question. You may then identify one or two of these themes as being potentially fruitful for further data exploration. More data will be collected in a way which seems likely, to the researcher, to illuminate these emerging themes. In this second stage of the research, the data may be collected from respondents who are different to the initial respondents. The research sample will tend to be determined by the developing theory. This is the origin of the term 'theoretical sampling'. The research may proceed through a considerable number of these phases, with the direction of the research altering slightly as the possibility of new themes or concepts develops. Ultimately, the purpose is to develop a theory which has explanatory and predictive value.

The difficulty with describing this type of process in the methodology chapter is that the data collection is intertwined with the data analysis. Much of the analysis will be explained in later chapters, when the results are outlined. However, in the methodology chapter you can still explain the essence of the procedure, without going into details about the results of the analysis. It is important that, having read the methodology chapter, your readers have a clear idea of the process by which the data was collected, and of the reasons for adopting that process.

Ethnographic research

Many of the same kinds of issues arise when writing about ethnographic research. When you first arrive in a new social context to collect data, there may be a large number of options in terms of the kind of data you first collect. If conducting an ethnography of a factory shop floor, there may be many ways in which you could begin the process of data collection. You could start with writing an overall description of the setting, or with interviewing some of the production workers, with talking to supervisory staff or with attending a union meeting. The options are extensive. However, in a situation such as this, you as a researcher would have taken a decision on how to proceed. There would have been a strong element of subjectivity in that decision, and it is important that the grounds for that decision are discussed in the methodology chapter. When describing the research process in your thesis, you should emphasize the logic of the process, and the grounds upon which you took decisions. It may not always be possible to determine each stage of a research project a long time into the future. However, it should always be possible to define the reasons upon which each procedural decision was based.

> ## Example – Justifying the data collection process
>
> It could be argued that in ethnographic research (and in other types of research for that matter), it is less important how you collect your data, but more important that you explain very clearly what you did, and why you did it. As long as you have clear, rational reasons for doing your research in a certain way, and you can explain those reasons to your examiners, then that is a very good start.

Ethnographic research is discussed in Gill and Johnson (2002, pp. 123–60), Creswell (1998, pp. 58–61) and Miller (1997).

Data analysis

When reading the methodology chapter, the reader does not expect to be presented with actual data you have collected, but hopes to understand the process by which you have collected the data and then analysed it. The actual data analysis and the results which derive from that process are presented in the later chapters. It is helpful if the data analysis process can be explained as lucidly as possible, and in particular that the procedure chosen can be related to the type of data on which it is used.

Statistical analysis

An example of this principle is the use of statistical tests. When students first start using quantitative analysis, they do not always realize that a specific statistical test is designed to be used with data of a particular kind. The chi square test, for example, is designed to be used with nominal data. In addition, different tests have advantages and disadvantages when compared with other tests. It follows from this that when designing a questionnaire it is essential to be aware of the type of statistical test which it is intended to use. The process of data analysis should be in your mind when you are designing the data collection instrument. This reinforces a theme which has recurred throughout this book, which is the need to treat the thesis as an integrated whole.

Example – Designing a data collection instrument

These principles can be summed up as follows: do not design your instrument and then work out what you will do with your data; think what kind of data you want and what you will do with it, and then design your instrument.

With statistical analysis, it is helpful to provide evidence of the way in which any questionnaire you used was coded. It is customary to include a blank copy of the questionnaire in the appendix, and the coding system can be shown on this example. Each detail such as this helps the reader to comprehend the entire research process. You may also have used a computer package to analyse your data, whether it is quantitative or qualitative. The use of computer analysis should not alter the outcome of the research, but again it helps your reader to understand the total process. It is usual to include only a portion of the total data output from a computer package in the actual body of the thesis, as the volume and detail of such output is usually too great. However, it is useful to include a few sample pages of data output in the appendix of the thesis to provide the reader with an idea of the extent of the analysis.

Example – Computer analysis of data

It is important to remember that data analysis packages will only do what you tell them to do! You still need to understand the theory of data analysis, whether qualitative or quantitative, before you start the computer analysis. Only then, will you carry out the correct procedures and be able to understand your results.

Action research

Every approach to research has its own distinctive pattern of data analysis, and it is important to explain this in the methodology chapter. Sometimes it is helpful to try to put yourself in the position of your reader or the examiner of your thesis. Try to imagine how they would respond to your results chapters if they were not given an introduction to the overall data analysis process. Would they be able fully to understand your results? Consider the features of the analytic process which would help them to understand the later chapters. Action research, for example, normally follows a type of cyclical procedure, involving the initial collection of data, followed by a period of analysis and reflection on that data. The period of reflection then conditions the next phase of data collection. This cyclical process may be adapted in different research designs, but you need to explain the process you have used, and the way in which it helped to address the original research problem. Action research is also an intrinsically democratic research process, involving the participation of a range of people involved in the original research issue. For example, if you were conducting an action research investigation into the issue of undergraduates leaving their degree programmes before completion, then you would probably want to involve students, lecturers, administrators, parents and others in the research. You would have to contact all of these different categories of people and explain the research project to them. In your methodology chapter it would be necessary to explain the process, and the various procedures you used to involve participants in the research.

Comparing quantitative and qualitative analysis

One final distinction should be made between the broad nature of analysing quantitative data and the analysis of qualitative data. By and large, analysis within the positivistic tradition attempts to be objective, and involves you standing back from the data during analysis. On the other hand, in the interpretative tradition, the respondent has a potentially much greater influence upon the analytic process. You and respondent engage in a much more interactive process, and during the data collection the respondent may in a variety of ways influence your ideas towards data analysis. If this has happened in your research, then you should try to reflect upon this process in as much detail as possible, and to write about it in the methodology chapter. These processes are often very complex, and it is not always easy to illuminate them, but again an attempt at this can help your reader to make sense of your analytic procedures.

Strengths and limitations of the methodology

When writing about methodology it is a good idea to discuss the limitations of the approach you have chosen. It is part of writing in a critical, academic style that you should be able to see both the advantages and the limitations of the chosen research perspective. The results of your research are conditioned as much by the limitations of your approach as by its strengths. It is therefore essential that you write with a balanced understanding of your perspective.

Ethnography, for example, depends very much on the researcher establishing an intimate contact with the research field or context. Indeed, one of the principal methods of data collection for the ethnographer is participant observation, implying that the researcher actually becomes a social actor within the setting which is being studied. When ethnographers are researching a setting with which they are not familiar, it inevitably takes them some time to orientate themselves towards the setting, and to determine the kind of observations they would like initially to make. As strangers in this social setting, it may take considerable time before they can regard themselves as participants in any genuine sense.

The opposite situation occurs where ethnographers decide to investigate a setting with which they are very familiar. This often happens in the tradition of teachers acting as researchers. When practising teachers are conducting ethnographic research in their own school, and particularly in their own classroom, they are certainly participants. They will be very familiar with the social setting, and will scarcely have the problem of getting to know the research setting. However, that very familiarity does bring some problems. Teacher-researchers often fail to note relevant social events simply because these have become part of their routine life as a teacher. They need to learn to mentally withdraw from the field, and to observe social interactions with the eye of a newcomer. On the other hand, there is the decided advantage that as they are familiar with so many different facets of the setting, they can often develop interesting lines of research based upon their sophisticated knowledge of the field.

An added dimension is the manner in which school pupils respond to the field researcher. Their response to those with whom they are unfamiliar will be different to those who they know as their teachers. In the latter case, it poses a methodological issue for the teacher-researcher to be able to change roles from teacher to researcher, and back again. These are clearly rather complex issues, and it is essential that they are discussed in the thesis. In a sense these are not problems for which there are absolute solutions. Rather, they are methodological issues of which you should demonstrate, in your writing, a sophisticated understanding. You should explain the strategies used to minimize the disadvantages for your research, and to enhance the advantages. The aim of your writing is not to show that you have resolved all the problems, but to show an awareness of the difficulties which may arise.

Writing about ethical issues

When you write about the methodology you have used, explain the steps you have taken to treat the research participants with care, sensitivity and respect for their status as human beings. The problems raised by research ethics cannot always easily be resolved. Ethical issues by their very nature are complex, and people have genuine differences of opinion about the manner in which they should be addressed. Moreover, although a consideration of the classical theories of ethics and of the writings of well-known moral philosophers do help in resolving ethical issues, such theories tend to provide only general guidance rather than absolute answers.

Informed consent

Although the area of research ethics does entail a certain element of ambiguity, there are some established procedural principles which are relevant to a wide range of social research. One of the best known principles is that of informed consent. This places upon the researcher the obligation to ensure that before respondents agree to take part in the research, they are made fully aware of the nature of the research and of their role within it. As a researcher you would be expected to comply with this principle, and in terms of writing your thesis you should explain carefully the steps you took to inform your respondents about the research.

The principle of informed consent is itself a complex concept. Some respondents may be rather impressed by the status of a researcher, or even by the word 'research', and may agree to take part without having a very good idea of the nature of the process. They may later come to regret taking part. Other people may take part in a research project, and perhaps suffer some degree of anxiety or stress when asked questions. Yet others may take part in a research programme without realizing that some of their responses would be published in a written report of the research. All of these situations are undesirable, and the principle of informed consent is designed to ensure that researchers provide respondents with all the information necessary for them to decide whether or not they wish to participate.

Example – Helping the respondent to understand the research

We have to accept that as researchers we often employ language which is complex and contains jargon. Potential respondents may simply not understand this type of language sufficiently, in order to understand your research. Consequently they will not be in a position to give their fully informed consent. You may have to simplify your description of your research, to a level which is understandable yet still accurate.

When you first contact prospective respondents you should provide them with a summary of the key aspects of the research. It may not be feasible to explain all aspects of the process, simply because of the pressures of time. There is clearly a matter of judgement here concerning the extent of the information which is relevant to their decision to participate. They may not be interested, for example, in all the theoretical considerations which were part of developing the research design. However, they probably would be interested in those aspects of the research concerning the way in which they would be expected to provide data, and the type of questions they would be asked. They would also probably want reassuring that they would not be named in connection with the research, and that there would be no way in which the opinions they expressed could be associated with them personally. There may be other areas in which they would like information about the research, but these are some of the main issues which might concern them.

In your thesis, then, you would be expected to describe those aspects of the research which you explained to potential respondents. You will also need to indicate the method which you used to convey the information. It could be seen as an ethical issue that you tried to ensure that everyone was given the same information. One way of ensuring this is to prepare an information sheet about the research and to distribute this to potential respondents. Respondents will be able to ask further questions, but at least this method provides standard information to all respondents. A discussion of the principle of informed consent may be found in Bailey (1996, p. 11).

Anonymity and confidentiality

Anonymity and confidentiality are in many ways related terms. In research, anonymity tends to refer to the wish of the person providing data not to be identified in the final thesis. Confidentiality, on the other hand, refers to the range of people who might have access to the data being provided. If the data were to be confidential to the researcher then only he or she would have access to the data. Clearly, in the case of a research thesis, this will not be the case. Certainly examiners and academic supervisors will read the thesis. The ethical issue here is therefore that in terms of informed consent, the research respondents have the right to know whether the data could be traced back to them, and who will have the opportunity to read the data.

It is not easy to offer absolute guarantees about these issues, but there are a number of established strategies which may be used. The most common method of trying to assure anonymity is the use of either fictional names, or letters or numbers, to specify respondents. In most cases this ought to be reasonably effective in securing anonymity, but there are one or two potential problems. If the work role occupied by a respondent is named, for example, 'Head of English' in a named high school, then it would not be too difficult to identify the person. If respondents reveal anything about themselves in their data, this may also reveal something of their possible identity. The writer of a thesis may therefore have to consider making both individuals and institutions anonymous in their thesis, and eliminating any data which may provide clues about identity.

Confidentiality may be a little more complex, since it is difficult to know who may finally have access to a thesis. In the first instance, the supervisor or supervisors will clearly read the thesis, followed by the examiners. For some master's theses, these may be the only people who have access to it. If, on the other hand, a thesis, whether master's or doctoral, is placed in an academic library, then a great many people may have access to the data. Many university libraries provide access to members of the public who are not enrolled as students, and thus a thesis placed in a library moves into the public domain. In principle, an unlimited number of people may have access to it, even though in reality relatively few actually read it.

What seems to be the important principle here is that the limits to anonymity and confidentiality are discussed with respondents before they actually provide data. They can then form a personal judgement about whether they want to go ahead with the research. Importantly, they can also decide on the extent and nature of the data which they may decide to provide. For example, if they are unsure about the certainty of their anonymity, and if they are being asked to provide data on, say, their workplace, this could affect the type of issue which they are prepared to talk about.

Interview ethics

It is an important element of the account of research ethics to explain the steps which you took to help make the respondent feel at ease, and to enable them to feel some degree of control over the data collection process. The interview process, for example, can be rather daunting for some respondents, and there are a variety of strategies which you can use to minimize this. You might have ensured that the interview was conducted in a pleasant and relaxing atmosphere, with sufficient privacy. You may also have provided a glass of water for the respondent. Most researchers prefer to tape-record interviews in order to have an accurate account of the dialogue, and yet this very process raises several ethical issues. Even if respondents are happy to be tape-recorded, there may be some questions to which they would prefer not to respond, or at least they would prefer not to have their comments recorded. You will need to describe your strategy for dealing with such situations.

> ### Example – Giving control to the interviewee
>
> Some researchers make sure that the tape recorder is within easy reach of the inter-viewee, and advise them at the beginning of the process, that if they are unhappy with the way in which the interview is developing, they can turn off the tape recorder. This can help interviewees feel that they are more in control, and that they are not simply passive participants.

In addition, some respondents may ask about the system for storing tapes and how long they will be kept before being destroyed. It is a good idea for you to have a clear policy on this in order to be able to reassure respondents.

Research ethics is an area of growing importance, and it is essential to provide a clear account of the steps you took to ensure that respondents were treated fairly and equitably, and were informed about all aspects of the research which were relevant to them. In research ethics, as in other branches of ethics, people will often differ concerning appropriate action or in ways of resolving ethical dilemmas. When you have selected your strategies in relation to research ethics, it is often a good idea to consult others, such as your supervisor, and submit your strategies to a formal university ethics committee for comment. In this way you might receive useful comments on ways of amending your strategy. At the very least, you will have the reassurance of knowing that you have submitted your ideas to peer review. If you have followed this approach, then you should certainly mention it in your thesis as evidence of your having sought formal approval for your approach to ethical issues. Research ethics are discussed in Sapsford and Jupp (1996, pp. 318–22).

Signpost to success – Ethics

Make sure that you discuss the variety of steps which you took to ensure everyone involved in the research was treated fairly.

The issue of incentives in research

When you approach people to help you with your research, and in particular to act as respondents who provide data, you will probably find that if they have the time, they will usually be happy to help. They will probably be interested in knowing about the background to your research, and the reasons for your approaching them to provide data. They will normally find the process of data collection – be it a questionnaire or interview – interesting in itself, and will want no further recompense other than the pleasure of being asked to take part. However, some researchers would argue that if we expect people to give up their valuable time in order to provide data, then we should at least offer to reward them in some way. A form of incentive may neither be expected nor necessary, if the data collection consists of a short interview or the completion of a short questionnaire. However, if you wanted your respondents to take part in a longer process, for example a series of tests in a psychology laboratory, then you may think it justifiable to offer them a small financial incentive.

The main argument in favour of this is that if we asked people to give up their time in any other walk of life, we would probably expect to pay them for their trouble. Why, then, should we expect them to give up their time to act as research respondents, without receiving any recompense in return? On the face of it, this seems a perfectly reasonable argument. However, there are one or two aspects of the research process which may not be entirely compatible with offering incentives.

We hope that research respondents will always act as objectively as they can when answering questions, and will not be influenced by any extraneous factors. This is important for you as a researcher to be able to collect data of high validity. If the respondent has no reason to help, other than one of personal interest in the research, then there is every chance that the responses will be objective. On the other hand, if there is a financial relationship between you and your respondents, then the latter may tend to be overly influenced by their potential income. They may try to provide the type of responses which they believe you want to hear, in order to extend the financial arrangement. It may be possible to avoid any threats to the validity of the data, by discussing the issue openly with respondents. However, on balance, it is better if respondents are happy to give their time, without receiving any incentives.

Should the methodology have been different?

At some place in the thesis you should review the overall success of the research design and of the strategy for collecting and analysing data. We tend to select the methodology on a number of grounds, including the nature of the aims and our judgement about the extent to which data of a certain kind may be available. For any particular research question there will usually be several different ways in which you might have tried to resolve it. Your chosen approach for your thesis may have been more or less successful. The examiners of your thesis will be looking for evidence that you have reflected on your overall strategy, and have carefully considered the extent to which it has been successful. They will expect to see a carefully balanced discussion of its apparent strengths and weaknesses. Moreover, they will expect to read an objective analysis of the way in which you might have amended the methodology, given the wisdom of hindsight. It may be easier, and more logical, to present this kind of discussion in the conclusion to the thesis, or there may be some elements of this analysis which could be placed in this chapter. What is important, however, is that you include in an appropriate place a careful discussion of these issues.

Ethical justifications of research

When explaining to potential respondents the nature of the research you are undertaking, it is worthwhile telling them why you are doing the research. The prime reasons may be, of course, that you wish to gain a research degree. This is a perfectly good rationale, but there may be additional reasons. You may be conducting an action research study during which you hope to resolve a particular social issue. Alternatively you may be interviewing people who are experiencing difficulties of some kind, and you may hope that the research conclusions will motivate others to try to improve the situation. In other words, there may be a direct moral dimension to the research aims.

Research may not, of course, have a directly moral purpose. It may be concerned with adding to the total of our understanding of an issue. It may be that a researcher aims to add to the sum of human knowledge, only to find later that someone uses that knowledge for a purpose which is unethical. This may not reflect at all upon the original research. However, it seems reasonable that a potential respondent, who is asked to take part in research, may want to discuss the ethical dimension of the project. They may wish to ask you about your understanding of the moral purposes of the research.

Therefore, when you write about the methodological aspects of your research, it is important to demonstrate that you have considered the many ethical aspects of your research design. It is important to show that you appreciate that research is rather more than collecting and analysing data. Research is an activity which involves the lives of others, and it is important to show that you have reflected upon the impact of your research on other people.

Sponsorship of research

One aspect which may impinge upon the ethical dimensions of research is that of funding. Many research students are likely to be self-funding; that is, they pay tuition fees to a university in the normal way. However, some research students receive a proportion of funding, directly or indirectly, from a commercial sponsor. This may occur because the leader of a research team, usually a senior member of university staff, has been successful in applying for financial support for a particular project. The additional finance may support the appointment of one or more doctoral students who will collect data for the overall project, but also use at least some of the data collected to write up their own thesis. The additional research funding may also be used to offset some or all of their tuition fees. The essence of the arrangement is that the commercial sponsor wants a particular issue, in which they may have a vested interest, to be investigated, and they are willing to pay a university research team to conduct the research.

While there is no reason that such funding may change any aspect of the conduct of the research, it is worth considering whether you should tell the respondents about the origin of the funding under 'informed consent' procedures. Some respondents may, for example, have an ideological or political objection to supporting research funded by some sponsors. It does seem reasonable that they should be informed about funding, in order that they can make an informed decision. The passing on of such information is something which you should then note in the thesis. The other aspect of the issue is that a failure to be absolutely transparent about the sources of research funding may leave you, and other research colleagues, open to accusations of bias in methodology or other aspects of the research. Such accusations may be completely without foundation, but even a slight lack of transparency may encourage unfair suspicion. It therefore seems reasonable to take all possible steps to inform people about funding sources. Again, you should note and explain it in your thesis.

Consulting respondents about their data

Many researchers feel that it is a good idea to guarantee to respondents that they will be able to read either the data analysis or the whole thesis, in order to check that the material included is accurate and a true reflection of what was said. It is understandable that this seems to be a sound ethical principle. After all, you may need to omit some elements of what is said during the interview, and this could conceivably distort the intended meaning. By allowing respondents to vet the presentation of the data, you can be seen to be following an essential ethical principle. However, it is a practice which can create several potential difficulties.

The first difficulty is one of logistics. In interview research, for example, you may first produce a transcription of the interview tapes. The intention may be to pass the tape and the transcription to each respondent in turn, and ask them to verify the transcription. If each of, say, 30 or 40 respondents were to do this, then it would be very time-consuming. With each respondent there may be minor disagreements about the nature of the transcription, and these would have to be discussed and appropriate action agreed.

If, on the other hand, the intention is to allow respondents to read the transcripts and the analysis, then the situation may become even more complex. Some respondents may not agree with the analysis and conclusions you draw. This might be because, if they are non-academics, they may not appreciate the analytic methods used, or it may be because they simply feel that the motives or meanings attributed to them are inaccurate. In either case, you are left with a major dilemma. In the interests of trying to act ethically and of consulting respondents, you have to either embark on a potentially major reworking of the thesis, or indicate that the comments of the respondents are noted, but that no changes will be made. In the former case, if parts of the thesis are rewritten, then there is the danger that the thesis and conclusions will lose coherence. In the latter case, there is the possibility that respondents will feel that having been asked for their views, these are subsequently ignored. Although this policy of consultation is motivated by the best ethical motives, the consequences may become rather unpalatable, and indeed by antagonizing respondents any ethical advantages may be subsequently negated.

This is a complex issue, but the logic of the situation seems to indicate that at some stage you have to take over complete responsibility for the data and the analysis, and beyond that point respondents are no longer consulted. Clearly, procedures for anonymity should as far as possible ensure that even if inaccuracies exist, these cannot be attributed to a named person. The debate then becomes one of determining the point at which you take over this responsibility.

It is possible that, even given anonymity, some respondents may say things during an interview, which on reflection they would prefer to have omitted. A compromise would be to hand over transcripts from each interview to the respective interviewee, and invite them to delete anything which they would prefer not to have included. After that, the data could be regarded as within the control of the researcher. The alternative would be to include in the informed consent protocol, a statement that as far as possible anonymity will be maintained, and that respondents may read but not change the final thesis.

The discussion of this issue demonstrates the complexity of research ethics. It is sometimes relatively easy to establish principles which appear ethically sound, but it can be more difficult to translate them into a practical course of action which does not make the research and writing process too complex.

Further reading

Crotty, M. (1998) *The Foundations of Social Research: Meaning and Perspective in the Research Process.* London: Sage.

Frankfort-Nachmias, C. and Nachmias, D. (2007) *Research Methods in the Social Sciences.* 7th edn. London: Macmillan (Worth).

McNiff, J. and Whitehead, J. (2009) *Doing and Writing Action Research.* London: Sage.

Miles, M.B. and Huberman, A.M. (1994) *Qualitative Data Analysis – An Expanded Sourcebook.* 2nd edn. London: Sage.

Silverman, D. (2004) *Doing Qualitative Research: A Practical Handbook.* 2nd edn. London: Sage.

Thomas, G. (2009) *How to Do Your Research Project.* London: Sage.

Walliman, N. (2005) *Your Research Project: A Step-by-Step Guide for the First-Time Researcher.* 2nd edn. London: Sage.

11

The Data Analysis Chapters

In this chapter we explore different strategies for the presentation of your data analysis. We discuss how to subdivide the data into chapters and also how to present both qualitative and quantitative data. We explore the issue of how you need to report the selection and rejection of data, in order that your account is open and transparent. In addition there is a discussion of the extent to which examples of raw data need to be included within the thesis.

Study Strategies

- Look at articles in a range of different academic journals, and note the different forms of tabular presentations and figures. Think about your own data, and the different methods you could use to present it. Qualitative data can also be presented in tabular form. Look for different examples, and consider how you might use those strategies. Would they help you in presenting your data? Would they help the reader to understand your arguments?

Defining a list of chapter headings

You are now embarking on the largest section of the thesis, which consists of the data you have collected, the analysis and the presentation of results or findings. This will probably be longer than the total of the first three chapters, and thus it is necessary to divide the presentation of data into different chapters. The actual number of chapters depends on the nature of the data, and on the manner in which you decide to subdivide it. You might typically require between three and six chapters. Each chapter should have a title which reflects the nature of the data within that chapter.

It is generally better to complete at least most of the analysis of your data before beginning to write these chapters. Without having conducted the analysis, it is difficult to decide on the themes of the chapters. When planning these chapters there are a number of factors to consider. If you have collected any quantitative data, for example from questionnaires, you will start with apparently a great deal of data in the form of completed questionnaires, but this will reduce rapidly after analysis to a relatively small number of descriptive statistics and statistical relationships. You may be able to convert the data from some of the questions into histograms or charts, but often in the case of inferential statistics the data reduces dramatically to a few estimates of statistical significance. Although such data may be of considerable importance, it is not always easy to discuss it at sufficient length to generate the number of words required for a long thesis. With qualitative data, there is often the opposite problem. Even a relatively small number of interviews, when transcribed, will yield a very large volume of data. Even if you are selective about the data which you finally discuss, you will probably find that you are seeking ways to restrict the final word length of the thesis, rather than extending it. It is partly for this reason that some researchers try to combine some quantitative and some qualitative data collection in their research design.

When identifying chapter headings it is preferable to relate these to the themes inherent in the data analysis, rather than using, for example, the names of the data collection methods. You may consider naming one chapter 'Interview data' and another 'Survey data'. However, quite apart from being a very mechanistic approach, it is likely that there will be some data from both types which will relate to a particular subject matter. For example, in a study of the management and administration of a high school, there may be some data on the role of meetings of various kinds in the management of the school. Such data may derive from various sources. If there is sufficient data, then it may be appropriate to construct an entire chapter around such data, and to name it, say, 'The role of meetings in school management'. The chapter titles should reflect the themes which emerge from the data, and which will ultimately be synthesized in the conclusion, to address the original aims of the research.

In the development of themes and concepts from qualitative data, it is important to try to be transparent about the process. As themes are developed, it is important to try to make connections between those themes, in order to have an understanding of an evolving theory. Some themes may be more significant, and will constitute the chapter headings, while others may be less important, and may be used as subheadings within the chapters. Readers of your thesis should be able to understand how the themes and concepts have evolved, and why they are grouped together. In the conclusion, it may be possible to show relationships between the themes in the form of an algorithm.

Selection from the data

In an ideal world a research project would be so carefully designed that all the data collected would be essential to resolving the research question. However, this is seldom the case, and you will usually find that you need to discard some of the data. You may not use all the data because some of it in retrospect appears superfluous to the research question, or simply because you have too great a volume of data. There are many factors which might affect the decision to discard some and retain other material. What is important is that you have a clear strategy for the selection of the data you use, and that you explain this strategy in the thesis. Such explanations are not always provided in theses or journal articles. The lack of such an explanation may leave readers wondering whether omitted data might contain some potentially interesting findings. Such dangers are easily avoided by being transparent about the strategy for selecting data for analysis. There are a variety of possible grounds for selecting data, and these are indicated in the summary.

Summary – Criteria for the selection of data

There are a variety of possible strategies which you could use to select some data for analysis, and to discard other data. Each of these strategies may be more relevant in some contexts than others.

- If a certain proportion of respondents all raise a particular issue, then that data may be selected.
- Some data may concur with findings from previous research.
- The researcher may take a subjective decision that certain respondents should be regarded as key respondents, and that data they provide should normally be included in the analysis.
- Where methodological triangulation has been employed, certain types of data may occur between methods.
- Respondents may themselves suggest a hierarchy of data, indicating that some issues are more significant than others.
- Some themes or issues may recur in data collected from a later sample of respondents, which is different from the earlier respondents.

The selection of data is often an important issue with qualitative data, such as that deriving from interviews or observational research. The volume of data is often so great in such cases that some degree of selectivity is necessary. Where this data is being used as part of a grounded theory study, it is important to clarify the criteria used for selection, since the nature of the theory which is ultimately developed depends very much on the data selection strategies used at each stage of the research. Sometimes, however, in social science research the intention is not to develop a theory grounded in the data, but to analyse the collected data within the framework of an existing typology. Such a typology often derives from the work of another research study, and consists of a range of concepts which are seen as being useful in analysing or interpreting data within a particular subject area. When such a conceptual framework or typology is used to analyse data, then some of the data may not fit the typology and may be discarded. This is not necessarily a drawback, but the analytic process should be explained to the reader in order that the process of utilizing only part of the data may be understood.

Example – Using a typology

If you decide to conduct this type of analysis, then you need to report very clearly why you have selected a particular typology. You need to make a connection between the original development of the typology, and its use within the context of your research. In other words you need to establish its relevance.

Writing about the analysis of qualitative data

If your research has involved largely qualitative data, then your data analysis chapters may be fairly lengthy, partly because of the number of extracts from the data which you will provide, but also because it takes a considerable amount of discursive writing to explain the analysis of the data. These chapters will be fairly long, and it will be easy for the reader to become slightly confused when reading them, simply because of the quantity of the material. It is important to have explained clearly the analytic process which you are using, and perhaps to return to that from time to time, as a reminder of the research procedures. The subheadings used provide another useful guide, in that they indicate the nature of the developing themes and analysis. It is worth noting that in a qualitative study, you should try to provide readers with as many 'signposts' as possible within the thesis. These are a reminder of what has gone before and the analysis which is to come. You might say, for example, 'this theme will emerge in the next chapter, when we further analyse some of the data from the teachers'. Alternatively, you could say, 'a large number of interviewees appeared to relate this concept to the theme of teaching style which was discussed in the previous chapter'. Such 'direction guides' help to indicate the connections within the data analysis chapters, and act as a preparation for the discussion in the concluding chapter.

Most of your writing about the data will consist of the analysis into themes and concepts. However, there are other issues which you might wish to mention. Some of the developing themes may be connected with findings from previous research studies with which you are familiar. It may be relevant to mention this in terms of providing support for your interim findings. Equally, your data may suggest new concepts you have not seen identified in other research. You may decide to mention this as supporting the continued investigation of the concept. In all cases you should try to provide evidence for your assertions, based upon quotations and extracts from your data. Bryman and Burgess (1994) and Dey (1993) discuss the analysis of qualitative data.

Presenting qualitative data

The presentation of qualitative data provides you with opportunities to exercise considerable initiative. The formalities of presentation are perhaps less precisely defined than with, say, statistical data, and it is possible to develop new and innovative ways to include data in the thesis. The main requirement is that the presentation should reflect as accurately and validly as possible the original data at the point of collection.

When writing about case study or ethnographic research it is usually necessary to describe something of the research setting. Whether this is a school, college, government department or commercial setting, the nature of the research field is essential to an informed appreciation of the research study. One of the difficulties of providing an accurate description of the field is that it may, in effect, divulge the identity of the research location. This in turn may compromise the anonymity of respondents. In order to guard against this it is usually sufficient to use a fictional name for the setting, and to be careful about referring to any of the distinctive identifying characteristics of the setting. Generally, however, it is very interesting for the reader to gain an idea of the location for the research, and it can help a great deal in understanding the nature of the data. The example takes the case of field research in a further education college, and lists some of the features of the college which it might be useful to describe.

> ## Example – Field research: describing the research setting
>
> If you have conducted research in a further education college, you might wish to write in a general way about some of the following features in order to explain the context of the research:
>
> - The general layout of the college, and its non-specific location (for example, the North of England).
> - The nature of the student catchment area.

- The number of students enrolled.
- The academic and management structure of the college.
- The range of courses offered.
- Relationships with neighbouring academic institutions.
- Numbers of academic and support staff.
- College resources.
- Distribution of student numbers between departments and courses.

Assuming that the name and immediate location of the college are anonymized, then there is no reason for the above details to reveal the college identity.

In accounts of field research it can also be useful to provide a sketch map of the setting and, even, photographs. These can again provide useful background information to the data. If prepared with care, they need not necessarily divulge the identity of the institution.

The most common form of qualitative data is that deriving from interviews. It is the norm to tape-record the interview, then to transcribe the recording, and to include short extracts from the transcriptions in the thesis. The extracts are usually indented and presented in much the same way as quotations from books or articles. This raises an issue of presentation and formatting, however, since some writers prefer to distinguish between these two types of extract. For example, perhaps the interview data is presented in smaller font size, whereas the quotations from articles are italicized.

The presentation of interview data does raise the issue of the accuracy of transcription from the tape recording. If you listen to a recording of an interview, you will probably notice that the interviewee (and the interviewer) exhibits a variety of pauses, stops and starts, repetitions, emphasis on certain words, and exclamations within the dialogue. Yet, an examination of research reporting in articles generally reveals a fairly standard transcription style, which notes relatively little of this variety of speech pattern. Yet it is within this immense variety of linguistic pattern that much of the meaning of dialogue is contained. This is worth commenting on, not necessarily as a criticism, but merely to note the norms of research reporting. The principal exception to this is in the case of ethnomethodological research, where it is normal for the lines of the transcript to be numbered, and for a range of diacritical marks to be employed to indicate the great variation inherent in the speech patterns. When reporting interview data there is no need for you to deviate from the accepted approach. However, it would be useful to explain briefly the system of transcription which has been used and the principles inherent in that approach. This does not necessarily need to be a long explanation, but it has the important advantage of setting some of the parameters to the validity of the data.

Example – Style of transcription

The style of transcription which you decide to adopt should reflect the type of analysis which you decide to undertake. If you wish to explore subtle nuances of meaning, then a detailed transcription system will be needed; on the other hand, if you are seeking broad concepts or themes, then a less detailed system will be satisfactory.

In ethnographic research where there may be a number of key respondents, it is useful to provide short biographical details of each. The nature of such details would vary depending upon the nature of the research, but would provide sufficient information to enable readers to identify with each individual. The fictional name of each respondent could also be attached to the biography. Such details could be included in the appendix or at the beginning of the thesis. These details often enable readers to imagine the research setting in a more realistic way, and to appreciate better the lives and interactions of the social actors.

There is, of course, a balance to be struck between providing useful contextual information about the research setting and key respondents, and the danger of disclosing identities. It is important to be aware of not providing personal details to the extent that the identity of a respondent could be discerned. The same issue can arise if codes are added to extracts of data to indicate something about the respondent.

It is common, when qualitative data is presented in theses, not to distinguish between the different respondents. The nature of the total sample is described, but within that sample all respondents are treated as if they were the same. Although this is often acceptable, one of the problems with the approach is that there may be far more data included from one respondent than from another. There may be few clues as to how much data has been rejected as unsuitable for inclusion. The data which is selected for inclusion in the thesis may not represent a balanced perspective of the total research sample. With this approach it can also be very difficult to identify whether one subgroup of respondents hold a particular view on an issue, while a different subgroup have a very different opinion. There may be many social or economic factors within the research sample which are related to their views on issues, but these connections may never emerge in the analysis. One of the solutions to this is to add codes at the end of the data extract, which reflect variables which are relevant to that respondent.

One of the most common types of code to be added to a data extract is one indicating the gender of the respondent. It is a simple matter to add 'M' or 'F' at the end of the quotation to indicate the gender. This then creates the possibility that the researcher can identify possible differences in responses between males and females. It may not be possible to say anything definitive about gender differences, but it may at least be feasible to indicate possible areas for future enquiry. The identification of codes should proceed from the original aims of the study and the overall nature of the research. For example, in research on the subject of teachers' careers, it may be necessary to identify the approximate age of the teacher. The researcher may group respondents into three broad age bands, for example, allocating the letter A, B and C to these age bands. Such a coding system may be used to suggest possible attitude differences between teachers of different ages. There are many other possible codes depending upon the research subject, but these could include such variables as ethnicity, educational history or employment.

The addition of such codes to data extracts can add further possibilities to the analysis, but there is also the problem that they reveal further detail about respondents. There is the remote possibility that this detail may compromise attempts at anonymity, and if there are any real concerns about this, then it could be discussed with respondents as part of informed consent protocols.

Finally, it is perhaps worth mentioning one issue which may involve qualitative research, and that is making comparisons between two research settings or two case studies. It is tempting in designing research to attempt to draw comparisons between, say, two schools, two industrial companies or any two organizations or settings. The fundamental difficulty with such designs is, however, that there will inevitably be many potential variables involved in such a comparison. It is extremely difficult to minimize or eliminate the effect of some variables in order to make a viable comparison using other variables. This is exacerbated in qualitative research where the richness and complexity of the data make it very difficult to isolate variables in any meaningful way. Consequently, although the above strategy of coding data is very useful when investigating a single setting or case study, there are numerous inherent problems when the strategy is employed to try to make meaningful comparisons between two case studies.

Writing about grounded theory analysis

The traditional approach to developing knowledge in a subject area involves the development of a hypothesis, or provisional statement, of the way in which variables interact. The researcher then collects data in order to try to shed light on the truth or falsity of this hypothesis. Such a deductive process remains the cornerstone of positivistic research. However, rather different approaches are typically used in the analysis of qualitative data. One of the main methods is termed 'grounded theory', and was first described in a well-known text by Glaser and Strauss (1967). The essence of this method is that rather than testing a hypothesis to develop social science theory, we carefully analyse our data in order to construct a theory. In other words, our theories are 'grounded' in our data, and emerge from that data. This process is known as induction, rather than deduction.

One of the main philosophical underpinnings of the approach, is that we try to reveal the nature of the world as understood and interpreted by our respondents. We are interested in the sense of meaning which people and objects have for them. In other words, we as researchers do not try to impose our own sense of understanding on our respondents. We are interested primarily in exploring the way in which our respondents see the world.

Example – The respondent's perspective

Most qualitative methodologies try to understand the world from the respondent's point of view. It is not to say that this is the only perspective which matters, but merely that qualitative research seeks to explore this view of the world. It sets out to understand what respondents think, rather than using social definitions derived from the researcher.

The way in which we can do this, is to meticulously examine the data we get from them, whether this consists of observations, conversational or interview data, or documents. Within grounded theory, the data analysis proceeds in parallel with data collection. At the beginning of the research within your chosen research setting, you have to make a decision about where to begin collecting data. The analysis of that early data, may suggest the collection of more similar data, or it may point in the direction of collecting slightly different data. This new section of data will then be analysed, and will probably indicate the next source of data. In other words, there is a continual interaction between the collection of sections of data, and the way in which you allocate meaning to that data. When you first start collecting data, you will probably find that it suggests various concepts or categories to you. These categories may help you summarize the data, or make sense of it. You may feel, however, that you need further data to help clarify or expand these categories. This process of using your categories to help suggest further data collection is known as theoretical sampling. As the sampling and data collection proceeds you will try to explore the relationship between the different categories. For example, you might try to understand how one category affects another, or perhaps which category exerts the most influence over the others. The connections between the different categories in effect constitute your evolving grounded theory. Eventually, you may reach a point at which there does not seem to be any more relevant data to collect, and you may wish to present your grounded theory as it stands. However, it is worth emphasizing that all such theories are provisional, and are only valid until such time as someone collects further data which appears to falsify them. In that case, you would need to amend your theory in the light of the new data, and then wait to see if someone else eventually collected some contradictory data.

Table 11.1 Tabular presentation: absolute numbers

Highest qualifications of teachers in the case study school, academic year 2002/3. (n = 86)

	First degree	Master's degree	Doctorate
Number of teachers	69	15	2

Examples of the presentation of qualitative data

There are many different theoretical perspectives which are used to analyse qualitative data. These include symbolic interactionism, phenomenology, ethnography, action research, grounded theory and participant observation. However, whatever the theoretical position being used, the majority of qualitative data collected in research consists of either observational accounts or interviews. Let us start with a fictional example of an observational account. This is of an undergraduate sociology class held in a college in the evening. All of the students are mature students, some of whom have come straight to class after work.

Example – Observational data

The class is supposed to start at 6 p.m. There are only about 10 students present by that time, and the tutor waits 10 minutes before starting teaching. If everyone is present there should be 22 students. The tutor asks the students present, whether they have seen the others. Eventually, he starts by recapping the work from the previous week. Students arrive between 6:10 and 6:40. Most are carrying bags as if they have come from work. Many have bought cups of coffee on the way, and start to eat sandwiches as soon as they sit down. This seems to be the norm. Without exception, those who are late, apologize to the tutor. They enter quietly so as not to disturb the class. Everyone is taking careful notes of what the tutor says. The tutor has said he will give them all copies of the projection slides at the end. None of the students asks any questions. From time to time, the tutor asks a short

(Continued)

(Continued)

question, apparently to check understanding. One student tends to respond to all of the tutor's questions. Sometimes the tutor asks 'Does anyone else have a view?' or something similar, but others seldom respond. There is the impression that the tutor would like people to engage in a debate. The class is scheduled to last two hours. At 7 p.m. there is a 5-minute break. Some students go up to the tutor to ask questions, and address him by his first name. There is a friendly atmosphere. When the teaching resumes, the tutor divides the class into groups, and gives them a topic to discuss. He then circulates to check they know what to do. A number of students ask questions about the essay which they have to submit the week after. Sixteen students have arrived in total, and the atmosphere in the classroom is one of diligent work.

If we were to adopt a grounded theory approach to analysing this account, we could start by considering the evidence of hard work in the group. Although some students are late for the class, the overall impression is one of a serious approach to study. Some students seem to come straight from work, even though they are tired; they bring their own drink and food; and they use available time to consult their tutor. We might decide to develop a concept which we call 'study diligence', to indicate the apparent seriousness with which these mature students take their studies. This is only a tentative concept at this stage, and we would need to collect more data, perhaps by interviewing some students, in order to examine aspects of their motivation. Here is a short fictional extract of interview data from one of the students:

Example – Interview data

Interviewer:	Most of you seem very motivated in the group . . . do you think you are keen on your studies?
Student:	Yeh . . . I would say so. We're a bit older than the average; so we're a bit keener.
Interviewer:	So . . . would you say it's a case of making up for missed opportunities?
Student:	A bit of that in it, I guess. In my case, I definitely messed about at school – so this degree is very important to me. I want to prove to my parents and my girlfriend that I can do this.

Interviewer: And to yourself?

Student: Sure. Definitely. I know I can do it. I've always got my nose in a sociology book. And I need to get out of the job I am in.

Interviewer: What do you do?

Student: I work in the parts department at a garage. I was always interested in cars, but I need to get out.

Interviewer: What will you do with your sociology degree?

Student: Well – it's well into the future, but I'd like to be like Dr . . . I'd like to be that good at the subject, I can teach it. That's what I want. I might make it.

This short interview appears to shed light on our initial concept of 'study diligence'. We have a provisional explanation that the student concerned may not have taken advantage of educational opportunities earlier in life, and hence is motivated to work very hard now. Then there are the issues of trying to justify oneself with relatives, and also the motivation to obtain a more rewarding job. There is thus some interesting data here, which could form the basis for further exploration. You would need to undertake more interviews, and then more observations of other classes. You should be able to build up a range of concepts, which may influence the level of motivation of mature students.

Writing about the analysis of quantitative data

The first requirement when discussing quantitative data is to ensure that you have explained the background to the collection of the data. You may have already done this in the methodology chapter, but it is essential to check that you have addressed such matters as the sampling procedure, the type of survey and data collection instrument, and the response rates.

A great deal of descriptive data can often be presented as histograms or line graphs. However, it is also possible to integrate quantitative analysis within your discussion, as in the following example:

The total sample consisted of 336 teachers, of whom 57% said they would not wish to be involved in taking children on residential activities.

Simple statistical data can also be included, as in:

> The teachers in the sample had a mean age of 37.5 years.

Sometimes you may not wish to use precise figures in your discussion, either because they would be too numerous and may distract the reader, or because the exact values may be reproduced in tabular form. In this case you may be able to use an approximation in your discussion, in order to explain the broad trend of your argument, and then refer to the exact figure in the table. An example of this approach is:

> About one quarter of those surveyed were undertaking some form of part-time postgraduate course (see Table 3.2).

Sometimes you may wish to mention quantitative trends in your discussion, which are derived from secondary sources and not from your own empirical data. For example, you might mention economic or fiscal trends in society. It is important to be able to distinguish such cases from your primary data. It is a good idea to check that you have provided detailed references for all quantitative data which is derived from secondary sources.

It is also worthwhile checking carefully that the variables you discuss in the data analysis chapters can be related easily by the reader to the data collection instrument such as the questionnaire. As the researcher and writer of the thesis, you often become very close to the analytic procedures, and it is easy to provide an account which makes assumptions of the reader, and which is really too superficial. Always try to put yourself in the position of the reader, and ask yourself whether you would understand the account. It is sometimes easy to be discussing a wide range of variables, and to forget that the reader may easily become confused and may not appreciate how these relate to the questions in the questionnaire. The most useful strategy is from time to time to refer the reader back to the questionnaire, thus reinforcing the relationship between questions and variables.

Presenting quantitative data

When presenting quantitative data resulting from analysis, it is not necessary to include in the text of the thesis the calculations which produced that data. Under certain circumstances examples of such calculations might be included in the appendix, but they are certainly unnecessary in the main text. It is only necessary to include the summary figures resulting from the calculations.

One of the commonest methods of presenting quantitative data is the use of tables. An example is given in Table 11.2.

When presenting such tables it is important to include the sample size (n), and to make clear the units of the numbers in the columns (in this case, percentages). It can also be

Table 11.2   Tabular presentation: quantitative data

Title: Teachers and residential activities
Those teachers (n = 145) who would be willing to take children on residential activities felt as follows:

	Yes	No	Unsure
	%	%	%
You would be willing to take children on outdoor pursuits courses, if you were adequately trained and qualified	81	17	2
You would be willing to take children on a trip overseas, assuming adequate staffing levels	69	21	10

useful to include tables which contain absolute numbers, as in the example. In terms of inferential statistics, it is not necessary to include any calculation of the test statistic. To take the example of a chi square test, you only need to include in your discussion the computed value of the test statistic, the degree of freedom and an indication of the level at which the statistic is or is not significant. For example, in a study of any gender difference between male and female pupils in terms of whether or not they handed in homework at the required time, the results might be reported as follows.

A chi square statistic was calculated to test the significance of the difference between males and females in the submission of homework, but no statistically significant difference was noted at the 5% level. (Chi square 3.06, df=1, p>0.05)

This system does enable you to present your results in a very succinct manner, but it does not provide the raw data which would enable the reader to check your calculations.

Placing sample data in the appendices

It is not normal in a thesis to include large quantities of raw data. This applies whether the data is quantitative or qualitative. Therefore, you would not normally include any of the completed questionnaires, unless there is a special reason for so doing. You would include, however, a single copy of an uncompleted questionnaire, in the appendix. This would provide an understanding of the method of collection of the data, and relate the questionnaire items to the variables discussed in the data analysis chapters.

Perhaps the main reason for not including completed questionnaires is that they take up too much space in the appendix. There is, however, an alternative. If you are using Statistical Package for the Social Sciences (SPSS) to analyse your questionnaires, then you could include in the appendix a printout of the SPSS data input sheet. This lists in the vertical columns all the variables which are derived from the questionnaire. The variables will have been coded from the alternative responses on the questionnaire. Thus, if you provide a single, coded questionnaire, and the data input spreadsheet, readers of the thesis can check any of your statistical calculations if they so wish. The questionnaire and data input sheet take up very little space in the appendix.

Signpost to success – Transparency of analysis

Try to be as clear and transparent as possible in the way you describe your data analysis. This will help to make your thesis more understandable.

In the case of qualitative data, because of the sheer volume of material involved, there is no comparable easy solution to the problem. The transcripts of interviews conducted for a typical piece of qualitative doctoral research would, for example, take up many pages. It is not the norm to include all these, but merely to include extracts in the text of the thesis. You could, however, select sample sheets for inclusion, in order to illustrate different elements of the interview dialogue. You might also be able to indicate the manner in which you selected certain data for inclusion in the thesis and discarded other data. This would certainly help to explain the analytic process which you have used. In addition, if you have used a system of diacritical marks to analyse linguistic data in detail, then examples of this would also be useful.

Further reading

Field, A. (2005) *Discovering Statistics Using SPSS*. 2nd edn. London: Sage.
Glaser, B.G. and Strauss, A.L. (1967) *The Discovery of Grounded Theory*. Chicago, IL: Aldine.
Hoy, W.K. (2009) *Quantitative Research in Education: A Primer*. London: Sage.
Mertens, D.M. (2009) *Research and Evaluation in Education and Psychology*. 3rd edn. London: Sage.
Richards, L. (2005) *Handling Qualitative Data: A Practical Guide*. London: Sage.
Silverman, D. (2006) *Interpreting Qualitative Data: Methods for Analyzing Talk, Text and Interaction*. 3rd edn. London: Sage.

12

The Conclusion

In this chapter we look at the essential content of a good conclusion. We discuss how to review the aims and how to stress the contribution to knowledge made by your research. We also consider how to write a reflexive discussion of the research process, and how to write the abstract. The chapter concludes with a checklist to help you write and structure your own conclusion.

Study Strategies

- Read a sample of research articles in academic journals, and consider any apparent ways in which the research could have been improved. Are these possible limitations mentioned or discussed in the article? If you had been conducting the research, how would you have addressed such limitations?
- The advantage of using articles rather than theses for this exercise is that it is so much quicker to read journal articles. However, you will need to apply to your own thesis the kind of critical skills which you develop through this exercise.

Drawing together the threads of the argument

Just as the introductory chapter of a thesis is crucial because it provides the reader with an initial contact with the research, the concluding chapter is important because it is your final opportunity to explain your findings to the reader or examiner. One of the basic functions of the conclusion is to summarize the progress which has been made in achieving the aims of the research. A thesis is a very long document, and by the time readers reach its conclusion they may have forgotten a good deal of the material. It is important then to give a reminder of the key points made so far.

Example – Summarizing the thesis

It will be very difficult for the examiners to absorb the entirety of your thesis in one reading. They will rely on your conclusion to remind them of the most significant elements of the thesis. Think of this as you are writing your conclusion, and stress the issues you want the examiners to remember.

In order to do this, you will need to refresh your own memory as to the key points you have made in the previous data presentation chapters and synthesize these into a coherent body of understanding. Wherever possible, try to show links between the key ideas. As you proceed with this process of summarizing, you may need to refer readers back to section or page numbers in order that they can locate the part of the thesis where an issue was originally discussed. During this discussion, you may wish to include one or two extracts from the data or quotations from relevant academic works. However, these should be new quotations, not repeating material which has been included in previous chapters.

Examining whether the aims have been achieved

If examiners wish to make a very rapid judgement about a thesis, then they can read the aims, read the conclusion and consider the extent to which the latter meets the requirements of the former. This would provide a very inadequate picture of the thesis, but it would at least provide a check on whether the student had attempted to address the aims.

If the aims have been expressed carefully, they should encapsulate everything which you hope to achieve. Moreover, the manner in which the aims have been written should reflect the particular academic level of the thesis. If we imagine two theses on broadly the same subject, one at master's level and one at doctoral level, then the aims of the two theses should be expressed differently. That difference is often achieved by varying the verb at the beginning of the aim. For example, doctoral aims may require the student to 'analyse' or to 'develop a theory' or to 'test the hypothesis that . . . '. Aims written for a master's thesis may put rather more emphasis upon such verbs as 'explore', 'examine' or 'survey'. It is not possible to make rigid divisions here, but this indicates the spirit of the distinction.

If, on reflection, you feel that your aims have not been achieved in any respect, then it is essential to explore this theme. You should explain clearly where you have your reservations about the achievements of the research, and indicate precisely which element of the aims has not been achieved. You should then try to formulate reasons for this. The failure to meet the aims of a thesis is not, in itself, a serious drawback for your work. The aims may have been slightly overambitious, and there may have been many factors which militated against a successful completion. In a grounded theory study, for example, the aims may have assumed three cycles of data collection and analysis. It may have been that on completion of the second cycle, many of the respondents moved location for some reason, and you were unable to contact them to complete the data collection. This could have resulted in a more limited theory. It is perhaps a truism in research that while it may not be considered essential to meet all of your aims, it is essential to demonstrate an awareness of that failure, and to be able to articulate a rational explanation.

Emphasizing the contribution to knowledge

The exact wording of the criteria for the award of a doctorate may differ slightly from university to university. However, those criteria usually include a variant of the statement that the thesis should make 'an original contribution to knowledge in a particular academic field'. Such a clause is not usually associated with the criteria for a master's thesis, even though some master's theses may indeed add to our knowledge of an area.

It is not easy to clarify the concept of 'an original contribution to knowledge'. Individual academics may have slightly different understandings of the concept. However, it is worth exploring the term since, in one sense, the idea of a doctoral thesis rests upon it. One of the key words here is 'original'. In everyday language we tend to use the word original in two rather different ways. We speak of 'an original painting' for example. By this we tend to signify a work of art produced by the artist, and not a later print or reproduction. We might also speak of 'an original book edition' meaning a first edition and not a later one. Similarly we might use the phrase 'an example of original Tudor architecture'. This would imply that the building had remained in an unaltered state from when it was first built. These uses of 'original' suggest that original knowledge is knowledge which has been freshly developed, and does not represent an amendment of pre-existing knowledge.

The second use of 'original' in everyday language is when someone develops an unusual solution to a problem, or a new way of doing something. Then, we often refer to it as 'original', meaning innovative or unique. In this sense, we use it to convey a suggestion of an activity which is 'exploring a new area' or 'breaking into untried territory'. We can see how this meaning of original can be applied to an 'original contribution to knowledge'.

Signpost to success – Contribution to knowledge

Particularly in the case of a doctoral thesis, ensure that you provide a clear statement of the original contribution to knowledge made by your research.

However, if we apply these two uses of 'original' at the same time, we appear to have the requirement that a doctoral thesis should make a contribution to knowledge which is both the first of its kind and innovative. It may not be easy to envisage how your thesis will entirely meet these requirements, but you will need to address the matter in your conclusion. You should do your best to explain clearly how your research and thesis have contributed to knowledge, and evaluate that contribution in terms of originality. It is better to address this issue clearly, rather than avoiding it and hoping that everything is self-evident from the rest of your thesis.

Example – An original contribution

Some students have the impression that an original contribution to knowledge should be something major which perhaps changes the way we look at the universe! This is not so. It can be something very minor, and yet still be an original contribution. Do not worry if it does not seem to be world-changing, but do make sure that you explain your contribution clearly.

Developing practical recommendations

Many students like to conclude their thesis with a list of practical recommendations. You should normally avoid this, unless it constitutes a distinct part of the aims and, hence, you have clearly embarked on doing it. As we have discussed, at doctoral level the prime outcome is that there should be an original contribution to knowledge. This is more significant than trying to make practical recommendations. Indeed, the latter may well provide a distraction from the main outcome. At master's level a thesis may have a slightly more pragmatic orientation, and hence it may be more appropriate to include some recommendations.

If you decide that it is appropriate to include recommendations, it is essential that you clarify to whom the recommendations are made. In some theses, one finds a long list of recommendations, some of which might reasonably be addressed to, say, teachers, some to the government, some to a local education authority and some to any number of other people or organizations connected with the research.

Recommendations are normally directed to those individuals or organizations who are in a position to consider and implement them.

It is possible that the original contribution to knowledge in a doctoral thesis may imply in addition some practical recommendations, although these may not be an intrinsic element of the research. For example, if the original contribution to knowledge is that a particular way of teaching primary school children to use computers appears to speed up the acquisition of information technology skills, then it may be that the logical recommendation is that the approach be adopted in schools. However, it still may not be necessary to write a specific recommendation into the thesis. If the research findings are adequately disseminated that they move into the public domain, they may be taken up by policy-makers if considered appropriate. It is unrealistic to expect policy-makers seriously to consider all recommendations emerging from research theses. In any case, before any recommendations were adopted, it would be only reasonable to have the research replicated and the results thoroughly checked by other researchers. One could not expect policy-makers to adopt proposals based entirely on a single study.

Finally it should be noted that there are some types of research study which do set out to develop practical recommendations. Notable among these are action research studies. The philosophical pragmatism of action research owes a considerable intellectual debt to the writings of John Dewey and Kurt Lewin. The approach of action research has been to address practical issues and problems, often in the workplace, and to provide provisional solutions for those problems. It is therefore normally expected that action research studies will conclude with some practical strategies to address the research issue.

Example – Professional doctorates

The newer type of professional doctorates are normally related to a specific vocational area, and in such cases concluding the thesis with some practical recommendations may be more relevant. If you are working towards a professional doctorate, it would be a good idea to discuss the issue of recommendations with your supervisor.

Limitations of the thesis

Your examiners will not expect the conduct of your research to have been faultless, nor will they expect your thesis to be perfect. They will anticipate finding areas where they would probably have done things differently, and they will almost certainly identify sections of your thesis in which they would have provided more or less detail, or written in a different way. It is natural that they should feel like that. However, they will also expect you to have reflected on the limitations of your research, and to have discussed these in the thesis. Such reflections are probably best placed in the concluding chapter. To put this another way, the examiners will expect you to critique, or to be critical of, your work. This does not signify that you should speak in a derogatory way of it, but merely that you should think carefully and analytically about ways in which the research and the thesis might have been improved.

In order to achieve this, you should look back at the entire research project, starting with the aims, and consider any decisions or approaches which could have been altered for the better. Here are some examples of questions which you could ask yourself in order to identify possible improvements in the research.

Examiners will normally feel much more positively about your work if you can convince them that you have thought critically about your research and considered ways in which the process could have been improved.

Example – Thinking critically about the thesis

Look back on your research project and the writing of your thesis, and ask yourself the following questions:

- Should I have revised the aims?
- Are they too broad, or are they too narrowly focused and restrictive?
- Did I look widely enough for relevant literature?
- Are there areas of research at which I should have looked?
- Were there practical alternatives to the methodology which I selected?
- Did I employ the correct strategy for choosing my sample?
- Was there any way in which I should have been more careful in collecting my data?
- Were there ethical issues which I should have addressed more fully?
- Was I sufficiently rigorous in the data analysis?
- Did I explain my procedures sufficiently fully to the reader of the thesis?
- Are there questions of validity or reliability which I should have addressed?
- Do my findings meet the requirements for a thesis at this level?

Possibilities for further research

A research study is not usually thought of as an isolated piece of intellectual activity, separated from other similar studies. It is perhaps best seen as existing on a continuum. It adds to previous research, and acknowledges that other research will take place in the future in the same field. It is important that your thesis gives expression to this element of research activity.

In fact you have already addressed one part of this by writing the literature review chapter. This contains an analysis of the previous research in the field, and establishes the links with your current research. However, it is also important that you look to the future and indicate the directions for future scholars and researchers to explore.

This is, in a sense, another element to the issue discussed in the previous section. The acknowledged limitations of the thesis may well point to areas for further work. In order to help you consider the possibilities for further research, the following example includes some questions which you could ask yourself about your research.

Example – Further research

The following questions might help you clarify ways of extending your research.

- Could the subject of my research be addressed using a different methodology, which might reveal new insights into the issue?
- Were my findings incomplete in any way?
- Could such areas be explored by a new study?
- Was there insufficient data to explore certain themes or concepts?
- Might further research indicate links with other studies or fields?

When suggesting further areas of research you need not try to plan how such research might be carried out. You only need to provide a brief indication of the directions of enquiry.

A reflexive account of the research process

Within certain research traditions, notably ethnography and other interpretative approaches, it is often necessary to explain in the thesis the interactive process between you, as the researcher, and the respondents. Within interpretative research there is an appreciation that the research participants, the research field and yourself are involved in an interactive, dynamic process whereby each affects the others. Your intervention in the field or context of the research may have a significant effect. You cannot sit in a classroom and observe a lesson without expecting to change that environment in some way. Even if there were no apparent change in the behaviour of the pupils and teacher, one may reasonably suppose that even the awareness of a newcomer in the classroom transforms, in some way, the dynamics of the situation.

Suppose that you are collecting data in college staff rooms. You enter a staff room, sit down, and ask a question of one of the teachers. The question concerns the amount of evening teaching carried out in the college. The very fact that you select that topic, and ask the teacher to reflect on it, in a sense changes the social setting. Perhaps other staff members overhear what is said. They in turn start to think about the same issue. Perhaps a fresh conversation is started. What is more, you must have chosen to express the original question in a certain way. Perhaps that mode of expression reflected certain assumptions and preconceptions on your part. The manner in which you expressed the question will have conditioned to some extent the manner in which the teacher reflected on the issue. Similarly, the response of the teacher will have an effect upon you, and the way in which you articulate further questions. In short, you have an impact upon the social setting and the participants, and the participants affect your perspective.

Within interpretative perspectives it is acknowledged that the researcher does not act as an impassive, objective observer of the social world, but is continually making decisions about how to interact with the research field, the kinds of questions to ask, the issues to raise and the manner in which they will be raised. Simultaneously, researchers anticipate being asked questions by participants, and appreciate that those questions will affect the manner in which they view the setting. This dynamic interplay within social settings is known as reflexivity. It particularly involves a process of individual social actors reflecting on the social world and attempting to make sense of it. Interpretative researchers appreciate that there are a variety of factors in their own intellectual and social development which can affect the manner in which they relate to the social world, and interpret both their own responses and those of research participants. They also appreciate that it is often helpful to readers of their research if some of these personal factors are described and analysed, in order to help them appreciate the particular perspective with which the researcher approaches the research field, and the data which emerge from it. Such reflexive accounts have become increasingly common, particularly in ethnographic studies. It is interesting to consider the kind of issues which could be discussed in a useful reflexive account.

It is often interesting if you can discuss the routes you have taken in arriving at your current research topic. For example, it might be that jobs you have held in the past have caused you to be interested in a particular issue. If there is a connection between your employment experience and your choice of research topic, then it may be helpful for the reader to appreciate that perspective in your approach to the subject. The type of posts we have held and the level of those posts may have an influence upon the way in which we approach an understanding and analysis of data. It is also certainly relevant to discuss your academic history. For example, if you are writing a doctoral thesis on a particular subject, your first degree may have been in a variety of disciplines. A psychologist, for example, is trained to look at issues somewhat differently from a sociologist, and yet they may both be conducting research in education. It may be relevant to the research to discuss something of this disciplinary background. Personal interests may also play a part in the way in which we approach research. Flick (1998, p. 6) discusses reflexivity.

When writing a reflexive account it is important to consider your reactions to the research field and to the people from whom you collected data. This will involve you in a considerable amount of reflective thought, in order to try to analyse the factors which condition your perception of the data. However, even if such self-reflection is limited and rather difficult to accomplish, an account of your academic and personal history related to the research subject will certainly be an interesting part of your thesis.

Summary – Possible content of a reflexive account

The following are some features of your personal and intellectual history which you could consider incorporating into a reflexive account:

- The institutions at which you have studied, and the qualifications you have gained.
- The influence these have had, if any, upon your research interests and the selection of the thesis topic.
- The way in which your intellectual interests have developed over time.
- A discussion of your employment history and any connections with your research interests.
- The relationship, if any, between personal and leisure interests and the research topic.
- The impact which your research has had on you personally, and the things you have learned from that experience.
- Reflections on the interactions with research respondents, and a discussion of what has been learned from that.

Writing the abstract

It is generally best to complete your thesis, at least in first draft form, before writing the abstract. It is only then that you will have the complete information on which to base the abstract. This is the reason for discussing the abstract at this stage of the book.

The abstract is a précis of the thesis, which is usually bound into the thesis immediately after the title page. It is normal to restrict the length of the abstract to one side of typed A4 paper. However, some researchers type the abstract in a slightly smaller font or use a narrower line space in order to provide rather more detail. This should not be taken to extremes, and it should be possible, with 10 point or 11 point font size and one and a half line spacing, to fit the abstract onto one side of paper.

The abstract should provide a synopsis of every key aspect of the thesis. For the examiners or library readers it provides an overview, which helps them to relate to the detail of the actual thesis. The abstract is also used by librarians to catalogue completed theses, in order that future scholars can identify and locate those which they wish to consult. Writing abstracts is discussed in Brause (2000, p. 131) and Allison (1997, p. 10).

Writing a good abstract is a literary skill in itself, and before starting your own, you may find it helpful to read a number of abstracts from other theses. The style of writing should be succinct and precise. You do not need to go into great detail over any aspect; merely summarize the key contents of the thesis. Before starting the abstract, it is a good idea to

ABSTRACT

This study investigates the perceptions of key stakeholders in midwifery education concerning the involvement of service users in student assessment. It identifies the key stakeholders in specific interest groups, as expert professional and expert lay people, parents, student midwives, qualified midwives who mentor students in clinical practice and the heads of midwifery education in University Departments. The work starts from the premise that assessment is an underestimated means of enhancing students' learning and the development of competence to practise as a registered midwife.

The inquiry opens by examining the professional context in which maternity services are provided. It identifies the relationships that midwives form with the women and their families for whom they care.

These considerations are followed by an interrogation of the literature that reveals a rich variety of interlocking concepts that are apposite considerations in terms of the assessment of student midwives and the involvement of women in it. This firmly links the problem to previous research and provides a sound rationale for the conduct of the study.

Interpretivism is advanced as a suitable philosophical framework for the prosecution of the study that offers a methodological rationale for a pragmatic, mixed methods investigation. The study design presents a raison d'être for a phased approach to the work and data are accrued variously from qualitative and quantitative sources.

Although the focus of the work concerned the role of users of maternity services in student assessment and found considerable support for their involvement, what emerged has wider consequences for teaching and learning, the overall student experience and also for women as health service consumers.

Having examined the principle dynamics that influence student learning in clinical placements, the study concludes that there is a superficial disharmony between learning and assessment yet it claims the two are mutually complimentary. The inclusion of women in teaching and learning is seen as a potent means to add an extra element to the definition of competence and to add to the authenticity of its assessment.

Figure 12.1   Example of an abstract

skim through the thesis, noting down the main points of methodology, data analysis and conclusions. Then decide the best order in which to present these issues, and summarize them in a concise, descriptive style.

A checklist for the conclusion

Every thesis differs, and it is difficult to provide a definitive list of items which should be included in every conclusion. However, the following should help you to construct an effective concluding chapter to your study.

- ☐ Start by reminding the reader of the aims of your thesis.
- ☐ Evaluate the extent to which you have met these aims.
- ☐ If any have not been completely met, try to explain the reasons.
- ☐ Review the methodology which you employed, and discuss any problems which occurred.
- ☐ If your research involved testing a theory, to what extent do you now have confidence in that theory?
- ☐ If your research involved generating a theory, provide a clear summary of that theory.
- ☐ Explain what would need to be done to try to falsify your theory.
- ☐ State clearly the original contribution to knowledge which has emerged from your research.
- ☐ If you wish to make any practical recommendations deriving from your research, then state these clearly, and explain for whom they are intended.
- ☐ As a result of your research, are there any further studies which you would suggest be undertaken?
- ☐ If you feel that a reflexive account would be relevant, then this could be provided here, or as part of the appendix.

Further reading

Craswell, G. (2004) *Writing for Academic Success: A Postgraduate Guide*. London: Sage.

Gillett, A., Hammond, A. and Martala, M. (2009) *Successful Academic Writing*. Harlow: Pearson Education.

Murray, R. (2011) *How to Write a Thesis*. 3rd edn. Maidenhead: Open University Press.

Silverman, D. (2004) *Doing Qualitative Research: A Practical Handbook*. 2nd edn. London: Sage.

Thody, A. (2006) *Writing and Presenting Research*. London: Sage.

13
Completing the Thesis

In this chapter we consider the way you need to check your thesis when you have completed the first draft. We look at the proofreading process, the checking of references and page numbers, and the different aspects which your supervisors will normally check. Finally, we consider the ways in which theses are normally submitted.

Study Strategies

- Having read this chapter, and also reflected on the nature of your own manuscript, devise your own checklist and procedure for proofreading your thesis.

Producing the first complete draft

The completion of a thesis is a very large undertaking. Inevitably the task has to be divided into sections and written on different occasions. However, there comes the time when you need to combine these different sections into a unified whole. At this stage each of the individual sections or chapters will still be in initial draft form. Many of the chapters may have substantial omissions, where you have decided to leave issues to discuss once you have an impression of the overall thesis. Nevertheless, it is a very important event in the evolution of the thesis when you lay all the separate sections together on a table and for the first time have a sense of the whole study.

At this point you should really try to have all the sections present. You should print off a listing of your references to add at the end. You should assemble the documents you intend to put into the appendix, and prepare a title page and an abstract, and place these at the beginning. As you look at the assembled document you will have an idea of its size and scale. For the first time it will have the appearance of a book or a thesis, instead of disjointed computer files and printouts. You may have made notes of tables omitted, or of paragraphs which require adding, but at least it is all beginning to take shape!

Example – Taking your time

When you have completed the final chapter of your thesis, it is very easy to breathe a sigh of relief, and think that you have finished the task. However, in some ways, the work is only starting! If you rush the process of turning your thesis into a finished piece of work, then the most likely scenario is that the examiners will give you a long list of corrections which have to be made, before they will consider passing it. It is better to create as good a thesis as you can before the examination process, rather than prejudice your chances of passing.

You may feel that now the job is nearly finished. However, there is still a great deal of work to be done! There are many different ways in which you can proceed to transform this compilation of drafts into a finished, polished thesis, and I will now suggest some strategies to help you achieve this. The first stage is to turn over the pages, looking for major errors and omissions. The purpose of this is to refine the thesis to a point where serious proofreading can begin.

At this stage, you are not reading every word, but trying to identify poor formatting, text which appears to have been omitted, pages in the wrong order, and figures which probably require redrawing. Try to mark clearly on the relevant pages, using a highlighter pen, the additions and amendments which are needed. The summary lists some of the aspects of this rough draft which may need amending.

Summary – Amending the first draft

These are some useful checks which you can make at this stage to transform the thesis into a more finished document which can be proofread.

- Check that no additional preliminary pages are required. Write any missing sections, and complete unfinished or poorly finished figures.

(Continued)

(Continued)

- Ensure that all pages are numbered.
- Add page numbers to the contents section near the beginning of the thesis.
- Check that all figures and tables have numbers and titles.
- Ensure that these are included in the lists of tables and figures near the beginning.
- Check on the overall quality of the printing of the thesis.
- Make sure that no text has been omitted from printing, between the bottom of one page and the top of the next.
- Check that subheadings are in appropriate places on the pages, and are not located on the very bottom line of a page.
- Make sure that each chapter starts on a new page, and that each chapter heading and title are formatted in the same way.
- Ensure that the reference style is adhered to throughout.
- Check the reference list at the end for major errors, such as works not being listed in alphabetical order.
- Ensure that appendix documents are numbered, and that these are either listed in the contents, or a key is supplied within the appendix.

Some of the changes you are making at this stage may still require later amendment. It is best to add the page numbers now since, once you are dealing with the whole thesis, it is easy to get pages in the wrong order. However, as you proofread the thesis and add minor corrections, this may still alter the page numbering slightly. The addition of corrections can also have the effect of moving subheadings up and down the page. If a subheading is located very near the bottom of a page, you may need to correct this. The main purpose at this stage is to produce a manuscript which does not have any major presentational errors.

Checking for coherence and internal consistency

The next stage is to check for internal consistency in presentational matters. An important example of this type of checking is to ensure that all the citations in the text are listed in the references at the end of the thesis.

Again, you do not have to read the text of the thesis in order to make these checks. As you turn over the pages, look at each citation. It is quite easy to identify these as you glance down the page. In the case of citations in the text where you have merely indicated the importance of a writer without including a quotation, it is only necessary to cite the surname and the year of publication. On those occasions where you have included a quotation then it is essential to include also the page number from which the quotation was taken. In the case of each citation make sure that the work is listed in the references at the end of the thesis, and that the author's surname and the year of publication are the same as in the text. This is the important check of internal consistency. You will probably identify other minor errors and omissions in the way in which the works are cited at the end, but these corrections can be left until the next stage of proofreading. For the moment it is only necessary to ensure that the work is present in the list, and that the name and year are the same. Try to make sure that throughout the thesis the system of referencing is used consistently.

Look carefully at all the chapter numbers and titles, and cross-check these with the contents page. Equally, check the titles of all subheadings and make sure these are identical with the version in the contents section. Also, ensure that all page numbers for the start and end of subsections and of chapters are accurate in the contents section.

Example – Page numbering

The page numbering in your thesis should be one of the last things you check. Even very minor amendments to the text can alter the page numbering, by causing the creation of new pages in a file. In addition, you may have referred in your text to a table, for example, on a specific page. If your page numbers alter, such items will no longer be accurate, and this can be frustrating for your readers. Ideally then, it is best to check page numbers when all other amendments have been made.

Sometimes writers employ a system of annotation to identify different types of data. For example, in presenting qualitative or interview data, they may add the letters M or F to identify the extract as being from a male or female. Alternatively, in educational studies they may add, say, P or T to signify pupil and teacher. If you have used any such system, check that these symbols are used consistently throughout. The main purpose of this stage of the process is to try to ensure that elements in one part of the thesis are fully consistent with the relevant elements in other parts.

Proofreading

The reason for dividing the process of checking the thesis is that it is difficult to check for different types of error at the same time. For example, if you are checking for grammatical mistakes and the quality of argument at the same time, the grammatical errors interfere with the assessment of the arguments. As you read a sentence which has grammatical or punctuation errors, these distract you from the content of the sentence. Some people may be very proficient at checking simultaneously for formatting, consistency, typographical errors and academic content. If that is so, then you may be able to check the thesis in one process. However, if you do not feel confident in doing this, then I suggest you adopt this approach and check the thesis in stages.

Some people refer to proofreading as the general process whereby a thesis is corrected, but I am using it in this section to refer to the process of checking for grammatical, punctuation and typographical errors. For this stage, you need to read all the text very carefully, word by word. While you are doing this, you may identify potentially important academic issues which you want to discuss with your supervisor. It is best to keep a note of these issues and to mark their position in the text. Other than that, the main purpose of the proofreading process is to check for errors in the language of the thesis. Check the spelling of any words of which, in retrospect, you are uncertain. In addition, check carefully that the wording and structure of sentences conveys the meaning you intend. A common error is to write sentences which are unduly long. The sheer length of the sentence may make the argument or meaning seem very convoluted. One of the best ways to check on coherence of meaning is to read the thesis aloud. If you try to check the meaning by reading silently, it is very easy to overlook errors. On the other hand, when you are listening to the spoken word, it often seems easier to identify confusing sentences. It may be even better if you can arrange for someone to read the thesis to you. You should then be able to detect immediately any problems with sentence structure and meaning. The same method is useful for identifying punctuation errors. If you ask someone to read the thesis to you, exactly as it is punctuated, then again you should be able to identify errors. The reader should be advised, however, not to add their own punctuation when reading, in order to try to render the meaning more accessible.

Example – The importance of checking

Examiners read many theses during their career, and become very skilful at identifying proofreading and spelling errors. They can be the first things which they recognize on a page. Examiners are only human, and do realize that anyone can make minor errors in a thesis. However, if there are lots of errors, they can make it more difficult for the examiners to understand your academic arguments.

In a sense, this process is inseparable from that of identifying errors of logic or reasoning in the text. Errors of argument are often related to errors of grammar. However, we are only referring here to small-scale errors, and not to major omissions. If you are in any doubt about the broad trends of your arguments, or of, say, the way in which you have presented the methodology, then you should draw these to the attention of your supervisor.

The final part of the thesis which you will check under this section is the list of references at the end. You have already ensured that all the required references are actually present, but now it is necessary to check each entry line by line. You will be following a standard referencing system, such as the Harvard system, and will need to comply with this. Proofreading a long list of references can be a very demanding task. It is, however, very necessary, as examiners are usually adept at identifying errors and inconsistencies. The following are some of the errors which are easy to overlook in a list of references.

- The surname of authors is usually followed by the initials of their first names. In some cases you may have used their first name in full. As with all aspects of referencing, it is essential to be consistent.
- Even though you are adhering to, say, the Harvard system, different journals and books employ slightly different punctuation. Again, it is essential to be consistent with the use of commas, colons and full stops.
- The use of italics is sometimes an area where it is easy to deviate from consistency. The titles of books should be in italics, but for journal articles, check that you have italicized only the name of the journal.
- Sometimes students are inconsistent when naming the place of publication and the publishers at the end of the reference. It is normal to type the place of publication first, followed by the publisher. The place of publication should be a town or city, and not a county, state or country. In addition, when naming a publisher such as the Cambridge University Press, the place of publication should not be omitted, but included as in 'Cambridge: Cambridge University Press.'

Checks to be made by the supervisory team

When you have completed the above series of checks on the thesis, you should have a document which is well presented, with relatively few spelling or grammatical errors. You will also have identified any potential larger errors of content or argument. The thesis is now ready for handing over to your supervisor or supervisors. You will probably have submitted the individual chapters to them while you were writing the thesis, and they will have provided you with interim comments. However, from their point of view, it is difficult to provide a definite response to a small part of the whole thesis. They do really need to read the full document before being able to judge the overall quality.

If you have more than one supervisor you should provide them with sufficient copies of the whole thesis. It is not necessary to bind the thesis in any way as long as the pages are correctly numbered. They can be placed in a simple, cardboard folder. As you have by now given careful attention to the proofreading, errors of syntax will not act as a distraction to your supervisors when reading the thesis. They will be able to concentrate fully on the content and arguments. However, you may have to allow considerable time for your supervisors to read it, particularly if it is at doctoral level.

As they read, the supervisors will be asking themselves a range of questions. By now, they will have very firmly in their minds the forthcoming viva, and will be anticipating questions which you might be asked. They will be looking for any possible shortcomings, which might attract the examiners' attention. The example suggests some of the questions which the supervisors may ask themselves as they are reading your thesis.

Example – Checks on the thesis made by the supervisors

The following are examples of the questions which your supervisors may ask themselves about your draft thesis.

- Is the abstract clearly written and an accurate precis of the thesis?
- Does the introduction set out the research question clearly?
- Are the aims clearly stated and achievable?
- Is the literature review sufficiently comprehensive for the academic level of the thesis?
- Is the literature reviewed relevant to the subject matter of the thesis, and sufficiently contemporary?
- Is the research design relevant to the research aims?
- Does the account of the methodology demonstrate an adequate appreciation of research methods, relevant to the research design and subject of the research?
- Is the data sufficiently and appropriately analysed?
- Do the results and conclusions derive logically from the analysis?
- Are the ethical issues inherent in the study discussed adequately?
- Is the linguistic style of the thesis appropriate to the academic level?

Each supervisor will normally annotate the manuscript, noting positive issues and areas where the thesis could be improved. It is also normal for each supervisor to prepare a written statement noting the strengths and weaknesses of the thesis, and in particular the amendments which should be made before it is finally submitted. In the case of doctoral theses, where there are usually two or more supervisors, each will normally read the thesis independently of the others and prepare their own short report. It is almost inevitable that they will not entirely have focused on the same issues. However, if there are major deficiencies, it is to be hoped that they have all identified these, even though they may have slightly different views on the steps to be taken to correct them. In any case, the supervisors should certainly meet before they provide feedback to you. They should discuss any differences they have about the overall quality of the thesis, and should ensure that these are rationalized before they meet you. It is essential that you are given coherent advice by the supervisors. They need to agree on the main issues which require correction before the thesis is of an appropriate standard to formally submit. They may decide to give you their separate reports or to produce a single composite report. In any case, when they meet you they should explain clearly, point by point, the changes which they feel are necessary before the thesis will be ready for submission. If you are at all unclear about anything, then you should ask at this stage.

Your supervisors may structure their advice in terms of the things which in their view must definitely be altered, and the things which they would ask you to consider changing. If they felt, for example, that some very important works had been omitted from the literature review chapter, then they would recommend strongly that these be added. Equally, if they felt that the discussion of methodology was limited in some ways, they may also regard that as an essential change. On the other hand, concerns about, say, the way in which data is presented, or the order of arguments, may be drawn to your attention, but any changes left to your own discretion.

Checks to be made by supervisors, and those to be made by students

If your supervisors request some substantial changes to the thesis, then at least your main supervisor may want to read these changes. Note that sometimes your main supervisor has to give formal approval before a research thesis is submitted for examination. This is one of the reasons for your senior supervisor wishing to make a last check on your writing. He or she will certainly want to check any rewritten sections in which the meaning has been substantially altered. With minor amendments, your supervisor may leave the checking up to you. When all changes have been made, you are ready to arrange the printing and binding of sufficient copies for the examination process.

Signpost to success – Proofreading

Check your thesis carefully. Better to correct errors before the viva than have to do them afterwards!

Temporary binding

Universities differ slightly in their requirements for the binding and presentation of theses. The requirements will usually be published in the university handbook of regulations. A typical process is that you have your thesis bound in a temporary binding, in case there are amendments to make after the viva. The temporary binding will involve binding the pages together at the spine, but with a soft cover at front and back. You will need to provide the binders with a single definitive copy of the thesis. Just before you submit your copy to the binders, it is worth making a few last-minute checks, as in the example.

Example – Final checks before binding

Just before temporary binding, make a few rapid checks of the following:

- Is the exact wording of the title correct on the front page?
- Is the abstract included immediately after the front page?
- Check some pages at random, for page numbers in the correct order, and any blank pages included from the last printing.
- Check the appendices are included.

You should have been informed by your director of studies about the number of copies required. Normally it would be one copy for each of the examiners, one copy to be retained by the university during the examination process and one copy for your director of studies. You should also have one copy bound for yourself. You will need this to revise from before the viva, and to take into the viva to consult during the oral examination.

Procedure for submitting the thesis

Your director of studies will inform you of the formal procedure for submitting the copies of a doctoral thesis for examination. It may involve signing a formal declaration that you submit the thesis for examination for a specific award. It is normally a part of university regulations that you take sole responsibility for the submission of your thesis. Although it may well be the case that the director of studies approves the submission, this is no guarantee of success. You will be judged not only on the written content of the thesis, but also upon your defence of it in the oral examination.

Once submitted, there may be some considerable time until your viva. By now, your examiners will have been approved by the university, and you will have been told their identities. However, in order to preserve the impartiality of the process, it is important that you have no formal contact with them up to the date of the viva.

In the case of a master's thesis, the submission process may not be very different to that for a module assignment on the course. You may have to submit two copies of your thesis, and these, like the doctoral thesis, may only need to have some form of temporary binding. Once the assessment process has been completed, and any necessary amendments made, then the thesis is permanently bound and a copy usually placed in the university library, and/or an electronic copy uploaded to the university repository.

Further reading

Churchill, H. and Sanders, T. (2007) *Getting Your PhD: A Practical Insider's Guide*. London: Sage.

Craswell, G. (2004) *Writing for Academic Success: A Postgraduate Guide*. London: Sage.

Hart, C. (2004) *Doing Your Masters Dissertation*. London: Sage

Silverman, D. (2004) *Doing Qualitative Research: A Practical Handbook*. 2nd edn. London: Sage.

Thody, A. (2006) *Writing and Presenting Research*. London: Sage.

14

Publishing Findings During Preparation of the Thesis

In this chapter we examine some of the advantages and disadvantages of trying to publish an academic article while working on your thesis. We advise you on how to select a subject for your article, how to choose an appropriate journal, and how to meet their requirements. Finally we discuss the refereeing process typical of academic journals.

Study Strategies

- Select several journals which you feel would be relevant for your article. Consider writing a brief letter to the editor of each journal explaining that you are a research student seeking to publish some of your research. Ask if the editor can send you either a list of criteria used to assess submitted articles, or if any general pieces of advice can be given. This should help you with the writing of your article.

Advantages and disadvantages

When your thesis is successfully completed, a copy will be placed in your university library. It will be consulted by students, researchers and members of staff, and indeed may be requested at other universities through the inter-library loans system. Your thesis may also be included in the references of other theses and of books and articles. However, your research will probably not in this way reach a very wide audience.

Some students decide to publish some of their research either during the writing of their thesis, or after they have gained their award. We are here concerned with the advantages and disadvantages of publishing findings during the research, although much of the advice about the mechanics of publishing will also be relevant once your thesis has been completed. In this, as with other aspects of thesis writing, you should look carefully at any relevant university regulations.

Writing a thesis can be a very protracted process. In fact, it may be so protracted that it is very easy to become demotivated because of the very magnitude of the task. There are also no intermediate targets and rewards for the thesis writer. When you are studying on a taught course, in which the curriculum is subdivided into modules, you have the target of submitting assignments at the end of each module and, hopefully, of passing the module. With a thesis there are none of these incremental rewards. Therefore, the act of writing a short journal article can be quite an exciting activity, which can motivate you to greater enthusiasm for the thesis.

The journal article will also provide you with the opportunity to analyse a portion of your total data. In a sense, this can be a practice for the complete analysis. You will be able to identify a small section of your data, and explore the findings you are able to develop from that data. In addition, it is a useful exercise in academic writing. The article is a self-enclosed piece of academic writing, with a beginning, a middle and an end. One can think of it as the thesis in microcosm. To that extent, it is a useful opportunity to catch a glimpse of the finished piece of work.

It is also a very useful discipline to have to write in order to comply with certain predetermined requirements. Most academic journals include a section entitled 'Notes for contributors', specifying the format of submissions. It is instructive to have to write according to these requirements, and to begin to appreciate some of the formal requirements of academic writing as practised by professional academics.

If you are successful in publishing your article, then not only is there the personal satisfaction, but the article may also indirectly enhance your thesis. Universities normally expect that you will make mention of your publication in the thesis, and indeed include a copy at the end of the thesis. Depending upon the regulations, this might be bound within the actual thesis, perhaps in the appendices, or it might be attached in some way within the back cover of the thesis. It is a debatable matter whether such a publication should be assessed as an intrinsic element of the thesis. If it is bound within the appendices, then presumably it should be assessed. If it is simply appended at the back of the thesis, then it may be read, but perhaps not formally assessed. Nevertheless, the fact that you have had the initiative to publish some of your research while completing the thesis can scarcely make a detrimental impression upon the examiners. Journal articles are independently refereed, and it demonstrates that probably at least two other academics, and the journal editor, thought that your work was worthy of publication. Another important advantage is that if you are working towards a doctorate, and aspire to a career in higher education, then a published academic article is very useful to include in your curriculum vitae.

Example – Your academic career

While you are working on your research, you will naturally be preoccupied with the successful completion of your thesis. However, at the same time, it is also worth reflecting on how you will use your qualification to develop your career. If you are wanting an academic career, then publishing in academic journals is an important asset. It will be worthwhile to reflect on the kind of issues you might write about, and how such articles might relate to your work on your thesis. Then, gradually, you will develop your own area of academic expertise.

Having said this, there are some potential disadvantages to attempting to publish a journal article while working on your thesis. An academic article may seem very short when compared with a thesis. However, at, say, 6,000 words or more, it still requires an investment of time. If it is to meet the quality standards for publication, then you will need to spend a good deal of time in writing and proofreading it. Some supervisors may feel that this is an unnecessary distraction from the core business of completing the thesis, and may advise you against it. If you decide to embark on writing an article, then it is advisable to think long and hard about whether you can allocate sufficient time, and not fall behind with the thesis schedule.

The other potential disadvantage is that you may not select the most appropriate journal in which to publish your article. Journals may be divided for convenience into two main categories: professional journals and academic journals. The dividing line between the two is not always precise, and so the following brief discussion is inevitably a generalization.

Professional journals are normally associated with a professional body within a particular vocation such as teaching, social work or the medical profession. They may include some research-based articles, but also articles which discuss current themes and issues within the profession. They will typically contain relevant photographs, and may also contain commentaries by leading figures in the profession. They may also be published in association with a body such as a trade union or a management organization.

Academic journals tend to have a more formal appearance and to publish research-based articles. The articles will have a fairly standard appearance, as defined by the guidance notes for contributors which are usually printed inside one of the journal covers. Such journals are regarded as an outlet for formal research articles written by academics. The articles are usually read by referees before being accepted for publication. It is normal for referees to suggest a number of amendments before the editor finally accepts the article. Such journals tend to have a higher status than professional journals, within academic circles. What is more, some academic journals tend to be regarded as of higher status than others. For example, some journals which are associated with the more prestigious universities may have a higher status. It may be commensurately more difficult to have an article accepted by the very high-status journals.

Example – Advantages of being published

Apart from the central issue of having your article published, there are a number of other potential advantages about having your name in a journal. Other researchers and academics may contact you to discuss your research, or to let you know that they are working in a related field. You may receive an invitation to present some of your research at a conference, or to work with people in other ways.

Having explored the broad differences between journals, publication in a professional journal would not be appropriate if you intended to attach the article to your thesis. Equally, the more prestigious the academic journal in which you published, then the more impact the article would be likely to have when attached to the thesis. However, it would be counter-productive to try to publish an article within a very high-status journal, if you were continually unsuccessful. It would be best to seek the advice of your supervisor concerning the most appropriate journals in which to aspire to publish. There are thus both advantages and disadvantages in terms of trying to publish an article while writing the thesis. It should be stressed, however, that it is not necessary to do this in order to be successful with your thesis.

Selecting an element of the findings

It is not normal to try to distil an entire thesis, especially a doctoral thesis, into a journal article of, say, 6,000 words. It is more typical to take a small section of the data and to analyse this for the article. The same strategy is often used by professional researchers who are engaged in a large study. They may try to subdivide the research into manageable sections, and to report on these sections in different issues of the same journal or in separate journals. In this way, their research reaches a wide audience.

When deciding on the specific section of your thesis or research to try to transform into a journal article there are a few factors to take into account. A good initial plan is to read several different journal articles in order to gain an impression of the way in which they are structured. The prime controlling factor on the structure of a journal article is usually the restriction upon length. Although it is difficult to generalize, you may find that first there is a brief introduction which explains the context of the research, and perhaps the connection with a larger study. There may then be a short literature review, making mention of indicative references and particularly very recent or contemporary research. This is followed by, usually, a very brief indication of methodology and sampling, followed by the data, data analysis and findings. You will normally find that you have very little space in which to present your data and analysis. There are several strategies which you could use to select data for the article. If you are using qualitative data in your thesis, then you might be able to select several respondents to use as case studies or key respondents. On the other hand, you may be able to extract a section of interview data, which is concerned with a specific theme within the research. If the data is quantitative or derived from a questionnaire survey, then you may be able to use the data deriving from a group of questions on the questionnaire. The questions would all need to be connected by a common theme or research issue. It is important to remember, however, that your respondents probably gave their original agreement to participate in the research on the assumption that the data would be written as a thesis. Depending upon the nature of the data which you use, you may feel it is necessary to obtain further approval to use data for a journal article which may receive wider circulation. Woods (1999, pp. 112–27) discusses the publication of articles in academic journals.

Selecting a suitable academic journal

As we have discussed, there can be considerable differences between a professional journal and an academic journal. However, not all academic journals are alike and it is wise to give careful thought to the journal to which you submit an article. Some students and writers tend to write an academic article and then submit it to the journal which seems most appropriate in terms of subject matter. While this may result in the article being accepted, it is perhaps not the most precise and best planned strategy for achieving publication.

An alternative broad strategy is to select carefully the journal which seems most relevant for your research, and then to write the article, structuring it as closely as possible to examples previously published in that journal. When selecting a journal, the principal criterion is normally subject matter. Journals do tend to specialize in terms of subject area, and their title is an indication of this. However, an examination of articles published in a single journal often indicates a wide range of subjects. Some may be directly connected with the core subject of the journal, while others may appear to be only tangentially connected. It is also a good idea to look at the authors of articles in previous issues. If most of them appear to be professors from prestigious universities, then you may feel that a different journal may be more appropriate. Ideally, you should locate a journal which is in your subject area, and which appears to have published articles by research students, either with or without their supervisor's name attached.

The next step is to look at the format of previous articles and ensure that the journal publishes articles of the type you intend to write. Some writers do consult the journal editor prior to submitting an article, to check whether it is the type of article which might be considered. However, normally the type of article published by a particular journal should be reasonably evident from the previous copies of the journal.

At this stage it might also be a sensible idea to discuss your proposed article with your supervisor. Not only are supervisors able to suggest suitable journals, but they may also be willing to collaborate with you on the article. Supervisors may suggest that their name be added to yours on the article. This is perfectly acceptable, on the assumption that they make a contribution to both the intellectual content of the article and the writing of it.

Signpost to success – Selecting an academic journal

When you are writing your article, think carefully about the journal to which you will submit it. Ask experienced academics for advice on the most suitable journal.

Following style notes

When you have selected the journal to which to submit your article, you should do your best to comply with the requirements of the journal in terms of presentation. You will be able to discern the main requirements by reading examples of previous articles. However, most journals publish in each issue a list of guidance notes for contributors. It is wise to follow these as closely as possible.

You may be asked to submit both a paper and an electronic copy of your article. It is important that the two versions are identical. If you are required to make amendments to the article before publication, you may need to submit both amended paper and electronic versions. The notes for contributors will usually specify a desired word length for the article. You should try to adhere to this, since editors and publishers usually have a conception of the number of articles they would like to include in each issue. You may be asked not to type your name on the title page of the article, but to attach it on a separate piece of paper. The reason for this is to preserve the anonymity of the writer when an article is sent to a reviewer by the editor. It is possible that a reviewer would know a journal author personally, and the preservation of anonymity helps to ensure that the article is read objectively.

Guidance will be provided on the referencing system the journal would like you to use. It is best to comply with this. Articles which are produced in a non-standard format will not create a good initial impression with the editor and, while amendments can be made, it will involve both yourself and the journal staff in a considerable amount of later work.

The refereeing process

When you submit your article, the journal editor will probably acknowledge receipt and then send it to referees for comment. Academic journals usually have a panel of academics who have experience and knowledge of the subject matter of the journal, and who have agreed to read and comment upon submissions. This panel is usually known as the editorial board. The members are usually lecturers or professors at a range of universities around the world. The referees are the key to the quality standards of the journal. They read articles and judge them according to the agreed criteria for the journal. They will write comments on the article manuscript, noting where amendments appear to be desirable. The journal will probably require them to complete a written assessment of the article, and a final judgement on whether the editor should accept the article, accept it subject to specified revisions or reject the article.

The editor will usually send a copy of the article to at least two reviewers. They should not normally know the name of the writer of the article. This is the reason for submitting your name on a sheet of paper separate from the article. The two referees complete their reports independently, and return them to the editor. If the two referees have reached similar conclusions, then it is easy for the editor to convey a formal decision on publication to the author. However, if the referees differ in their judgement then the editor may need to arrive at some form of compromise decision. The journal's final decision will be conveyed to you by the editor.

Academic journals certainly do reject some articles, and different journals may have different rejection rates. However, if you have written your article carefully, and tried to comply with the standards of previously published articles, then you can reasonably hope that your article will be accepted subject to minor amendments. When you have made these changes, your article should be accepted, and will be allocated to a particular issue for production. When it is finally published, most journals send authors a copy of the issue and a number of copies or offprints of the article. It is one of these that you could bind into your completed thesis.

Most serious academic journals advertise themselves as 'fully refereed' journals. This indicates that they follow the kind of refereeing system indicated above. This system does ensure that only articles which comply with the broad standards of academic scholarship are accepted for publication.

However, individual journals can differ in terms of the detail of their criteria, and indeed in the manner in which such criteria are applied. If your article is rejected by one journal, you should not be too despondent. It does not follow that you will not be able to have it accepted by another journal. If you do receive a rejection, then you will probably also receive some constructive comments from the editor. Try to take these into account, and perhaps amend your article slightly. Then submit it to another suitable journal and try again. In the meantime, it might be helpful to let your supervisor read the revised version and comment on it.

Checking upon the progress of your article

The system outlined above has many virtues, but like all systems it is not perfect in practice. One of its less desirable features is that it can be very time-consuming, and this is very frustrating for writers, particularly so since journals generally prefer you to submit your article to only one journal at a time. When you have submitted your article, you should receive an acknowledgement by post or email within a few days. If not, then it would be sensible to request an acknowledgement of the safe arrival of your article. After this, you will need to allow time for the refereeing process to be completed. However, if you have not received any feedback within four to six weeks, it would be sensible to contact the editor for a progress report. After this, you could make an enquiry every two to three weeks, until you receive a decision.

One of the fundamental difficulties with the system is that usually the editor, deputy editor and editorial board members are all employed as university academic staff, and carry out their journal functions as an addition to their core duties. As they need to give their prime attention to such matters as teaching, research and assessment, delays are occasionally inevitable.

Further reading

Craswell, G. (2004) *Writing for Academic Success: A Postgraduate Guide*. London: Sage.
Gilbert, N. (2006) *From Postgraduate to Social Scientist: A Guide to Key Skills*. London: Sage.
Silverman, D. (2004) *Doing Qualitative Research: A Practical Handbook*. 2nd edn. London: Sage.
Thody, A. (2006) *Writing and Presenting Research*. London: Sage.
Wilkinson, D. (2005) *The Essential Guide to Postgraduate Study*. London: Sage.

15

The Oral Examination

In this chapter we discuss the nature of the viva voce examination. We explore the ways in which your supervisors help you prepare for the viva, and the kind of preparation work you yourself can do. The chapter explains the normal structure of the viva, and the type of questions often asked. We also suggest various strategies for interacting with the examiners during the viva. Finally, we analyse the different possible results of the viva process.

Study Strategies

- Talk to former research students about their vivas and the kind of questions which were asked.
- Bear in mind, however, that no two vivas are the same!

The role of your supervisor

The viva voce or oral examination is the culmination of the process of preparing a research thesis. We should however note at this stage that there are slightly different practices for individual awards. Generally speaking, most degrees classified as 'research degrees' involve a viva as the final stage of the assessment process. Hence, generally there is a viva for MPhil, EdD and PhD degrees. However, some universities, for example, do not have a viva for the Master of Philosophy. For most master's degrees which include a taught element, there is no viva of the kind conducted for a research degree. The thesis is examined in the written form by either one or two examiners who teach at the university concerned, and then the thesis may also be read by the external examiner for the course. Sometimes the external examiner routinely meets several students on an individual basis to discuss their thesis with them. This may be referred to as a 'viva', but it is usually a less formal event than the research degree viva. In other cases, the external examiner will rely entirely upon the written thesis to make any judgements. The discussions in the remainder of this chapter relate to a research degree viva.

We have already discussed, in Chapter 4, the general mechanisms by which examiners are appointed. Your main supervisor will have had a central role in ensuring that the examiners have been appointed in accordance with the regulations and procedures of the university. Once they have been officially appointed, then you may be informed of their identities. However, in order not to prejudice the impartiality of the process, it is important that you do not have any contact with the examiners before the viva.

Example – The academic background of examiners

Once you have been informed officially of the identity of your examiners, it might be both interesting and useful for you to explore their personal research and publications. This will give you an idea of their research interests, and although not an infallible guide to the kind of questions they may ask, it may suggest certain issues they could raise.

It is normal that there will be at least one examiner from a different university (the external examiner) and one from the university in which you have been studying (the internal examiner). Sometimes there may be a third examiner. Once they have been appointed your supervisor will ask you to suggest convenient dates for the viva, and will then arrange a date which is convenient for everyone concerned. The viva will take place in the university at which you have been studying. Your supervisor, with the help of other staff, will ensure that a room is reserved and that refreshments are booked. Arrangements will be made to meet and transport the external examiner to the university. The examining team will usually meet for private discussion before the viva, and the viva will start when they have completed these discussions.

Supervisors are usually present in the university on the day of the viva, but normally do not participate in the actual event. However, regulations sometimes allow for the supervisor to be present in the viva if you request it. However, the supervisor takes no part in the discussion. Your supervisor will probably arrange to meet you prior to the viva, in order to support you and offer a few reassuring words.

The role of the internal and external examiners

All of the appointed examiners will be sent a copy of your temporarily bound thesis. They will read the manuscript and probably make a variety of notes in the margins. They will also probably be required to complete a written report on the thesis and submit this to the university prior to the viva. Along with the report, they may have to indicate whether or not they regard the thesis as being of adequate quality to proceed to the viva stage. It is conceivable that a thesis may be of such poor quality that it requires extensive revision before it would be appropriate to hold a viva. This eventuality is unusual, although the examiners may still be asked to formally confirm that a viva should be held.

The examiners need not communicate with each other prior to the viva and normally do not do so. In fact, university regulations may require that they complete their initial assessments of the thesis independently of each other. At this stage it is not particularly significant if they differ in their judgement of the thesis. It is only important that they all feel that the thesis should proceed to the viva stage. The examiners will be able to share their views about the thesis prior to the viva. It is important to remember that the final judgement by the examiners is based upon both the quality of the thesis and your performance in the viva.

Strategies for rereading the thesis

By the time of your viva, you will probably not have read your thesis for some time. A few weeks before the viva it is important to reread it, and to make notes of any problematic issues which occur to you. At about this time your supervisor will also probably arrange your final tutorial, in order to brief you on the structure of the viva, and what may typically happen. Also, normally at this stage your supervisors will arrange a 'mock' viva. They will try to replicate the viva process, and will ask you some typical questions in order to help you prepare for the actual event.

When rereading your thesis it is important not to do so in a passive manner. You will take your thesis into the viva with you, and so it is not necessary to read your thesis with a view to memorizing every section! The first purpose in rereading it is to familiarize yourself broadly with the content, and to be able to locate the sections on particular topics. In the viva, however, when the examiners ask you a question on a particular part of the thesis, they will usually refer you to a paragraph or several sentences on a specific, numbered page. You will be able to turn immediately to that section in your copy.

The second main purpose in rereading the thesis is to try to identify areas where it is less than clear. As you will not have read the thesis for some time, you may find this easier now than when you were constantly revising it. You should be able now to 'distance' yourself from the writing and read it much as if you were reading it for the first time. You may find that you have omitted a fairly obvious feature of the research setting or context. You may notice that you have not included as many quotations in the literature review as you thought that you had done. As you read the methodology chapter you may notice that you did not mention the proportion of questionnaires which had been returned. There is no need to worry about such things, partly at least because examiners do not expect a thesis to be perfect. The main thing is to try to identify omissions and to make sure that you mention them during the viva.

Example – Reading in a questioning manner

When you reread your thesis, try to do so in a sceptical, questioning manner. Ask yourself whether your arguments are logical and plausible, and whether the evidence you adduce, genuinely seems to support your arguments. Ask yourself whether you have chosen suitable references to illustrate your arguments. In short, be challenging towards your own work. In that way, you should prepare yourself for the kind of issues likely to be raised by the examiners.

On rereading, you may notice that the research works mentioned in your literature review are not as recent as you would wish. The final stages of writing a thesis take so much time that it is almost inevitable that you will omit the most recent publications. As further time elapses between the completion of the thesis and the date for the viva, there is again the possibility that more recent work will have been published. It is conceivable that during the viva, the examiners may mention some of the very latest research in your subject area, and that this is not included in your thesis. It is therefore a good idea to spend a little time in the library prior to the viva, ensuring that you are familiar with the latest publications.

Anticipating questions

It is clearly not possible to predict every question which may be asked in a viva. However, the nature of an academic thesis is such that it is very likely that the examiners will focus on certain topics, at least part of the time. They may be interested in the broad relevance of the subject you have chosen to investigate. They may ask you directly why you chose this particular topic. This should not be a difficult question for you to answer, and they may ask this near the beginning of the viva in order to help you to relax.

The examiners will certainly wish to satisfy themselves that you have a sound knowledge of the background literature to the research subject. They may ask you to expand on a particular study to which you have referred in your literature review, or they may wish to explore the extent to which your research has added to the existing body of knowledge. The examiners will almost certainly engage you in detailed debate about your methodology. There are many issues here which they could choose to raise. They may ask a general question about the reason for your choice of methodology, or they may focus upon detailed aspects of your method. Most research involves sampling issues of one sort or another, and they may well enquire about the manner in which you selected your respondents. They may challenge you on that strategy, or they may ask you about the extent to which you feel it is legitimate to generalize your findings.

It is quite common for examiners to enquire about the validity and reliability of your data. They may ask you about your views on any potential validity threats, and the steps which you took, or could take, to minimize these. The subject of research ethics is also an area on which examiners can easily ask questions. There is very little social science research which is not likely to raise ethical issues. You should expect to be asked a question about your strategies for data collection and the ways in which you considered ethical issues. The issue of strategies to ensure anonymity and confidentiality may arise here.

The examiners will certainly look very carefully at the ways in which you have analysed your data. If your data is quantitative, they will have checked your statistical procedures and formed a judgement about your choice of statistical tests. They will look very carefully at the way in which the statistical results have informed the conclusions you have drawn about your research. They may well ask you about these issues. If your data is qualitative, they may ask about your strategy for selecting the data which is included in your thesis. They will certainly examine the analytic processes you have employed, and will wish to assure themselves that the data is analysed appropriately for a research degree.

Finally, if yours is a doctoral thesis, then they will almost certainly ask you about the perceived original contribution to knowledge. This question may be asked in a variety of different ways, but you should be prepared to explain clearly the manner in which your research adds to the knowledge in your subject area.

Example – Kinds of questions which may be asked in a viva

The following is a brief selection of the type of question which examiners may ask:

- Why did you select those two schools in particular for your sample?
- When you were collecting your observational data, what sort of impact do you feel you had on the research field?

- What would you regard as the most significant previous piece of research on this subject?
- With hindsight, if you had the opportunity to revise your questionnaire, what changes would you make?
- Some of your data was collected from school pupils under the age of 16. What ethical issues did this raise for you?
- You employed three separate cycles of data collection. Did the data from one cycle affect your data collection strategy in the next?
- What impact do you think your research findings will have upon this subject field?

The structure of the viva

The examiners will meet prior to the viva to discuss the thesis and share their views of it. They will almost certainly not hold exactly the same views, but will discuss their points of difference. One examiner may feel that there is a deficiency in one part of the thesis, while another examiner may not be very concerned about this. After a good deal of discussion, they will draw up a list of questions and issues they wish to raise. They will probably allocate the questions among themselves, so that each examiner has several to ask.

The examiners may decide on one of their members to act as the chairperson for the proceedings. This will usually be one of the external examiners. The chairperson will welcome you at the beginning and announce the result to you at the end. When the examiners are ready they will invite you into the room. Remember to take your copy of the thesis with you. There should be a desk available for you, so that you can easily turn the pages of your thesis, depending upon the questions which are asked. There should also be a glass of water for you. If there is not, then it would be a good idea to ask for one. You may be talking for some considerable time!

The examiners should normally introduce themselves and then ask one or two straightforward questions to help you to feel at ease. They may, for example, ask you to provide a brief overview of the thesis, much along the lines of the abstract. They may also ask you about your original reasons for embarking on this research. After these preliminary questions, they will then proceed with the predetermined questions. The viva will normally take between one and two hours, although it is possible for it to be shorter or longer. When the examiners have completed their questions, they may conclude by asking if you have any questions to put to them.

They will then ask you to withdraw from the room, while they consider their conclusion. Such discussions may take half an hour or longer. There is no need to feel perturbed if the discussions seem to be taking a long time. They may have decided that you only need to make very minor amendments to the thesis, but they may be coming to an agreement on the exact nature of those amendments. When they have made their decision and determined exactly the action they wish you to take, you will be called back.

The chairperson will announce the decision. Most doctoral candidates need to do some additional work to the thesis. However, this can range from amending a few typographical errors, to a major reworking of a number of chapters. Whatever the decision and the work to be done, the examiners are usually very sympathetic and supportive. They will also usually provide you with clear instructions about the work to be done. If you need to do a large amount of work, they may also call in your supervisor and explain the details of this. Your supervisor will then be in a position to help and advise you with amendments. You will also be advised about the timescale within which you need to make the amendments, and the mechanism for assessing the amended thesis. The doctoral oral examination is discussed in Rudestam and Newton (1992, pp. 142–4).

Coping strategies for questions

Many of the questions you may be asked will be specific to your thesis, and hence it is difficult to offer advice. However, there are certain general types of question which can arise, and one can at least develop broad strategies for coping with them. For example, sometimes an examiner might ask a question of the type 'The recent research by Dr X and Professor Y on this subject is very interesting. What did you think of that?' This is of course a perfectly easy question if you have just read the work of Dr X and Professor Y. If you have not done so, you should certainly not feel nervous if asked such a question. Try saying, 'Actually, I have not read that piece of work. Could you explain the findings briefly, and I will try to relate them to my own research'. You then have the opportunity to engage in a discussion with the examiners, rather than just feeling awkward because you are unfamiliar with the article they have mentioned.

Sometimes you may be asked a question, and you may simply not understand it or not grasp the purpose of raising that particular issue. Under these circumstances, you should not automatically assume that the lack of understanding is your fault! Examiners may sometimes express themselves less than clearly. It is best not to try to answer a question about which you are unclear. This may simply exacerbate any lack of clear communication in the viva. Simply explain that you have not fully understood the question, and ask the examiner to rephrase it.

Another example of the same issue is if an examiner says, 'I noticed on page Z that you argued as follows. Could you explain how that paragraph relates to what you suggested on page X?' Under these circumstances you should certainly not rush to provide an answer. If you are absolutely certain of what you argued, then you can provide an immediate answer but, if not, you should say, 'Could you just indicate exactly the paragraphs you are referring to, as I would like to refresh my memory about exactly what I wrote'. Then read the paragraphs carefully, before providing an answer. Try not to let yourself be rushed.

Examiners may ask you difficult questions, but they are normally not confrontational in the manner in which they ask them. They appreciate that a viva is a potentially stressful situation, and they normally try to be as supportive as they can. It is also worth bearing in mind that there are seldom clear and precise, single responses to research issues. For example, an examiner may formulate a question such as, 'I see that you decided to do X under those circumstances; would it not have been better to do Y?' You should not assume from the form of this question that the examiner actually believes that Y would have been a better alternative. It is simply that the examiner would like to hear your explanation for not adopting procedure Y. It is sometimes easy under such circumstances to find yourself in something of a confrontation as you try strenuously to defend your approach. You should really try to avoid this. It is advisable to adopt an approach which concedes that there are some virtues in the idea suggested by the examiner, but which then outlines the justification for the strategy which you adopted. You might say something such as, 'Ah yes, I see what you are suggesting. I am sure that would have worked well, but on balance, there were a number of factors which influenced me to do X'.

Defending the thesis

The idea of 'defending' a thesis in an oral examination is a very common concept in doctoral education. Having written the thesis, you are expected to defend what you have said. In logical terms, the concept of a defence implies also the concept of an attack. In this sense, the attack comes from the examiners and consists in asking you questions which are designed to probe your deeper awareness of how you carried out your research. They are interested in whether you are aware of alternative strategies you could have used. They want to understand the full reasons for you conducting the research in the way in which you did.

The most appropriate approach to take when confronted by such questions is to stand by the actions which you took, but within the context that you concede that there were viable alternatives. This is definitely not the same as agreeing with all the criticisms made and accepting that you could have done it better! This would be an inappropriate stance to take, and would not be in accord with defending your thesis.

When you are asked a question concerning the reason for conducting a part of the research in the manner in which you did, try to think back to your reasoning prior to taking the decision. You will probably be able to reconstruct these reasons in your mind. Remember that you put a lot of thought into planning your research, and that you had valid reasons at the time for most of the things you did. Try to think out those reasons, and to articulate them clearly to the examiners. There is no harm in conceding that there were alternatives, but try to provide, in a confident manner, the reasons for your actions.

It is also worth remembering that you are likely to know more about your thesis than the examiners. They may have greater specialist knowledge of some aspects of the methodology, and they will have a good knowledge of the broad subject background of the research topic. However, they may not have much experience of the specific topic of your thesis, nor of the methodological issues created by that topic. You, on the other hand, have probably been wrestling with these problems for the last four or five years. While this is not to underestimate the expertise of the examiners, there is no reason for you to be excessively in awe of them.

Signpost to success – Defending your thesis

If you have planned your research and writing carefully, have confidence in what you have written and in your ability to defend your thesis!

Overall strategy for the viva

Quite apart from trying to develop responses to anticipated questions, it can also be very useful to develop a general approach to the viva. For example, it is possible to project a particular image of oneself.

The viva can be viewed as a social interaction within a small group of people. Two or three of those people are relatively powerful within the interaction, and one, the candidate or student, is much less powerful. The former tend to ask the questions, and the latter responds. The former tend to determine the tone and atmosphere of the interaction, and the latter tends to adapt to that tone. The former tend to plan and control the layout of the room, and the timing and scheduling of the interaction, while again the candidate tends to comply with whatever has already been arranged. As a very broad, and perhaps often inaccurate, generalization we might perceive the examiners as being 'active' and the student as 'passive' in this interaction. However, this does not necessarily have to be so.

Many doctoral students try to rely entirely upon a calm rationality in the viva, assuming that the simple strength of their arguments will win the day. While that may be so, and perhaps in a perfect world ought to be so, situations may arise in the viva where a more assertive approach may be necessary. For example, one or more examiners may not either understand your argument, or accept its line of logic, and they may try to move the discussion on to another subject. If you sense this, then you may wish to keep the discussion going to clarify your viewpoint – 'Before we move on, I would just like to make another point with regard to this . . .'.

For example, let us suppose that the examiners challenge the size of your sample, then the discussion may proceed as follows:

Examiner: I was just slightly concerned about the size of the sample. Did you not consider collecting data from some teachers as well as students? It could have added richness to the data.

Candidate: Yes, I appreciate what you are saying, but the title of the thesis emphasizes the views of students.

Examiner: Well, yes, but we just have to consider what would have made the best study. Anyway, if colleagues are ready, we can perhaps discuss the analysis.

Candidate: But just to stay with that point for a moment, I set out the aims very clearly on page 17, and those specify that the study is concerned with the views of students. I think, having established the aims, I had of necessity to use those as the basis of the sample. I appreciate teacher views would have been of interest, but I still feel that on balance they are outside the parameters of this study.

There are no actual 'rules' for the conduct of the viva! If you wish to ask a question of the examiners during the discussion, then you should do so. You might want to say, for example, 'Well, in that section, I was trying to expand on this argument, and illustrate it with examples. Did that make sense to you?' In other words, you are really engaging with the examiners in a discussion, not simply responding to their questions. By adopting this approach you are demonstrating personal confidence, and the ability to initiate aspects of the discussion, rather than simply reacting where necessary. Many examiners actually like students to demonstrate a confidence in their own ability, and to show that they really want to develop into serious researchers and academics. It is possible to strike a balance between being respectful towards the examiners, and at the same time to show that you are confidently engaging with them on their level.

In the past, the doctoral viva has tended to involve simply the examiners and the candidate, with sometimes the supervisor being present at the invitation of the student. However, there is an increasing debate about the importance of having an additional person present, to monitor the conduct of the viva and to ensure that the examination proceeds according to the established regulations and procedures. Such individuals would usually chair the event and be independent of the assessment process. This neutrality is an important factor in reassuring candidates of the fairness of the proceedings, and of arbitrating in the case of any disputes over the conduct of the examination.

The viva should be a serious academic debate. Almost inevitably, that debate takes place within a certain academic linguistic register, which usually involves the use of a considerable number of long, technical words. Academics are familiar with the use of such words, and incorporate them easily into their dialogue. Now we might regard some such words as being jargon, but the reality is that they form the regular vocabulary of professional researchers and academics. Hence it is absolutely necessary that the doctoral candidate develops the habit of using such terms easily and fluently. In a sense, it gives out signals that you are part of the research community, that you speak its language, and think in the same way as the examiners. On its own, this will not ensure that you are successful in the viva, but it will be an important element in the impression which you are trying to create.

Example – Using terminology

It may be useful, prior to the viva, to make a note of twenty or thirty specialist terms which you intend to use in the discussion. Make a mental note of how you might introduce them, and practise the type of phrases you might use. This will help you feel more authoritative during the viva.

Also remember that the doctoral thesis is a very complex document. It is extremely difficult to read it and internalize and understand all of the data, analysis and arguments. Yet this is what examiners try to do. Nevertheless, with the best will in the world, they will sometimes misunderstand things, not follow the line of argument intended by the student, or forget issues which the student regards as crucial. It is therefore important that you reflect, before the viva, on the key issues which you hope to emphasize during the discussion. In a sense, it does not matter whether all of these issues are raised by the examiners, but you must ensure that you somehow bring them into the debate. It is really a matter of you deciding in advance on a few elements of the thesis which you regard as particularly interesting, or making a special contribution to the debate within the subject area, or perhaps making a noted contribution to our understanding of an issue. You may decide on perhaps four or five areas. Then, during the viva, you will need to keep bringing these issues into the discussion, even if the examiners have not raised them. Moreover, it will probably not be sufficient to simply mention them once. You should keep returning to them to make absolutely sure the examiners have understood and fully absorbed what you were trying to say. In this way, irrespective of whatever other opinion the examiners may have formed, you will at least feel confident that they have understood the central arguments you have advanced. For example, in a study of student choice in higher education, you may consider that your research shows that students in the sample do not feel that they have the choice of modules within their degree programme that they might have expected. The discussion in the viva might proceed as follows:

Examiner: Yes there were some interesting points in the analysis, though I felt that Chapter 7 did not perhaps separate out the issues sufficiently clearly.

Candidate: Well, I certainly tried to, but it is true that the issues are complex. Still, I think that the central question emerging of the students' perception of a lack of choice is very important, and has consequences for educational planners in higher education.

Examiner: Of course modular programmes have brought many advantages, including arguably a clearer approach to curriculum design.

Candidate: Oh certainly, but it was a system introduced at least partly on the grounds of increasing student choice; and I think it is one of the key contributions of my research to show that students do not largely perceive that choice as being reflected in reality.

Examiners also usually like to have a vision of a thesis within a time sequence. They like to have an idea of how the research project started and where it is likely to lead. They may not specifically ask about the original inception of the research, but it is worth making it clear to them how and why you first had the idea of the research. This is an opportunity to say something about yourself, your own research interests, and how these led into the research project. At the same time, it is also worth mentioning how you see your thesis stimulating fresh research projects, and how it might motivate other researchers. In this way, you are setting your study within a temporal sequence of other work, and it demonstrates that you have a vision of your research as part of the natural development of other studies in the subject area.

Example – Personal ambition for your research

A viva is also a golden opportunity for you to have the undivided attention of two or three senior and influential academics. You should take advantage of this! Explain to them how you see your thesis contributing to your future plans for research and publications. If you would like to try to publish the whole thesis as a book, then say so. They may be able to provide suggestions for publishers. It would do no harm to ask them directly if they have suggestions for how you might publish part or all of the thesis. This will also create a positive image for yourself, as a forward-thinking scholar.

Finally, and very importantly, it is essential that you have a clear understanding of the way in which your research study makes an original contribution to knowledge. This remains perhaps the central criterion by which a doctoral level thesis is judged. For the thesis to be considered to be at doctoral level, it must make an original contribution to knowledge. By the time of the viva you should be absolutely clear about the nature of this. You will have no doubt thought about this at length, and it should certainly have been discussed with your supervisors. Out of these discussions should emerge a very clear conception on your part of the precise contribution, and this should be clearly described in the thesis. There can sometimes be a fairly long gap between submitting the thesis, and the actual viva. If on reflection you are not totally happy with the explanation of the original contribution, then you should rephrase this in your own mind, and make certain that you explain this in the viva. The examiners may not ask you about this directly, but may ask questions which allude to the issue obliquely. However it is approached, you should state, and if necessary restate, your feelings about the contribution your research makes. This not only emphasizes to the examiners that you understand the significance of this criterion, but that you also have confidence in your own work and the conclusions which you have drawn.

Possible results of the viva

When you are invited back into the examination room, the chairperson will announce the result. The examiners have a number of options open to them. First, they can recommend that the research degree be awarded and that the thesis does not require any amendments. This is a relatively unusual circumstance since most theses require at least one or two minor amendments. Secondly, the examiners may recommend that the degree be awarded but subject to a number of minor amendments being made to the thesis. Minor amendments may involve such matters as corrections to the typing, the addition of brief sentences here and there or additions to the list of references. When the corrections have been made they are usually checked by a designated internal examiner, who signs a form indicating that they have been correctly made. It follows from this that minor amendments are usually issues which the examiners feel do not require a substantive change to the meaning or content of the thesis. If this were the case, then it would probably not be appropriate to leave the checking to one examiner acting alone. In practical terms, the examiners will usually provide clear written guidance on the sections which require amendment. They may also hand over their annotated copies of the thesis to the candidate, in order to help with the correcting process.

However, if the examiners feel that fairly substantive changes are required to the thesis, then they may refer the thesis for resubmission, usually within 12 months of the date of the viva. In some cases they may feel that a completely new viva is required. In other cases, they may be happy to see the thesis alone. In the case of referral, it is normal for all the examiners to see the revised thesis. The examiners will usually provide the candidate with a written account of the deficiencies of the thesis, although this will probably not indicate the required changes in a very precise manner. In the case of referral, the amendments needed are usually such that a measure of rewriting is necessary. Hence it is only possible to indicate the broad nature of the amendments required, rather than the detail. The written account should be sufficiently precise, however, for the candidate to have a clear idea of the general nature of the additions to be made.

In some cases, the examiners may feel that the thesis is not sufficiently good for the award for which it was submitted, but that a lesser award be recommended. This may happen in the case of a doctoral thesis, where the examiners may recommend the award of MPhil. In some extreme cases, the examiners may fail the thesis, without allowing the possibility of resubmission. Universities may differ in the detail of their assessment regulations, but these are generally the range of decisions available to examiners.

Once the necessary amendments have been made to a thesis, and it has been approved by the examiners (either in the case of minor amendments or a referral) then a nominated examiner confirms this in writing to the university administration. The candidate then arranges for the permanent binding of the thesis, and submits a copy for deposit in the university library. The appointed university officer will then sign a letter on behalf of the senate or relevant university body, indicating conferment of the award. You will also subsequently receive a formal certificate indicating the award.

So that could be the end of the story; or perhaps not. Many people feel such a sense of relief on getting their award, that they do not want to do any more study or writing. But before long, it often happens that people begin to miss their studying, and the thesis proves to be not the end but the beginning of fresh academic ventures. Some embark on sponsored research, or writing articles or a book. Once caught by the excitement of the academic journey, it can be hard to resist new journeys and, fortunately, the road is almost inexhaustible in terms of fresh challenges.

Further reading

Churchill, H. and Sanders, T. (2007) *Getting Your PhD: A Practical Insider's Guide*. London: Sage.

Murray, R. (2003) *How to Survive Your Viva: Defending a Thesis in an Oral Examination*. Buckingham: Open University Press.

Rudestam, K.E. and Newton, R.R. (2007) *Surviving Your Dissertation: A Comprehensive Guide to Content and Process*. 3rd edn. London: Sage.

Silverman, D. (2004) *Doing Qualitative Research: A Practical Handbook*. 2nd edn. London: Sage.

Wellington, J.J., Bathmaker, A. and Hunt, C. (2005) *Succeeding with Your Doctorate*. London: Sage.

References and Further Reading

Allison, B. (1997) *The Student's Guide to Preparing Dissertations and Theses*. London: Kogan Page.

American Psychological Association (2012) 'PsycINFO®', available at: www.apa.org/psycinfo/ (accessed 8 November 2012).

AMICUS (2012) AMICUS available at www.collectionscanada.gc.ca/amicus/index-e.html, accessed 21 November 2012.

Anderson, G., with Arsenault, N. (1998) *Fundamentals of Educational Research*. 2nd edn. London: Falmer.

Arksey, H. and Knight, P. (1999) *Interviewing for Social Scientists: An Introductory Resource with Examples*. London: Sage.

Bailey, C.A. (1996) *A Guide to Field Research*. Thousand Oaks, CA: Pine Forge Press.

Barnes, R. (1995) *Successful Study for Degrees*. London: Routledge.

Berger, A.A. (1993) *Improving Writing Skills: Memos, Letters, Reports and Proposals*. London: Sage.

Brause, R.S. (2000) *Writing your Doctoral Dissertation: Invisible Rules for Success*. London: Falmer.

British Library (2012) 'EThOS, Electronic Theses Online Service', available at: http://ethos.bl.uk/About.do (accessed 13 November 2012).

British Standards Institution (1990) *Recommendations for Citing and Referencing Published Material*. BS 5605. London: British Standards Institution.

Brown, A. (1997) *Gaining a Master's Degree*. Oxford: How To Books.

Bryman, A. and Burgess, R.G. (eds) (1994) *Analysing Qualitative Data*. London: Routledge.

Clough, P. and Nutbrown, C. (2002) *A Student's Guide to Methodology: Justifying Enquiry*. London: Sage.

Copac® (2012) 'Copac®', available at www.copac.ac.uk/ (accessed 21 November 2012).

Creme, P. and Lea, M.R. (1997) *Writing at University: A Guide for Students*. Buckingham: Open University Press.

Creswell, J.W. (1998) *Qualitative Inquiry and Research Design: Choosing among Five Traditions*. Thousand Oaks, CA: Sage.

Cryer, P. (1996) *The Research Student's Guide to Success*. Buckingham: Open University Press.

Delamont, S., Atkinson, P. and Parry, O. (1997) *Supervising the PhD: A Guide to Success*. Buckingham: Society for Research into Higher Education and Open University Press.

Denscombe, M. (2002) *Ground Rules for Good Research: A 10 Point Guide for Social Researchers*. Buckingham: Open University Press.

Dey, I. (1993) *Qualitative Data Analysis: A User-friendly Guide for Social Scientists*. London: Routledge.

Drew, S. and Bingham, R. (2001) *The Student Skills Guide*. 2nd edn. Sheffield: Sheffield Hallam University.

EBSCO (2012) 'SocINDEX™ with Full Text', available at: www.ebscohost.com/academic/socindex-with-full-text (accessed 11 November 2012).

Elsevier B.V. (2012) 'SciVerse®Scopus®', available at: www.info.sciverse.com/scopus/about (accessed 12 November 2012).

Erickson, B.H. and Nosanchuk, T.A. (1992) *Understanding Data*. 2nd edn. Buckingham: Open University Press.

Fairbairn, G.J. and Winch, C. (1991) *Reading, Writing and Reasoning: A Guide for Students*. Buckingham: Society for Research into Higher Education and Open University Press.

Flick, U. (1998) *An Introduction to Qualitative Research*. London: Sage.

Gash, S. (1989) *Effective Literature Searching for Students*. Aldershot: Gower.

Gill, J. and Johnson, P. (2002) *Research Methods for Managers*. 3rd edn. London: Sage.

Glaser, B.G. and Strauss, A.L. (1967) *The Discovery of Grounded Theory*. New York: Aldine de Gruyter.

Google Scholar (2012) 'Google Scholar', available at: http://scholar.google.com (accessed 11 November 2012).

Institut de l'Information Scientifique et Technique (2011) 'OpenGrey', available at: www.opengrey.eu/about (accessed 19 November 2012).

JSTOR® (2012) JSTOR® available at www.jstor.org/ (accessed 21 November 2012).

Jupp, V. (2006) *The Sage Dictionary of Social Research Methods*. London: Sage.

Levin, P. (2005) *Excellent Dissertations!* Maidenhead: Open University Press.

Leonard, D. (2001) *A Woman's Guide to Doctoral Studies*. Buckingham: Open University Press.

Maker, J. and Lenier, M. (1996) *Academic Reading with Active Critical Thinking*. Belmont, CA: Wadsworth.

Miller, G. (1997) 'Toward ethnographies of institutional discourse: proposal and suggestions', in G. Miller and R. Dingwall (eds), *Context and Method in Qualitative Research*. London: Sage. pp. 155–71.

Murray, R. (2003) *How to Survive your Viva*. Maidenhead: Open University Press.

Murray, R. (2006) *How to Write a Thesis*. 2nd edn. Maidenhead: Open University Press.

Murray, R. and Moore, S. (2006) *The Handbook of Academic Writing*. Maidenhead: Open University Press.

NDLTD (2012) 'Networked Digital Library of Theses and Dissertations', available at: www.ndltd.org/ (accessed 13 November 2012).

Northedge, A. (1990) *The Good Study Guide*. Milton Keynes: The Open University.

O'Hara, S. (1998) *Studying @ University and College*. London: Kogan Page.

OCLC (2012) 'WorldCat®', available at: www.worldcat.org/ (accessed 21 November 2012).

OpenDOAR (2010) 'The Directory of Open Access Repositories', available at: www.opendoar.org/ (accessed 13 November 2012).

OpenThesis (2009) 'OpenThesis', available at www.openthesis.org/ (accessed 13 November 2012).

Phillips, E.M. and Pugh, D.S. (2000) *How to Get a Ph.D*. Buckingham: Open University Press.

Preece, R. (1994) *Starting Research: An Introduction to Academic Research and Dissertation Writing*. London: Continuum.

Punch, K.F. (1998) *Introduction to Social Research*. London: Sage.

Punch, K.F. (2006) *Developing Effective Research Proposals*. London: Sage.

QAA (2004) *Code of Practice, Section1: Postgraduate Research Programmes*. London: QAA.

RefWorks (2009) 'RefWorks', available at: www.refworks.com/ (accessed 29 October 2012).

Research Councils UK (2012) 'Postgraduate training', available at: www.rcuk.ac.uk/researchcareers/postgrad/Pages/home.aspx (accessed 25 September 2012).

Rudestam, K.E. and Newton, R.R. (1992) *Surviving your Dissertation: A Comprehensive Guide to Content and Process*. Newbury Park, CA: Sage.

Rugg, G. and Petre, M. (2006) *A Gentle Guide to Research Methods*. London: Sage.

Sapsford, R. and Jupp, V. (eds) (1996) *Data Collection and Analysis*. London: Sage.

Sharp, J.A. and Howard, K. (1996) *The Management of a Student Research Project*. 2nd edn. Aldershot: Gower.

Silbergh, D.M. (2001) *Doing Dissertations in Politics: A Student Guide*. London: Routledge.

Steier, F. (ed.) (1991) *Research and Reflexivity*. London: Sage.

Thomson Reuters (2012) 'EndNote', available at: http://endnote.com/ (accessed 29 October 2012).

Turabian, K.L., revised by Grossman, J. and Bennett, A. (1996) *A Manual for Writers of Term Papers, Theses and Dissertations*. 6th edn. Chicago, IL: University of Chicago Press.

Turner, J. (2002) *How to Study*. London: Sage.

Wallace, M. and Wray, A. (2006) *Critical Reading and Writing for Postgraduates*. London: Sage.

Walliman, N.S.R. (2005) *Your Research Project*. London: Sage.

Wolcott, H.F. (2001) *Writing Up Qualitative Research*. 2nd edn. London: Sage.

Woods, P. (1999) *Successful Writing for Qualitative Researchers*. London: Routledge-Falmer.

Wyse, D. (2006) *The Good Writing Guide for Education Students*. London: Sage.

Index

978-1-4462-0325-5

978-1-4462-0287-6

978-1-44620-710-9

978-0-85702-932-4

978-1-84920-562-7

978-1-84920-794-2

978-0-85702-928-7

978-1-4462-0932-5

978-1-4462-0143-5

For more study skills information, multimedia resources
and special offers visit **www.uk.sagepub.com/studyskills.sp**

SAGE STUDY SKILLS - GIVING STUDENTS THAT EXTRA EDGE!